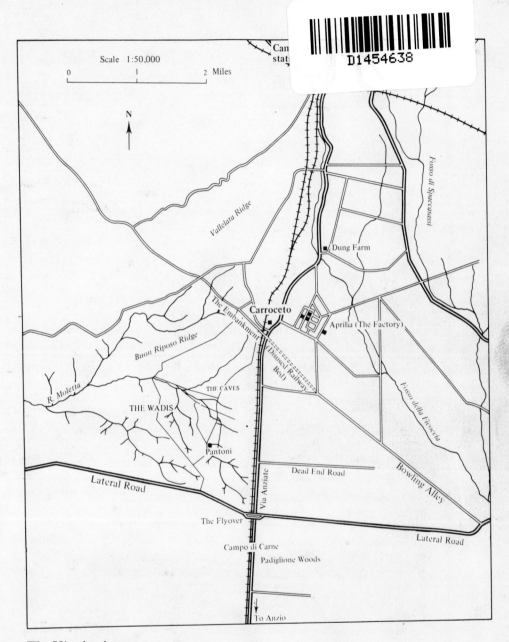

Scale 1:50,000

0   1   2 Miles

N

Camp... stat...

Vallelata Ridge

Fosso di Spaccasassi

Dung Farm

The Embankment

Carroceto

Aprilia (The Factory)

Buon Riposo Ridge

(Disused Railway Bed)

R. Moletta

THE CAVES

Fosso della Ficoccia

THE WADIS

Pantoni

Lateral Road

Dead End Road

Via Anziate

Bowling Alley

The Flyover

Lateral Road

Campo di Carne

Padiglione Woods

To Anzio

The Via Anziate

B13

mgm

VERNEY, Peter

Anzio 1944

6.   940.5421

ANZIO 1944:
An Unexpected Fury

Peter Verney

B. T. Batsford, Ltd
LONDON

First Published 1978
© Peter Verney 1978

ISBN 0 7134 1323 9

Filmset by Elliott Bros. & Yeoman Ltd.,
Speke, Liverpool L24 9JL
Printed and bound in Great Britain by
Redwood-Burn Ltd, Trowbridge and Esher
for the publishers B. T. Batsford Ltd,
4 Fitzhardinge Street, London W1H 0AH

'We was like fleas in a blanket seein' no more than the next nearest wrinkle.'
  (*Anonymous Irish Guards private in World War I*)

'I had hoped that we were hurling a wild cat on to the shore, but all we had got was a stranded whale.'
  (Winston Churchill, *Closing the Ring*)

Acknowledgements

I would particularly like to thank Mrs D. C. C. Dixon for graciously allowing me access to the papers of her late father, Major-General Sir Ronald Penney, KBE, CB, DSO, MC; Major Nick Straker for a great deal of help over German material; Lieutenant-Colonel James Acland for advice and assistance of every sort, and Colonel Stewart Carter for his invaluable midwifery.

I would also like to thank the following for their help, and in many cases their hospitality: Lt.-Gen. Sir Terence Airey, KCMG, CB, CBE; Capt. H. R. R. Attwooll, MC; Maj. J. C. Beadle, MBE, MC, RM; Maj. M. K. Beadle, MBE; Capt. J. P. Bolongaro; Col. John G. Bourne; Maj. H. Brown, MBE; Col. W. P. Careless, DSO; Maj.-Gen. T. B. L. Churchill, CB, CBE, MC; Capt. A. D. N. Clark; Col. J. Cleghorn; Brig. A. F. L. Clive, DSO, MC; Maj. R. Close-Brookes, DSO; Mr B. C. Cortis; Maj.-Gen. K. C. Davidson, CB, MC; Col. The Rt. Hon. Viscount De L'Isle, VC, KG, GCMG, GCVO; Maj. A. J. Donald, RM; Mr J. Dunne, DCM; Col. R. C. Evans, MC; Maj. Sir George FitzGerald, MC; Sir Edward Ford, KCB, KCVO; Maj. R. A. Fortnum; Mr Gunther Friedrich; Lt.-Gen. Sir George Gordon-Lennox, KBE, CB, CVO, DSO; Brig. I. H. Good, DSO; Maj. T. A. Gore Browne; Maj. J. Graham, MC; Sir Peter Henderson, KCB; Maj. T. S. Hohler, MC; The Hon. Edmund Howard, CMG, MVO; Sir David Hunt, KCMG, OBE; Mr M. J. Hussey; Brig. T. de F. Jago, OBE; Brig. F. D. Jones, MC; Mr M. R. Jones; The Hon. Lord Keith; Lt.-Col. J. J. Kelly, OBE; Maj.-Gen. S. E. Large, MBE; Col. A. T. Law, DSO; Maj.-Gen. F. A. H. Ling, CB, CBE, DSO; Lt.-Col. S. J. Linden-Kelly, DSO; Col. P. Mansell, DSO; Maj. P. L. Mercer, MBE, MM; Mr Malcolm Munthe; Lt.-Col. J. Oliver-Belasis, DSO; Maj.-Gen. J. M. S. Pasley, CB, CBE, MVO; Lt.-Col. J. Peddie, DSO; Mr J. L. Quarrie; Brig. G. A. Rimbault, CBE, DSO, MC; Maj. Sir Hugh Ripley, Bt; Maj. A. Robotham, MC; Maj. W. I. Rooney, MBE, MM; Col. S. Rubens; Maj.-Gen. Sir Peter St. Clair-Ford, KBE, CB, DSO; Maj.-Gen. J. Scott-Elliott, CB, CBE, DSO; Col. J. W. Sewell; Mr W. Stewart; Sir James Stuart-Menteth, Bt; Maj. A. R. Taylor, MBE; Field-Marshal Sir Gerald Templer, KG, GCB, GCMG, KBE, DSO; Capt. A. Thorne; Brig. G. E. Thubron, DSO; Maj. A. F. Tuke; Brig. B. W. Webb-Carter, DSO, OBE; Maj. G. J. Williams, MC; Maj. J. C. Williamson, OBE, MC; Lt.-Col. J. F. Winn, OBE, MC; Dr. P. L. E. Wood, DSO; Brig. H. L. S. Young, DSO; and I am particularly grateful for the unfailing co-operation of the headquarters of those regiments who fought at Anzio. Without their help this book could not conceivably have been written.

The author and publishers would also like to thank the following for permission to reproduce illustrations: the Imperial War Museum (figs 1, 2, 4, 6, 7, 8, 14, 15, 16, 19, 20, 23, 24, 26, 27); the Robert Hunt Library (figs 5, 10, 13); the US Department of Defence (figs 3, 9, 11, 17, 18, 21, 22, 25).

6

Contents

List of Maps

List of Illustrations

Important Dates

November 1942: invasion of French North Africa by Anglo-American Forces (Operation Torch).

13 May 1943: all Germans clear of the North African shore.

July 1943: the invasion of Sicily (Operation Husky).

8 September 1943: invasion of Italy at Reggio.

9 September 1943: landing at Salerno (Operation Avalanche).

Dramatis Personae

Alexander, General the Hon. Sir Harold. Commander-in-Chief Allied Central Mediterranean Force (ACMF). On 9 March 1944 Commander-in-Chief, Allied Armies in Italy.

Clark, Lieutenant-General Mark Wayne. Commanding General 5th U.S. Army.

Eagles, Major-General William W. Commander 45th U.S. Infantry Division.

Evelegh, Major-General V. Deputy Commander 6th U.S. Corps from 17 February.

Frederick, Brigadier-General Robert T. Commander 1st Special Service Force.

⋆Gräser, Lieutenant-General Fritz-Hubert. Commander 3rd Panzer Grenadier Division.

Gregson-Ellis, Major-General P. G. S. Commander 5th British Infantry Division.

Harmon, Major-General Ernest N.·Commander 1st U.S. Armoured Division.

Hawkesworth, Major-General J. L. I. Temporary Commander 1st British Infantry Division.

⋆Herr, General Traugott. Commander 76th Panzer Corps.

⋆Kesselring, Field Marshal Albert. Commander-in-Chief Southwest and Army Group 'C'.

Lowry, Rear-Admiral Frank J., U.S.N. Commander Allied Naval Assault, Anzio, and Force 'X' for the landing.

Lucas, Major-General John P. Commander 6th U.S. Corps.

⋆Mackensen, Colonel-General Eberhard von. Commander 14th Army.

O'Daniel, Brigadier-General John W. Commander 3rd U.S. Infantry Division from 17 February.

Penney, Major-General W. R. C. Commander 1st British Infantry Division.

⋆Pfeiffer, Major-General Helmut. Commander 65th Infantry Division.

⋆Schlemm, General Alfred. Commander 1st Parachute Corps.

⋆Schlemmer, Brigadier-General. Appointed to command Anzio area 22 January (D-Day); handed over to Schlemm that evening.

Templer, Major-General G. W. R. Commander 56th British Infantry Division.

Troubridge, Rear-Admiral T. H., R. N. Commander Force 'P' Anzio landing.

Truscott, Major-General Lucian K. Commander 3rd U.S. Infantry Division to 17 February. Deputy Commander 6th U.S. Corps 17–22 February. Commander 6th U.S. Corps until end of Anzio operation.

*Vietinghoff, Colonel-General Heinrich-Gottfried von. Commander Tenth Army.

Walker, Major-General Fred I. Commander 36th U.S. Infantry Division.

*Westphal, Lieutenant-General Siegfried. Chief of Staff to Kesselring.

*German commanders

Introduction

There is a road running south across the plain. It twists down the gentle lower slopes of the Alban Hills, past farm and vineyard, factory and shop, and the ubiquitous hoardings which proclaim the wares of an international market. Near the hamlet of Campoleone it straightens out and goes arrow-like towards Anzio and the sea. It is difficult to picture this scene thirty-four years ago, when every fold in the ground held its quota of vehicles, every farmhouse was occupied by hidden watchers, when it was death to travel this same road in daylight.

A sign to the right points to Campoleone Station, a goal and a will o' the wisp to the Allied troops in the beachhead and never reached until the great break out four months after the landing. To the left is what became renowned as 'Dung Farm'—curiously, by both Allies and Germans alike—now reconstructed, it is neat and well-stocked, yet in its time a scene of fighting as fierce as any at Anzio. Beyond is Aprilia—the 'Factory', the British and Americans called it—now a completely rebuilt and thriving community of square functional architecture; only the beautiful bronze statue of Saint Michael remains of the Factory which the Allied troops came to know and hate. Here new high-rise apartments command a view over the Campo di Carne (the Plain of Flesh)—now called the Campo Verde—a name which was to gather a unique and sinister connotation in the spring of 1944. Nine miles from the sea is the Flyover.

The Flyover, one of the few places of shelter and observation over the otherwise featureless plain, is soon to be, and may already have been, removed. To the side is a new and dominating factory which hides the Buon Riposo Ridge from view. The wadis have largely been bulldozed in, and those that remain seem innocuous valleys of peace and repose, but to the veteran they embodied all that was foulest at Anzio. Other places are harder to identify. The Bowling Alley, the Embankment, has become the bed for the new Appian Way. The Padiglione Woods, which once hid the Allied gun-lines and mighty administrative echelons for the invading forces, have been largely destroyed to make way for development and carefully tended fields.

Along the road—the Via Anziate—where once were dire warnings bidding drivers take heed, there are now ambling tractors carrying in season the red and green grapes of the district. Sometimes cars and mopeds hurry noisily along bearing Romans to the twin seaside resorts of Anzio and Nettuno, with their rash of new buildings, obtrusive sea-view villas, and rebuilt town centres. Only a few of the older houses show the marks of war, bullet holes and shrapnel scars, which tell that this was not always the peaceful seaside setting it appears today, with the blue Tyrrhenian Sea lapping sandy beaches.

Looking back from these beaches it is still possible to sense something of what those who landed here in those far off days of January 1944 must have felt: the calm sea, the soft pines and cork oaks stretching away inland, while behind to the north are the Alban Hills, so near and so dominating, and beyond, only a little more than thirty miles away, is Rome.

Along the road to Rome, set back from the bustling Via Anziate, a little of the great Padiglione Woods remain around a place set apart. Here is one of the British Military Cemeteries. Surrounded by wisteria-covered pergolas and pyramid-clipped rosemary, the serried ranks of headstones in their setting of evergreen, of cypress and a background of the flat canopy of the umbrella pine, create an indelible memory. It is a sobering experience to walk here, where so many young men are buried; some only eighteen years old, most in their early twenties, not only British, but Commonwealth as well—New Zealanders, Indians, South Africans and Australians. One patch is set aside for the graves of Canadians of the 1st Special Service Force, who with their American comrades fought and died on the far side of the beachhead among the marshes and fields by the Mussolini Canal. At the end of the beautifully tended cemetery is a small monument to the men of the 655th Squadron of the Air Observation Post Squadron, R.A.F.—the forerunner of the present Army Air Corps—the eyes of the beachhead, who flew slow and very vulnerable aircraft, spotting the fall of shot and reporting on movement behind the German lines.

Most of the graves show the regiment, name and religion of those who lie buried, but some are anonymous. Perhaps all identifying marks were lost amid the mud, blood and carnage of war. Then the text is only 'Known unto God', and above 'A Soldier of the 1939–45 War.'

For Anzio was a soldiers' battle, perhaps the most bitterly fought of all engagements in World War II, and this book is dedicated to all those of whatever nationality, who fell in the battle of the beachhead.

Anzio is still a place vibrant with memories—it is some of these memories, while they are still remembered, that I have sought to capture in this book.

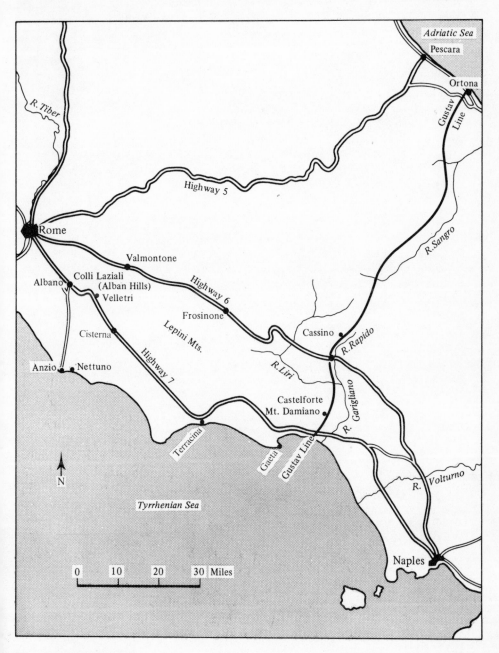

The following labels appear on the map:

Adriatic Sea

Pescara

Ortona

R. Tiber

Gustav Line

Highway 5

R. Sangro

Rome

Valmontone

Colli Laziali
(Alban Hills)

Albano

Velletri

Highway 6

Frosinone

Cassino

R. Rapido

Cisterna

Lepini Mts.

R. Liri

Anzio

Nettuno

Highway 7

Castelforte
Mt. Damiano

R. Garigliano

Terracina

Gaeta

Gustav Line

R. Volturno

Tyrrhenian Sea

N

0   10   20   30 Miles

Naples

The campaign in Italy

1

Prelude

By the end of 1943 it was clear that the advance of the Allied armies up the shin of Italy was slowing down. The first landings on the mainland of Europe had taken place only two months before, yet to the troops fighting among inhospitable mountains against a dogged enemy and bad weather, it might have been an age.

Ahead lay the Gustav Line, an immensely strong chain of defensive positions stretching the width of Italy. It had not been appreciated how strong it was until the advance of General Mark Clark's 5th U.S. Army on the left came to a grinding halt in freezing weather opposite Cassino; and General Montgomery's British 8th Army advancing parallel on the east coast found further progress impossible. Winter now took over in Italy—and deadlock ensued.

It was to break this deadlock that an amphibious assault had first been mooted—a left hook to get behind the German lines and cut their communications with the north. As early as the previous autumn a plan had been devised for such a landing by a single division: this was in conjunction with a major thrust on the western side of Italy by the 5th Army, to aid a final triumphant advance up the Liri Valley and Highway Six to Rome, and only to be undertaken when General Clark's forces had reached the town of Frosinone. By December 1943 the 5th Army was nowhere near Frosinone and the project was cancelled.

But the problem of Italy was no nearer solution. The highly mechanised troops of the 5th and 8th Armies found themselves in a struggle to which they could find no quick solution: a mountain campaign in the depth of winter, against an enemy skilfully led and fighting in country where natural defensive features abounded. By December they were up to the line of the Garigliano, the Rapido and the Sangro Rivers, and facing them across these formidable waterways, now swollen by winter rains, lay the Gustav Line. Once again the idea of an amphibious landing to break the constraints of weather and terrain was in the air.

The trio of conferences which took place in November and December 1943, at Cairo, Teheran and then once again in Cairo, encompassed the final defeat of the Axis Powers. While returning from the last session at Cairo Churchill became gravely ill and while the body was confined to bed the restless mind began to ponder on the Italian campaign, bogged down and soon to be pushed into the background as plans for the great invasion—Operation Overlord—became uppermost in men's minds. How great was the appeal of breaking the impasse in that country. How enticing to put an end to the Allies' inch-by-inch advance 'like a harvest bug' up the leg of Italy. This was strategy on the grand scale, a swift decisive move to quell the opponent, to attack from an unexpected quarter to send him scuttling. These were actions his great ancestor the Duke of Marlborough would have approved of, the modern counterpart to the miracle marches before the Battle of Oudenarde or that which broke the deadlock in the Low Countries and led to the siege of Tournai before the bloody contest of Malplaquet. The prizes were the elimination of the German forces south of Rome and the capture of the Eternal City itself, the final crushing of Mussolini's dream and a fitting and triumphant conclusion to the campaign in the Mediterranean before all eyes turned towards the great Second Front. The timing was right, the resources were there, the prizes beyond price.

Over Christmas he conferred with his military advisers, but it was generally agreed that nothing less than a two-divisional landing would suffice. But would there be enough landing craft?

A principal preoccupation at previous conferences had been the allocation of that most precious commodity of all, the landing craft needed for Operation Overlord, the greatest amphibious adventure known in history—principally the LST. (Landing Ship Tank). These remarkable craft, 350 feet long, drawing nine feet astern and next to nothing under the sloping bows, were designed to run on to a beach or into shallow water to discharge their loads. They were built in huge numbers in the United States, and sent in convoys across the Atlantic, skippered by college graduates, or anyone capable of reading a chart. A placid ship when the weather was calm, in the slightest swell the front of the craft would slap down violently. When the swell became a sea, the LST would all but stand on her stern and come down on her flat bottom with a shudder and vibration which made every rivet hum, caused cups to dance on the messdecks and had been known to throw men from their bunks. Because of their amazing versatility they were in high demand in every theatre of operation and guarded by the theatre commanders like gold-dust.

It was clear that nothing must be done to prejudice 'the greatest event and duty in the world' as Churchill called Overlord. Permutations of time and distance were thrashed out. The only way in which Operation Shingle, as the projected Italian landing was called, could be mounted was to delay the departure of the LSTs from the Mediterranean. There were 105 craft there at the time, and of these 68 would be required for

Overlord. This would leave only 37 in the Mediterranean Theatre. A minimum of 88 craft would be required for the two-division lift which the planners agreed was obligatory unless the force was to be so weak that it would be unceremoniously pushed back into the water as soon as it landed. The only way the necessary LSTs could be found was to delay the departure of those destined for England to the last possible moment. A few weeks here or there would not prejudice Overlord. The craft from the Mediterranean would still have over three months to recrew and refit on return, but to withhold them was quite contrary to what had been agreed between the Prime Minister and the President weeks before. A signal was sent by Churchill to Roosevelt and then the Prime Minister retired to Marrakesh to convalesce. A few days later 'with delight not unmingled with surprise', as he wrote, he heard that Roosevelt had agreed to delay the departure of the LSTs provided that Overlord remained the 'paramount operation'. Churchill replied, 'I thank God for this fine decision which engages us once again in wholehearted unity upon a great enterprise. I have heard from the British Chiefs of Staff that the Admiralty can conform to the conditions . . . Meanwhile here the word is "Full steam ahead." '* Shingle was under contract, but not later than on or about 20 January. Thus the scene was set for what some consider the greatest missed opportunity of the Second World War.

After the original plan had been mooted, extensive examination had been undertaken of all the likely beaches from south of the Garigliano to Civitavecchia north of Rome. It was a gloomy exercise. 'There is no place on the west coast where a full enemy division cannot be concentrated against us in twelve hours,' the planners uncompromisingly reported. Yet of all the places examined, the area around the twin towns of Anzio and Nettuno seemed the most promising. To the north and south of the towns lay sandy beaches, and good roads were not far from the coast, while due north from Anzio a good main road, the Via Anziate, ran towards the Alban Hills and subsequently to Rome. Near Anzio the beaches looked good, and investigation showed that apart from one or two hazards they were good. Anzio itself possessed a respectably-sized port and was within effective range of fighter aircraft operating from airfields in the Naples area; it was also no more than 100 miles from Naples by sea. Behind Anzio, the hinterland was flat with good cover until the broad flat plain of the redrained Pontine Marshes was reached a few miles inland. Most promising of all, both the two main German supply routes—Highway Seven, the renowned Appian Way, and Highway Six, the Via Latina—lay within reach. Highway Seven from Rome and passing

*Winston S. Churchill, *Closing the Ring*, Cassell.

through Albano, Velletri, Cisterna and Terracina on its way to the south, was no more than fifteen miles from the proposed landing place; and Highway Six less than twenty miles further inland.

It was decided to use two divisions in the initial assault, the 3rd U.S. Infantry Division under Major-General Lucian K. Truscott, and the 1st British Infantry Division under Major-General W. R. C. Penney. The importance of securing Anzio port at the earliest opportunity was obvious, so three battalions of U.S. Rangers were deputed to take it in the first wave. As a follow-up force the British 2nd Special Service Brigade of Number 9 Commando and Number 43 Royal Marine Commando were to land after the first wave and link up with the Rangers. Subsequent reinforcement for the operation would be provided by part of the American 1st Armoured Division, entitled Combat Command 'A', and later by the 45th U.S. Infantry Division. This reinforcement was dependent upon how quickly the landing craft could unload—it was reckoned that, dependent on good weather, the turnround could be effected in three days. From the outset, the pace of the Allied build-up relative to that of the Germans became a determining factor in both the tactics and the success of the operation. It was originally intended to provide supplies for seven days only, but General Clark was adamant that this was not enough. Should his force find themselves stranded without reinforcement, maintenance or succour and involved in a long-drawn-out campaign on a hostile shore, there would be only one result—resounding and conclusive defeat. He won his way.

At first, various embellishments were added to the basic plan. A diversion in Rome itself was considered. Insinuating a force of commandos into the Italian capital while the landing was in train would undoubtedly cause havoc. They could land at Ostia and drive to Rome. But there were landing craft for only 250 men, with room only for jeeps and trailers, hardly enough for an enterprise of this nature. There was only one road to Rome, which meant the force would be advancing against unknown opposition on a one-vehicle front. And what would they do when they got there? To destroy the bridges, communications centres and other vital points would be an invitation to the Germans to destroy the city; anyway Rome had been declared an Open City. Besides, the bridges were, for the most part, massive stone structures which would require hours of preparation before they were ready for demolition. The plan, to everyone's relief, was turned down.

Originally, too, it had been intended to air drop the three battalions of the 504th U.S. Parachute Infantry Regiment behind the beach defences, an operation of less hazard and more immediate return. This plan, too, was abandoned for to have transport planes in the sky at the same time as the Germans might be heavily attacking the assembled shipping was to court, if not disaster, very considerable fire control problems. The proposed dropping zone was later discovered to be densely wooded.

It was unsatisfactory to have both nations involved; either an all-British effort or an all-American operation would have solved many problems of administration and command. But the only corps headquarters not already committed to battle was that of 6th Corps, and the only divisions available were those earmarked. Besides, General Alexander considered both nations should share the risks, and the glory.

This was a far from ideal solution for either nation. The military ways of the one were not the ways of the other. To the British, the Americans appeared casual; the conduct of their battles was an ever-deepening source of mystery and amazement. On one occasion a British general approached his American opposite number and asked what was his plan for a certain operation, only to be greeted with the reply, 'General, we don't plan, we overwhelm.' Such an approach to war was totally foreign to a small nation which had been involved in bitter conflict for nearly four years and was suffering from a dearth of manpower. It is true to say that few Americans appreciated how this drastic shortage of reinforcements in the theatre dictated the day-to-day British conduct of war. To them the British reluctance to leave things to chance and their over-dependence on well-tried stereotype battle procedures stifled individual initiative.

Yet when battle was joined against their common enemy the individual fighting men had the greatest admiration for their comrades in arms: the British for the GI's toughness, the Americans for the stubbornness of the British soldier in adversity—and each developed a strong partiality to the other's rations. It was at the higher echelons that the frictions were most apparent and where methods of command differed so decisively. Here it was noticeable that there was little mutual confidence, and no mutual understanding. It was to prove a cause of considerable dissension in the days that followed.

Major-General John P. Lucas was in command of 6th Corps. An elderly man with the appearance of a kindly country doctor and forever smoking a corn-cob pipe, he was highly thought of in American military circles—General Marshall's verdict was that Lucas possessed 'military stature, prestige and experience'. He was a warm-hearted man, a cautious, careful and deliberate soldier, and everyone seemed to like 'Johnny' Lucas. After serving as Eisenhower's personal deputy in North Africa as adviser on tactical matters he was given command of the American 2nd Corps in Sicily, and on the dismissal of General Dawley after the near-disaster at Salerno had taken over 6th Corps. He was six years older than his immediate superior, Lieutenant-General Mark W.

Clark, commander of the U.S. 5th Army. Clark's career had been meteoric. First company commander and then a staff officer in World War I, in World War II he was briefly commander of the 2nd U.S. Corps in Britain until made Deputy Commander-in-Chief of the Allied Forces in North Africa. In January 1943 he became commander of the 5th U.S. Army and commanded the Salerno expedition—a brutal baptism—but he was otherwise without experience of high command in battle. A tall, gangling man with great personal charm, he was loyal to his subordinates and they in turn trusted him. He was highly ambitious, with a fine brain, compelling personality and drive, but it was his love of personal publicity with which his critics, of whom there were many, found fault. Wherever he went the eagle-beaked Clark was surrounded by a bevy of photographers and pressmen. His flamboyant approach was anathema to many, but he was commanding an army in a theatre which many in the States, and elsewhere, thought a fundamental mistake. To the people of America, smarting from the humiliation of Pearl Harbour, the defeat of the Japanese was paramount. The war in Europe was of secondary importance, and the campaign in the Mediterranean little more than a side-show. Under such circumstances, flamboyance and newsworthiness were a very necessary ingredient to command, and Clark was the right man to provide them.

A very different personality was the commander of the 3rd U.S. Infantry Division, Major-General Lucian K. Truscott. 'Old Gravel Mouth' his men affectionately called him, for he suffered from a throat infection for much of his time at Anzio and this emphasised his rasping way of speaking. A deep-thinking man, with a forthright manner, he was at heart a quiet personality. Clad in a leather jacket, cavalry boots and with a pearl-handled pistol at his belt and a silk scarf round his neck, and a varnished helmet on his head, to his British contemporaries he appeared as the archetypal American general. He was liked, admired and tremendously respected by all who served with him. He had been sent to England shortly after the United States joined the war, and at Combined Operations Headquarters he had gained a closer insight and knowledge of the British method of conducting war than most of his colleagues. He had commanded the 3rd Division in Sicily and turned it into what its members felt, and with some justification, was the finest division in the U.S. Army. Truscott was to prove one of the outstanding American field commanders in the Second World War, and before the Italian campaign was over he was to succeed Clark as commander of the 5th Army.

Truscott had a great and growing respect for his commander-in-chief, General Alexander, and their way of thinking was very similar. For Truscott, too, had the ability of stripping a problem of its inessentials. He had the gift, and understood the paramount need in a great Allied enterprise, of getting on with all those with whom he came in contact; he was above and beyond all an outstanding fighting general with a remarkable 'feel' for the battle.

In command of the British 1st Infantry Division was Major-General W. R. C. Penney. First commissioned into the Royal Engineers, in 1921 he transferred to the Corps of Signals, and it was as Chief Signals Officer during the North African campaign that Penney had made his mark. It came as a surprise to him, as to many other people, when he was given command of the 1st Division. An immensely conscientious and meticulous man, he was apt to strike awe into his subordinates. Yet at heart he was a kindly person, deeply religious and a good friend. He was, however, keenly aware of his own lack of experience of the infantry battle, and this led some of his American colleagues to comment on his pessimistic attitude and lack of self-confidence. Yet his commanding officers liked and trusted their divisional commander. He was to command under almost impossible conditions and with great distinction in the days that followed.

The great Allied invasion of North Africa—Operation Torch—had provided an invaluable initiation for the planning staffs. The unopposed landing on the island of Pantellaria by the British 1st Infantry Division had been a forerunner for the massive invasion of Sicily, the successful landing on the toe of Italy and the near-disaster of Salerno. There were only three weeks in which to plot and plan the landing at Anzio, to resolve the obscure formulae of men and vehicles to available landing craft, to determine the supporting tasks of the Air Forces and the Navy, and to set in motion the complicated machinery of the most intricate of military operations; yet three weeks was considered long enough—a remarkable tribute to the skill and experience of the inter-Allied and inter-service planners, many of whom were before long to find themselves concerned in the mightier operation Overlord, or Operation Anvil—the landing in the South of France. Much of their expertise and many of the techniques they had perfected during the previous amphibious operations were to prove invaluable in the great invasion of Hitler's 'Fortress Europe'.

It seemed an age since the 1st British Infantry Division had first practised assault landings on the west coast of Scotland in mid-winter. Many of those officers and men who had enjoyed the dawn delights and bitter weather of Argyllshire in mid-January two years before now found themselves preparing for another amphibious operation. In the interim they had served in North Africa, and after the defeat of the Axis there they enjoyed some months bathing, guarding prisoners of war, and training, particularly mountain training, before carrying out the assault on the island of Pantellaria. In the early days of December 1943 they quitted the warmth and peace of Tunisia for the cold of Italy. They were destined to join the 8th Army which was methodically working its way up the east coast of Italy. Shortly before Christmas a number of senior officers were informed that another move was in the air.

Security was paramount—and in the event wholly successful. The switch, from the east coast of Italy to Naples on the west coast, was surrounded by impenetrable secrecy and was not without its dramas. It was a nightmare journey across the spine of Italy, which even after the span of thirty-odd years, is vivid in the memories of those who took part. It grew colder and colder and the sleet turned to snow as the great convoys of vehicles climbed high towards the peaks of the Appenines. Dispatch riders leading the way had to be lifted bodily from their motor cycles when they were changed, which took place every few hours, and then placed in the back of trucks where their frozen limbs could be rubbed until the circulation returned. The drive was at night, and without headlights.

One Scottish unit moved at Hogmanay. The commanding officer, who had gone ahead, enquired of his adjutant if the move had proved any trouble. 'None at all, Sir,' came the reply. 'I assembled all the teetotallers and they loaded the others in stiff.' There was nothing more conducive to clearing heads than a rough, cold drive across Italy in mid-winter. When the travel-worn battalions awoke the next day, it was to warmth, and orange groves with a background of Vesuvius capped with snow.

On New Year's Day the 1st Battalion Irish and the 5th Battalion Grenadier Guards of 24th Guards Brigade, moved into Gragnano, a small town just south of Pompeii. The locals, experienced in the ways of *molti soldati*, shrugged their shoulders, but their faces of gloom deepened as more and more soldiers began arriving to find billets in the cavernous macaroni factories, which were well-built, snug and warm. The 2nd Infantry Brigade, comprising the 6th Battalion the Gordon Highlanders, the 2nd Battalion the North Staffordshire Regiment and the 1st Battalion the Loyal Regiment who, it transpired, were to provide the spearhead of the assault of the 1st British Division, with the 2nd Battalion Scots Guards borrowed for the occasion from the Guards Brigade, found themselves at Salerno. The 3rd brigade of the Division, the 3rd Infantry Brigade—consisting of the 1st Battalion the Duke of Wellington's Regiment (the Dukes), the 1st Battalion the King's Shropshire Light Infantry (the KSLI), and the 2nd Battalion the Sherwood Foresters (the Foresters)—had foreseen an unpleasant New Year's Day with the 8th Army at Ortona and were still wondering at their reprieve as they enjoyed the scenery around Naples.

In bewildering succession amphibious and other training followed, including driving on and off landing craft and becoming accustomed to the ways of the sea. Such training was interspersed with visits to Naples or Pompeii or Vesuvius. Concert parties and entertainments which catered for all tastes were arranged. A diarist in the 80th Medium Regiment, Royal Artillery (The Scottish Horse), wrote 'The chaps are in terrific form, whatever's coming it's going to be a change.'

What was coming was quite clear from the myriad of landing craft of all shapes and sizes which had gathered in the harbours along the coast from Pozzuoli to Salerno. It was clear too that it was going to be in the fairly near future. But where? The fanciful spoke of the south of France, the optimistic that they were sailing to England. Even when it was pointed out that the landing craft were not suited for such a voyage, they remained unconvinced. Not until most of the troops were embarked were they told their destination.

As conference succeeded conference in the great Palace of Caserta outside Naples—a cavernous place which one staff officer described as the only house where he had had his hat blown off indoors—the final shape of the plan began to emerge. There was a need to capture the port of Anzio as early as possible, for the meteorological experts could only promise one favourable day in seven for beach operating. The beaches themselves were giving cause for concern, particularly the sandbar off Peter Beach, the most northerly beach it was intended to use and where the British 1st Division was destined to land. It was clear that pontoons would be required at this beach on to which the larger landing craft could unload direct. All the beaches were fully exposed, so permission was given to ground up to four merchant ships to create a breakwater, if deemed expedient. For there was every indication that the port of Anzio would not be able to be used at all. A surreptitious but careful watch by aircraft over the past weeks had shown that the Germans made no use of the harbour facilities, scanty as they were, and it appeared that vessels had been sunk across the only channel. Hanging over all the preparations was the imperative need for the bulk of the LSTs to leave the Mediterranean theatre on or before 3 February. This was immutable; the landing would have to take place soon, or not at all.

A complex cover plan was devised to give every indication that Civitavecchia north of Rome was the chosen landing place. Troops and landing craft were to be ostentatiously assembled in Sardinia and Corsica. A naval force was to bombard Civitavecchia itself and a widespread bombing programme devised to sever or severely interrupt the flow of German supplies from the north of Italy by road and rail, and to suggest that landings might be made in Northern Italy or even in the south of France. The Luftwaffe, now reduced to a negligible size, was not considered a major factor in the landing, which was to go in under massive air cover from five American fighter-bomber groups—three of

Kittyhawks and two of Mustangs; three British Spitfire groups, and a British light bomber group flying Bostons. In addition, six medium bomber groups equipped with Marauders and Mitchells were in support and under the command of the Tactical Bomber Force; also on call were the Flying Fortresses of the Strategic Air Force.

The final conference took place on the evening of 15 January 1944 at Caserta. It had been decided that the proposed parachute landing must be cancelled, partly because it was too hazardous, partly because the Intelligence forecast was for negligible resistance. Instead Nos. 9 and 43 Commandos, released from the forlorn hope escapade to Rome, were deputed to take the feature behind Anzio town. The 504th Parachute Infantry were offered to Lucas as a follow-up force. Did he want them? 'Sure,' he replied, 'I'll take anybody who can even heave a rock.'

Some who attended that conference were full of optimism, over-optimism the realists thought. To some extent this optimism was justified. Here, at last, was a way out of the impasse into which the Italian campaign had fallen. By this one blow the entire German defensive system would be unhinged, their supply routes cut; even the El Dorado of Rome would be attainable. It was dangerous thinking and prevented a sober assessment of whether the operation was really practicable with the forces and the landing craft available. General Truscott, whose 3rd Division had been originally chosen to undertake the first Shingle proposal, was apt to describe in colourful terms what he thought would have been the result. Now he wrote to General Clark's chief of staff, Major-General Alfred M. Gruenther, 'I believe that you know me well enough to know that I would not make such a point unless I actually felt *strongly* about it. If this is to be a "forlorn hope" or a "suicide sashay" then all I want to know is that fact—If so, I'm positive that there is no outfit in the world that can do it better than me—even though I reserve the right (personally) to believe we might deserve a better fate.' Colonel William O. Darby of the Rangers put it slightly differently: 'They think it's gonna be all love and nickel beer,' he was heard to say, 'but I don't think it will be.'

Throughout those days, Lucas appeared apprehensive and was in a quiet, almost sombre mood. Never far from anyone's thoughts was the near-disaster at Salerno. Lucas had also studied the Gallipoli campaign with some care and the lessons from that and his own experience at Salerno told him that to push ahead and over-stretch himself before he was strongly ashore would be fatal. The Operations Order of 5th Army uncompromisingly asserted that the 'Advance was not to take place unless it can be synchronised with operations of the remainder of 5th Army in close vicinity of the beach-head.' Consolidation was the key and 'consolidation' was open to different interpretations. On Lucas's interpretation hinge the rights and wrongs, the conduct and the subsequent controversy, and the conclusion of the Anzio landing.

There was time for only one rehearsal. The British version, Exercise Oboe, could hardly have gone worse. The assault brigade were landed two and a half miles from the correct beach. Of the Gordons, the right assault battalion, half were landed well to the north, the other half well to the south of where they should have been. In general, the ships were in the wrong order, the capacities of some of the landing craft had not been calculated correctly and a number of vehicles were on the wrong vessels. In short, Exercise Oboe was a fiasco.

If the British rehearsal had been bad, the American, appropriately called Exercise Webfoot, was a disaster. In order to approach the landing beach from the correct angle, the force sailed far out to sea and then turned towards the coast. The sea was rough, the visibility none too good, and these may have been the reasons why the invading force transferred into their landing craft too far from the beaches. In the darkness, the DUKWs were launched into rough seas, where twenty were immediately swamped and the better part of two battalions' worth of guns and signals equipment lost. Few of the troops landed where they should have done, all landed late and some never landed at all. Not until hours after the first of the infantry had reached dry land were there any artillery, tanks, anti-tank guns or tank-destroyers to support them. As the morning progressed, a few did manage to struggle ashore and join the infantry battalions, but far too late. It was a gloomy augury. Everyone wondered what would have happened had there been real Germans opposing them. Truscott was appalled. Lucas and he asked for another rehearsal, but were told there was no time.

The assault battalions remained on board their craft, waiting for the invasion fleet to collect. Their mood was not bright as they analysed the failure of the rehearsal, sipping the orange juice which was the only stimulant most of the LSTs had on board and wondering if the real thing would be so grim. Elsewhere at Pozzuoli, Castellamare, Naples and Salerno, the regalia of war assembled and the invasion fleet began to gather and to load.

The loading did not go without a hitch. One of the last LSTs to be filled was found unserviceable, and its contents were crammed on board two previously loaded craft. The method of loading is that last on is first off; thus it was that a full field kitchen was one of the first items of equipment to hit the Anzio shore, and a piano with accompanying hymn books followed the assault waves into action. The captain and crews of the LSTs did their best to make their guests comfortable, but to the mildly apprehensive eyes of one officer there seemed to be a shortage of rafts and lifeboats on his ship. 'What do we do if we sink?' he rather hesitatingly asked. 'We can't sink,' came back the uncompromising reply. 'But if we do?' he insisted. 'Well,' the seaman

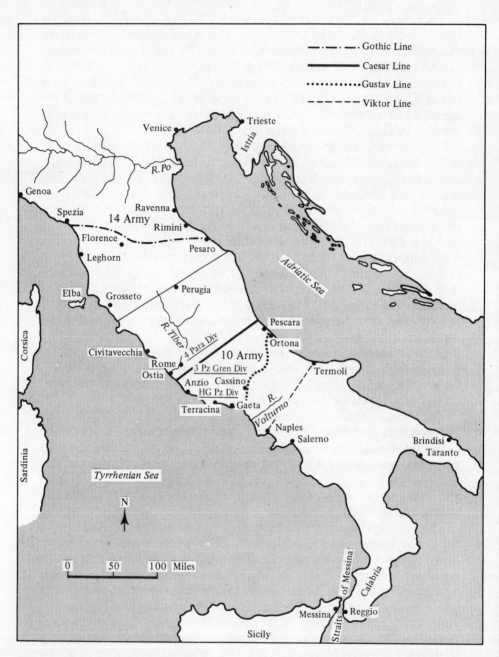

Gothic Line
Caesar Line
Gustav Line
Viktor Line

Trieste

Venice

Istria

R. Po

Genoa

Spezia

Ravenna

14 Army

Rimini

Florence

Pesaro

Leghorn

Adriatic Sea

Elba

Grosseto

Perugia

Corsica

R. Tiber

4 Para Div

Pescara

Ortona

Civitavecchia

Rome

10 Army

3 Pz Gren Div

Termoli

Ostia

Anzio Cassino

HG Pz Div

Sardinia

Terracina

Gaeta

R. Volturno

Naples

Salerno

Brindisi

Taranto

Tyrrhenian Sea

N

0   50   100 Miles

Straits of Messina

Calabria

Messina

Reggio

Sicily

German dispositions, 22 January

replied, 'I don't know what you do, but our orders are to save all sailors!'

The Irish Guards marched out of Gragnano to the Regimental Quick March 'Saint Patrick's Day' played by their Regimental band which was touring Italy at the time. They marched past their commanding officer, Lieutenant-Colonel C.A. Montagu-Douglas-Scott DSO, who was standing on the pedestal of a statue taking the salute. The Grenadiers borrowed the Irish Guards' band for the occasion and marched to the port. The Scots Guards' Pipers led off their battalion, while the 3rd U.S. Division embarked to the strains of their divisional tune, 'The Dog-face Soldier'.

> I'm just a dog-face soldier with a rifle on my shoulder
> And I eat a Kraut for breakfast ev'ry day——
> So feed me ammunition, keep me in the Third Division,
> Your dog-face soldier boy's Okay.

It was all very stirring, but the cynics might have wondered what it foreboded.

There was a spring-like feeling in the air and one of adventure and excitement. The Gordons, as they waited on board, were besieged by Italian bum-boats selling oranges and wishing them luck. Ashore, the troops waiting in embarkation camps were treated to film shows—staccato affairs as the picture was frequently interrupted to call forward men for embarkation. Out to sea, waiting for the invasion fleet to collect, minesweepers ploughed to and fro, while corvettes and destroyers looked busy and very reassuring. Overhead, planes kept a ceaseless vigil to spot and chase away intruders. On board, rumour succeeded counter-rumour.

'What we want,' General Penney of the 1st British Division, on board Admiral Troubridge's headquarters ship *Bulolo*, wrote in his diary, 'is good weather, reasonable beach expectations and a measure of surprise, guts and sound judgement.' Of most immediate import were two imponderables, the weather and the Germans. Just before they were due to sail the meteorological officers gave promise of thirty-six hours' calm weather with a possible extension for a further twenty-four hours. The fickle weather of an Italian January seemed set fair. But what of the Germans? As each day passed and the mass of shipping assembled in convoys off Naples it seemed inconceivable that the Germans did not know what was afoot, and were waiting to pounce.

September 1943 was a month of trauma, catastrophe and not a little confusion for the Germans in Italy. On 3 September Montgomery's 8th Army carried out an unopposed landing across the Straits of Messina from Sicily to Reggio and began the long advance up Calabria, the 'toe' of Italy, against negligible resistance but a lot of mine-strewn obstacles and elaborate delaying devices. On 8 September a task force of warships carrying the 1st British Airborne Divison sailed towards the port of Taranto. This they entered without opposition the next morning. Also on 8 September the Italian Government capitulated.

The defection of the Italians from the Axis cause, although not unexpected, nevertheless added a new and unwholesome dimension to German problems in Italy. At a blow, their late allies became at best passive, at worst hostile to their former comrades-in-arms. For most Italians the Armistice was the signal that their war was over, and they allowed themselves to be disarmed without trouble.

On the night following the announcement of the Armistice the Germans surrounded Rome, but not so successfully as to prevent the King and the Italian royal family from escaping to Pescara on the Adriatic and from there by boat to Brindisi, which was by then in Italian occupation and where subsequently an anti-Fascist Italian Government was established. On 9 September took place the great Allied landing by General Mark Clark's 5th Army at Salerno, and immediately a crucial situation developed. Hastily rushing forward reinforcements, over the next few days the Germans all but threw the Allies back into the sea—indeed plans had already been drawn up by Clark for a wholesale evacuation. At length, after a week of bitter fighting, the landing was established and the Germans began their long, skilfully-executed withdrawal up the leg of Italy. The burning question now was how far south should they hold the line against the Allies as the British 8th Army on the east and the American 5th Army on the west, worked their way slowly and painfully up the long Italian peninsula.

The further south the Germans held, the further away were reinforcements and the longer their tenuous supply chain which was subjected to heavy and sometimes crippling air attacks from Allied air fields in Sicily and southern Italy. To the north lay the economically and strategically vital Po Basin with its mighty industrial complex. Further south lay the essential communications hub of Rome, with its attendant emotional and political significance. All the way up Italy lay a succession of east–west river lines and forbidding mountainous terrain of unrivalled defensive potential—to abandon these would be a military absurdity.

On 21 November, Field-Marshal Kesselring became Commander-in-Chief South West, responsible for all German forces in the Italian theatre. His was a daunting prospect. On the southern front the Allies were closing on the Gustav Line, with Montgomery's 8th Army about to force a crossing over the River Sangro, and Mark Clark's 5th Army across the River Volturno and ready to push forward. In all seventeen Allied divisions were opposed by a mere eight German, and by no means all of these were at full strength. Some had been pulled out of Africa at the last minute and were still only partially re-equipped and retrained; others had been engaged until recently on the Russian front and had little time to reorganise. There were an additional thirteen divisions in northern Italy, but these were for the most part weak, untrained units, short of equipment and so low on transport as to be almost immobile; in any case they were earmarked as reinforcements for the East. Outside the immediate theatre there were few troops available—any that were would be needed against the Second Front which the Germans knew was imminent. Thus Kesselring was forced to fight a long delaying action largely with the forces he already possessed.

As casualties and sheer exhaustion whittled down the German divisions opposing the Allies in the mountains, the army in north Italy became a pool of men for the south and a place where battle-worn troops could rest, refit and retrain, replacing fresh combat-ready divisions previously enjoying the more relaxed scenery of Piedmont, Lombardy or Liguria. This shuttle was wearying of men and material. Although Allied air attacks hindered the two-way movement and made travel by night almost obligatory, air interdiction never precluded the transfer of units altogether.

The troops in north Italy had the unpleasant task of containing an increasingly restive civilian population, for already substantial numbers of partisans were springing up in what was beginning to be viewed by a good few as Occupied Italy. Many Allied prisoners in Italy had escaped during the days of confusion following the Italian Armistice. Some made their way south, either to seek sanctuary in the neutral Vatican or to attempt the hazardous journey through the German lines to rejoin the Allied forces. Some made their way north and sought freedom across the Swiss border. Others stayed to help organise the partisans who were beginning to create serious problems for the Germans in north and central Italy.

In addition to the scarcity of fresh troops and the need to guard their long lines of communications, the most pressing problem for the Germans was the continuing threat of an amphibious landing anywhere along Italy's immense coastline. The five most likely sectors were considered to be Genoa, Livorno, Istria, Ravenna and Rome. Contingency plans were drawn up should any of these landings come to pass—that for the Rome area was called Case Richard. The coast was guarded by obstacles and small mobile units between the principal sectors. In addition, further defence lines and delaying positions were constructed or planned. At the beginning of October 1943 a line from Naples to Termoli—the Viktor Line—had been built; but the Allies breached this later in the month. Thereupon the Germans slowly pulled back towards the Bernhardt or Gustav Line running between Gaeta on the west coast and Ortona on the Adriatic. Further back, between La Spezia and Pesaro, on the east coast, the Gothic Line was under construction. 200 miles behind this, in the foothills of the Alps, work was under way on the Voralpen Line, designed to create a barrier between the Swiss Frontier and Trieste. But if an amphibious landing was to be defeated, immediate action was essential, and this required strong mobile forces on the spot within hours. Thus the perpetual dilemma facing Kesselring was whether to take the risk of an Allied landing and denude the coast sectors—particularly that near Rome—in order to reinforce his hard-pressed southern front, or to risk defeat in the south in the interests of being able to oppose, and if possible eliminate an Allied landing before it could become firmly established ashore.

By fighting a stubborn rearguard action throughout November and December 1943, the Germans were able to impede the progress of the Allied armies up Italy. The longer the advance was slowed, the more time there was to complete the Gustav Line. By switching divisions from one threatened part of the front to another, a task aided by the obliging habit of the two Allied armies of attacking in turn, the Germans were able to stabilise the southern front with comparatively few divisions. It was a wearying process, particularly for the panzer and motorised divisions but it did enable appreciable reserves to be held back, particularly in the Rome area, ready to oppose a landing, for it had been clear since early December that a considerable force of ships and landing craft had been gathering in the ports around Naples.

In broad terms, the German forces were divided into two armies: 10th Army commanded by General von Vietinghoff controlling the southern front, and 14th Army, under General von Mackensen responsible for Italy north of a line through Perugia. At the beginning of the New Year, 10th Army was in the throes of reorganisation: 3rd Panzer Grenadier Division, which had been recuperating south and east of Rome for some time, were due to go to the Adriatic front to oppose the British 8th Army and relieve 90th Panzer Grenadier Division; 29th Panzer Grenadier Division were to move to the Rome area instead. In addition, the Hermann Goering Panzer Division, which had been severely mauled in the fighting around Cassino, was also scheduled to be pulled back to the southern slopes of the Alban Hills. The situation on the southern front did not permit them to recuperate further afield than that, nor for very long.

Thus, by the middle of January the German dispositions north of Cassino and south of Rome were in a state of some flux. 3rd Panzer Grenadier Division were about to leave for the Adriatic front, although they had not yet moved, the Hermann Goering Panzer and 90th Panzer

Grenadier Divisions were on the way in. In addition 4th Parachute Division, weak and largely untrained, were being activated north of Rome.

On 12 January 1944 a series of major attacks were mounted by the 5th Army on the Garigliano front. Four days later after fighting forward with great skill, speed and courage, General Juin's French Expeditionary Corps had eliminated most German resistance and were masters of the heights overlooking the Rapido River. On the night of 17 January the 10th British Corps on the left of the 5th Army crossed the raging Garigliano and by daylight on 18 January were well established beyond the river and attacking the formidable heights on the far side.

Kesselring viewed the pressure building on his southern front with increasing alarm. With the continuing reports of Allied preparations in the Naples area, it was highly undesirable to denude the Rome sector of troops; thus other areas must be stripped first. However, the success of the Garigliano operation at first surprised and then alarmed the Germans. They deduced, and correctly, that the attack by the 10th British Corps was only the preliminary to a major offensive down the line of the Liri Valley towards Rome. As reports came in of Allied success and of their own defence beginning to totter, it became clear that a real breakthrough on the southern front was not only possible but highly likely. An immediate counter-attack on the Garigliano was imperative, and this could only be undertaken by the 29th and 90th Panzer Grenadier Divisions in the Rome area. The German command visualised a quick redressing of the situation on the Garigliano and that the two divisions could then return to their counter-landing role once again. It was also considered that the Garigliano effort would so preoccupy the Allies that any amphibious landing, if any was imminent, would have to be postponed.

German Intelligence categorically stated on 20 January that no invasion was imminent, that the vast collection of craft of all types which had congregated in the Naples area were still there and unlikely to be committed until the situation on the main front had stabilised. It was a grave and nearly fatal miscalculation. On 19 January the redeployment began; on 20 January, the 2nd U.S. Corps started to force a crossing over the Rapido River in the centre of the 5th Army front, and German reinforcement became a matter of the utmost urgency. Thus by 21 January both panzer divisions had nearly all been moved and were poised to counter-attack on the main front. The Rome area had been dangerously denuded of troops. To cover nearly 100 miles of coast only small elements of the two panzer divisions could be spared. The weak 4th Parachute Division was to the north of the city, but otherwise there were only a few miscellaneous units and a number of anti-aircraft battalions of the Luftwaffe—who were to undertake a significant role in the days to come.

It is clear that Kesselring was fully aware of the risks he was running, but the immediate crisis was on his southern front. If the 5th U.S. Army succeeded in breaking through on the Garigliano, the threat to Rome would be as great as that posed by any landing. So uneasy was he though that he ordered a stand-to for all units in the area for the night of 19/20 January. In response to the entreaties of his staff, that he was unnecessarily tiring the troops, the stand-to was lifted for the fateful night of 21/22 January.

By act of Providence, the Germans had played into the hands of the Allies. Could they exploit it?

2

The Landing

22 January

It was a pitch dark night, there was no moon, the sea was like glass with barely a ripple. At 1925 hours, two Folbots* were lowered from a U.S. Submarine Chaser (USSC). The USSC towed the craft, each with its crew of two, slowly ahead, parallel with and about one mile off the coast of Italy. Then, at 2030 hours, they were cast adrift and were on their own.

The crews of the two Folbots knew the water, and more important the beaches they were to mark, for on the night of 17/18 January they had made a previous reconnaissance, the third since December. The first had been undertaken by three British Folbot teams during the night of 2 December; this had provided useful information, confirmed by an American party at the end of the month. During both these operations, a Folbot with its crew had been lost, but it was believed there had been no compromise although the fate of the crew was still unknown. The last reconnaissance had passed off without a hitch and now the two crews were returning to seas which were at least familiar to them.

The water was cold and so was the air as they made their way towards the dark mass of the shore, their paddles barely breaking the surface for fear of showing phosphorescence to watchers on the shore, but the shore remained silent.

For weeks past the beach profiles which the Folbot crews had obtained had been studied minutely by the planners. Thus it was known that off Peter Beach where the 1st British Infantry Division, together with some supporting troops, were to land, there was a prominent sand bar sixty yards offshore with a depth of water of two feet. This would be enough for the smaller landing craft to clear the sand bar, but not enough for the heavier, fully loaded LSTs and other vessels in the assault waves. Careful study of air photographs had shown that there was on average 100 yards of sandy beach rising to thick scrub-covered dunes. On the three beaches, Peter Red, Peter Amber and Peter Green exits looked scarce and difficult, but the most

*A collapsible canvas boat.

promising were those behind Peter Green Beach only 400 yards from the metalled coast road to Anzio. On X-Ray Beach—which was subdivided into X-Ray Red and X-Ray Green—where the 3rd U.S. Division were to land, the beaches too appeared poor but there was no menacing sand bar to contend with, instead a variable and generally unfavourable gradient which made it impossible for LSTs to unload. However, the beach was of firm sand, and behind were irregular low dunes and a rough sandstone road. The sea approach to this beach looked ominous, and it was felt that there was a strong possibility that shallow water mines and obstacles had been planted, although none had been spotted.

But this information was useless if the assault waves were landed on the wrong beaches. Experience at Salerno had shown how difficult it was to be wholly accurate about the positioning of an assault landing. The disastrous rehearsal in the Bay of Salerno had confirmed that even under virtually peacetime conditions the marking of a beach was one of extreme complexity. Now every precaution had been taken. As the last rays of the sun set beyond the Tyrrhenian Sea, H.M. Submarines *Uproar* and *Ultor* had taken a fix off Peter and X-Ray Beaches and then moved five miles off shore. When a channel had been swept by minesweepers, patrol craft would anchor to provide a lit path for the convoys. But the precise marking of the beaches themselves depended on the accuracy with which the Folbot crews found their bearings.

The two crews paddled slowly and carefully. H-hour was at 0200 hours, time enough, bar accidents. The shore came closer and clearer, but it was still dark, very dark. It was disturbing that they could see none of the familiar features they knew they would recognise; the Torre San Lorenzo, a tall, square tower 200 yards inland, or that of Torre Caldara, 2,000 yards south of the southern sector of Peter Beach and perched high on a cliff. Not even the most conspicuous feature of all on that coast, the gap in the trees behind the junction of Peter Red and Peter Amber beaches, and which denoted the precise centre of the Peter Beach complex as a distinct V-shaped cut against the skyline, was visible. Then, at 2230 hours, the crew in the leading Folbot spotted the tower of San Lorenzo; they were nearly there. Almost simultaneously an aircraft passed overhead and a flare was dropped over Anzio. The two canoes were turned out to sea to make them almost invisible from the shore. Their crews stopped, heart in mouth. But all remained quiet, and after a few moments they renewed paddling, a little later parting company. One hour later Folbot 'N' anchored three-quarters of a mile off Peter Red Beach; twenty minutes later Folbot 'S' anchored on its station off Peter Amber Beach. The markers were now in position and the Folbots tossed gently on the almost calm sea. Still the shore remained silent.

Throughout the early part of the night, five great groups of ships which had sailed from Naples, Torre Annunziano, Castellamare and Salerno converged on Anzio.

There were 374 craft in all, from four nations, although the British (210 ships) and the Americans (157 ships) provided the lion's share. Rear-Admiral Frank J. Lowry of the U.S. Navy, embarked in U.S.S. *Biscayne*, was also in overall command of the Task Force X-Ray responsible for the landings on the X-Ray beaches. Commanding the other half of the force, Task Force Peter, and flying his flag in H.M.S. *Bulolo* was Rear-Admiral T. H. Troubridge of the Royal Navy, who was in turn responsible for the British landings on Peter Beach. To deceive shore watchers and to avoid minefields, the convoys had at first sailed south, then, when darkness fell, had turned and headed north. Ahead lay 120 miles of peaceful, almost peacetime passage. The majority of craft had sailed during the night of 20/21 January, thus they were afloat on the Tyrrhenian Sea for a full day as they made their plodding way up the Italian coast. The faster convoys had sailed during the afternoon of 21 January, yet neither were spotted, for German aircraft sent out on the nights of 18/19 and 20/21 January had failed to return, and the main airfield for long-range reconnaissance aircraft at Perugia had been visited by Allied bombers on 19 January and put out of action. On 21 and 22 January the base was closed due to fog. Thus no German reconnaissance plane appeared in the sky, no lurking submarine came to have a look. Even in the insecure atmosphere of Naples, where rumour grew and flourished, and where it was obvious that an amphibious assault was under way, no inkling of the threatened invasion was passed to the Germans. Admiral Troubridge, in his concluding report on the operation, spoke of an assault landing being one of 'peculiar complexity and hazard' and seldom going as planned. 'Shingle', he added, 'was an exception.'

Shortly before midnight the force reached its appointed station. The larger ships anchored, the smaller waited for the channel to be swept by the minesweepers before moving closer to the shore.

The sea was still a flat calm, barely ruffled by a slight off-shore breeze. The sky was starry and clear and the visibility which had been poor earlier on had now improved. To the watching Folbot crews, the time had seemed to pass very slowly. Shortly after they had anchored there had been a few lights from the direction of Torre Caldara to the south, where air photographs had indicated there were German machine-gun positions, but after a few minutes these had been extinguished and the shore returned to darkness again. There was no positive sign of activity out to sea except a growing impression that something was doing. Shortly after midnight there had been some noise from what they had reckoned was an LCT, but this had died away shortly afterwards. From time to time, too, there were vague, indistinguishable flashes of light as one of the marker buoys placed by the minesweepers swung lazily in the wind. Certainly there was no inkling that a vast armada had crept up and was even now buzzing with activity five miles, and in some cases much less, from the coast.

At 0100 hours, one hour before H-hour, the two Folbots started flashing their marker lights at twenty-second intervals. The invasion was under way.

The LSTs had anchored three miles off shore, but the larger LSIs which had carried infantry and must now load them into smaller assault craft, a noisy job, were anchored five-and-a-half miles off the coast. But nothing, except the scare of some floating mines, cut loose by the minesweepers as they cleared the channel, disturbed the peace.

On board the LSIs *Sobieska*, *Glengyle* and *Derbyshire*, the assault battalions of the 2nd Infantry Brigade carried out their final preparations. It was a nervous moment. It seemed inconceivable that the Germans had not got wind of the assault and were even now watching the collection of ships with night glasses from the shore and holding their fire until they could annihilate the assault waves when they were at their most vulnerable. It was not a warm night, but many a man shivered more than the temperature alone warranted. It was the inaction that was the worst, and thinking about what might happen. The sea looked cold, the Italian shore black and uninviting. On the tank decks there was some singing; those on the upper decks spoke in whispers. Meanwhile the well-oiled machinery of an assault landing went into gear.

Inaction was brief. Almost as soon as the release point was reached and anchors dropped, the assault craft were loaded and lowered. Only the gentle throb from their engines was audible to the watchers on board as they moved away from the mother ships and towards the waiting submarine chasers whose stern-lights were to act as guiding stars for the long run to the shore. The lights were to be switched off a few hundred yards out. This would be the signal for the assault craft to fan out and make their own run to the beaches. Those on the deck of the mother ships could dimly see the small craft assembling in line ahead, then they were lost in the black of the night.

'It is difficult to describe one's feelings on that journey,' a Scots Guards officer later wrote. 'It was a beautiful starry night, moonless but with just that suggestion of breeze which made small waves lap noisily on the flat-bottomed bows of the craft. Everyone was very silent, we were packed like sardines in a tin, and the men rapidly got restive and stood up to relieve their cramp.'

On board the command ships there was an air of barely suppressed excitement. It was now less than one hour before H-hour and there was still no response from the shore. No warning shots rent the night, no sound nor sign of feverish activity broke out as the German defenders sprang to life. No tracer lit the night, no searchlight beams probed the sky or out to sea. German radar activity was reported as 'feverish', otherwise there was no indication that any Germans were aware that they were there. It seemed almost inconceivable that they had not been spotted and that complete surprise was theirs, but at the moment there was every indication that this was indeed so.

There was complete silence and no preliminary bombardment until, ten minutes before H-hour, with a spectacular eruption of orange-pink flame and a noise like tearing calico, a rocket ship (LCT(R)) discharged its rockets on the ground immediately behind X-Ray Beach. Three minutes later, opposite Peter Beach, another LCT(R) joined in, the target the machine-gun posts which air photographs showed were covering the beach approaches. The discharge lasted only ninety ear-splitting seconds and almost before the last monstrous firework had been discharged, the first were landing with devastating effect on a tight area behind the beaches. Each ship carried 792 rockets which were fired simultaneously and saturated an area 750 yards long by 250 yards wide. They were devastating weapons, immensely reassuring to assaulting troops, but behind Peter Beach they were largely wasted. For despite every precaution the Folbots were 800 yards off station. Instead of landing on Peter Red and Peter Amber beaches as intended, the assault waves landed on Peter Amber and Peter Green. In the event it did not matter, as the landing was unopposed, in fact it even proved a boon, for it transpired that the only good vehicle exit from the beaches was that behind Peter Green beach.

On the landing craft there was a feeling that the rockets would give the game away. Now there was an almost unnatural silence as the racket died down. Ahead the shore came closer and closer. But where was the searing fire they expected to meet from the enemy who must surely be thoroughly aroused, or the devastating mortar fire just off the beaches, the exploding world which they had all been expecting? But the shore remained silent. Then, with a shuddering grate, which knocked people off their feet, the landing craft grounded and they were off. The landing had begun.

On the left, on Peter Amber Beach, two companies of the 2nd Battalion the North Staffordshire Regiment stormed ashore in the first wave. To their right, the two leading companies of the 6th Gordon Highlanders landed simultaneously with an assortment of members of the Beach Group, who were to marshal the successive waves and organise the beach, and some sappers who were to deal with any coastal minefield that might be met.

It was a minefield on the junction of Peter Amber and Peter Red

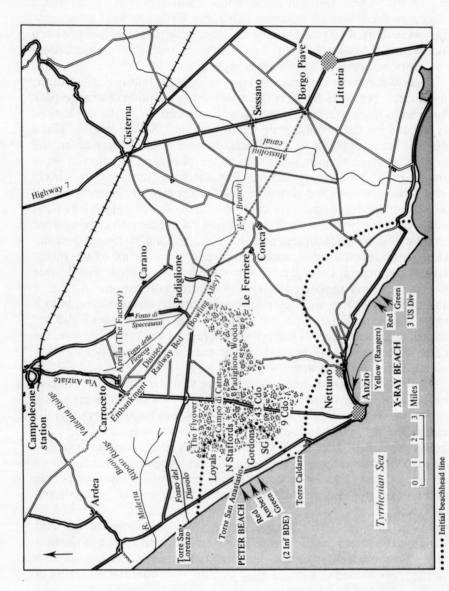

The landing, 22 January

•••••• Initial beachhead line

beaches which caused the first casualties. Forty yards deep, it stretched along the shore, part in the sand and part on the edge of the scrub beyond. There was no indication on the mine detectors of what was lurking beneath the sand until one unfortunate trod on one of the mines, for they were of the wooden Italian variety; to locate them involved the tedious business of probing gently with the bayonet and then gingerly prising them out to disarm them. Progress was at a snail's pace, and dangerous. Six men were killed and fourteen wounded before a narrow single-file lane was cleared.

The second wave, consisting of the rest of the North Staffords on the left and the other two companies of Gordons on the right, had been due to land fifteen minutes after H-hour. They were to be followed by the two leading companies of the Loyals and the Scots Guards, respectively behind the North Staffords and the Gordons. The fourth wave, due to land at 0345 hours, was to have brought the rest of the Loyals and Scots Guards ashore. Thus, within two hours of H-hour, the whole of the 2nd Infantry Brigade were to have landed and been fighting their way inland towards their first objectives. It was not to be. As the delay on the minefield drastically hindered the timings of the subsequent waves, what was described as a 'car park of formidable and ever-increasing dimensions' was collecting off shore.

In a steady procession the small DUKWs carrying the follow-up troops proceeded to beach in waves of twenty-two at a time. By 0320 hours the leading elements of the Scots Guards were ashore and half an hour later the first waves of the 1st Battalion the Loyal Regiment had landed north of the North Staffords, who together with the Gordons had already reached the coastal road and reported no opposition. On the beach, a second path was cleared through the minefield and the waiting troops, now released from what could have been a massacre on the beaches had the Germans opposed the landing, or manned the machine gun posts which covered the exits, shot out of the constricting area of the beach like a cork from a bottle.

Out to sea the Folbots were having an unhappy time. 'The DUKWs seemed to take an unholy delight in trying to ram us,' the Folbot commander somewhat plaintively reported later. Indeed Folbot 'N' off Peter Amber Beach was rammed by one of the first wave and had no sooner recovered from that than they were caught amidships by an LCT of the second wave. With the landing now properly under way, they withdrew with relief, their task completed.

Meanwhile those in the following waves were landing without interruption, but not always in the right place. The first waves of the supporting Scots Guards found themselves 1,000 yards south of where they should have been and faced with an almost impenetrable barrier of thorny scrub. It was to be some time before they extricated themselves and struggled through to join their second wave further north and who had landed on the correct beach. Earlier, some landing craft carrying the second wave of North Staffords had landed well to the north of where they should have been and it was some time before they too could join up with the rest of their battalion. The landing craft carrying the command element of the 6th Gordons duly grounded and with commendable zeal the Intelligence Officer cast himself off into the water to sound it for his commanding officer, only to fall flat on his face in six inches of sea. The experiences of a gunner officer who found his own craft aground on the outer bar were not so pleasant. He, too, jumped off expecting to find that he could wade ashore, only to fall into water well above his head. To add insult to indignity, the loss of his weight forward was enough to free the landing craft from the sand-bank and the officer was propelled ashore with the landing door firmly fixed under his steel helmet.

Elsewhere along the coast the Americans were making excellent progress. On X-Ray Beach General Truscott determined to simultaneously land the combat elements of all three of his infantry regiments so that the fighting portion of his division would be ashore as quickly as possible. Accompanying the leading waves were other small parties, heavily armed and very mobile. It was their task to make their way inland as quickly as possible and secure the crossings over the Mussolini canal which marked the right boundary of the initial beachhead line. Here they were to prepare the bridges over the canal for demolition and hold on against any enemy pressure until the main body of the division could come up.

To the left of the main X-Ray beaches, on the sands between Anzio and Nettuno on what was called X-Ray Yellow Beach, the 1st and 4th Ranger Battalions were to land and storm forward as quickly as they could to secure the town. They were accompanied by a strong team of sappers, whose task it was to defuse any demolitions they might meet on the way. The key points in Anzio were the railway bridges, the waterfront and the port, which would need to be made operational as soon as possible. While on the higher ground behind the town was a coastal battery which could cause havoc to the assembled shipping if not captured without delay.

If the disastrous rehearsal had one merit, it had put the navy on its mettle. The X-Ray Beach landing went, as Truscott put it, 'Like clockwork, word perfect.' The assault battalions were put down at the right time, on the right beach and in the correct order. There were no hold-ups and no beach defences were discovered either behind the coast or in the shallow water. Only one minefield was located, at the extremity of the beach, and obligingly well marked by the Germans. Within one hour of landing, five boat waves were ashore and the assault battalions of the three regiments were well on their way inland, while the first sleepy Germans, some captured still in bed, were being escorted back for interrogation.

The landing by the Rangers was as successful. Briefed until, as one man put it, 'I could pick out the home of the town bootlegger,' theirs was the most hazardous landing of all. Their beach was narrow and sandy and immediately behind lay a sea-wall surmounted by barbed wire. Overlooking the beach were stout stucco buildings, each a potential strongpoint, and each with fields of fire which could have made their landing place a charnel house. Here and there were some gun positions, well-sited and covering the beaches with enfilade fire. From the maps and air photographs the landing looked distinctly unhealthy were it to be opposed by anyone who knew their business. In the event, none of the waterfront buildings or the gun emplacements were manned. Without opposition the Rangers stormed over the beaches, scaled the sea-wall and raced through the town. There was no resistance until the 4th Battalion came across some manned machine guns guarding the railway bridge on the northern outskirts; these they rushed and captured losing one man killed. By three o'clock in the morning, only one hour after H-hour, the reserve battalion of the Rangers, the 3rd Battalion, had passed through their comrades and were well on the way towards the battery behind the town. They captured this later without opposition, the gun crews having prudently withdrawn by then.

It was incredible, wonderful, miraculous, the landing had evidently been a complete surprise to the Germans. A slightly bewildered news photographer who had accompanied the leading waves and been expecting to photograph grim and bitter battle commented, 'This isn't right, I don't like it.' To which his GI companion quickly replied, 'It ain't right all right, but I like it.'

Dawn revealed barrage balloons floating over the convoy, busy beaches where desert track was being laid over the sand and bulldozers hard at work. It was a scene of almost uninterrupted serenity. Out to sea, the vast armada lay at peace, the guns of the warships pointing inland, but silent. Lesser vessels scurried about their business like energetic beetles, and it became almost monotonous to watch the steady shuttle of the LCIs, DUKWs and smaller craft from the larger ships full-laded to the beach to unload and back again.

From time to time a splash would occur in the sea, to remind those who needed reminding that their activities were not going wholly unremarked, but no one paid much attention. And throughout, the sea remained calm.

Peter Beach, though, was proving a worse landing site than anyone expected. For two sand bars were discovered. The outer was 200 yards off-shore and covered by six to nine feet of water; the inner, a bare sixty yards from the beach, was only covered by two to three feet of water. It had been anticipated that only the shallower draft landing craft would be able to run on to the beach itself and that DUKWs would have to convey the support weapons ashore. Anything larger would have to use pontoons anchored on the beach and stretching out to sea to make a floating bridge. By 0745 hours one was working, by 1100 hours a second was operational, and by 1800 hours that evening, 1,000 tons of stores had already been brought ashore over the open beaches.

From the ships waiting to disembark their human and material cargoes it was now possible to pick out the landmarks made familiar by frequent study of maps, air photographs and silhouettes issued before landing. The long, low lines of the dunes were easily recognisable with their scrub and coppice behind. The neat white farmhouses and symmetrical fields were clearly visible in the distance on the slopes of the Colli Laziali, the Alban Hills. If one looked hard, behind the beaches it was possible to see the apparently snail-like progress of the assault battalions as they made their way through the scrub to the coast road. Shortly after eight o'clock in the morning the first German aircraft swooped low over the beaches and damaged one of the pontoons. It was driven away by the fire of every available gun on the beachhead, and thereafter there were raids every few hours, usually by single aircraft. These were irritating rather than damaging, but they did tend to keep people on their toes.

The landing was proceeding far better than the most optimistic had forecast. After the initial delay with the minefield on Peter Beach, 2nd Infantry Brigade was pushing fast inland. On X-Ray Beach, the 3rd U.S. Division was already well on their way towards the initial Beach Defence Line, and the mobile patrols had begun to secure the crossings over the Mussolini Canal. To their left the Rangers, after a little excitement with enemy armoured cars which roamed the streets of Anzio, were masters of the town and by 0930 hours of the port as well. By noon eighteen Germans had been captured and forty killed. The Rangers had already linked with men of the 9th and 43rd Commandos who had been given the task of securing the higher ground behind Anzio and filling the gap between the Rangers and the 2nd Infantry Brigade behind Peter Beach.

Shortly after seven o'clock the 2nd Brigade were fully ashore and were soon joined by some Sherman tanks, whose LCT had been able to negotiate the sand bar by driving full tilt at it, and a group entitled Baker Force of the 1st Reconnaissance Regiment equipped with some dozen armoured cars. It was the specific task of this force to make for the bridge over the Moletta River on the extreme left of the beachhead and protect a party of sappers while they destroyed it to prevent any

44

unpleasant interference by the Germans coming down the coast road from the north.

On this flank the Loyals were making excellent progress. Already they had pushed north through the tangled wilderness of cork oak and scrub which constituted the Selva di Nettuno towards the line of a prominent stream, the Fosso del Diavolo. Their only sight of the enemy had been an armoured car, which they destroyed without difficulty, and a staff car in which were three very drunk German officers making their way back to Anzio after a night in Rome. They were identified as being from 71st Panzer Grenadier Regiment of 29th Panzer Grenadier Division. But that was all, there was no sign of a counter-attack by the Germans.

To the Loyals' right, the North Staffords had completely reassembled after being widely separated on landing. They had suffered a few casualties in the minefield, but having negotiated that, had been able to push on inland without interruption and had covered two miles of scrubland without meeting any Germans at all. The Gordons could relate a similar story, and shortly after dawn they had negotiated the deep ditches near the Torre San Anastasio and secured the two prominent and important heights beyond. The many defences along and behind the beaches had proved to be completely unmanned, the sole prisoner they captured had been picked up in a farm. The only other incident had been when an armoured car had suddenly bolted from a barn and sped up the road pursued by a hail of shot—it escaped. The Scots Guards, on whom it had been impressed how utterly vital was the right flank of the 2nd Brigade landing, had soon struck inland and to the south to prevent interference from that quarter. But there was no interference. Apart from a convalescent German whom they found in a beach hut, the place seemed devoid of enemy. It was almost boring and rather eerie. The only group of enemy who approached them surrendered without a fight. It transpired that they had been sent out to shoot cattle for food, and were somewhat aggrieved at the way things had turned out.

The next brigade to land from the 1st Infantry Division was 24th Guards Brigade. At 0930 hours the 5th Grenadiers started to come ashore. The Irish Guards followed shortly afterwards, ferried ashore from the sand bar by the ubiquitous DUKWs. Their support company commander, Major H. L. S. Young, carried a large black umbrella with the air, according to their regimental history, 'of a missionary visiting a South Sea Island and surprised to see no cannibals'. In fact it turned out to be probably the single most useful piece of personal equipment on the beachhead, for apart from keeping its owner dry in a trench, when pulled down like a mushroom it also acted as a marker even on the gloomiest of nights for anyone seeking out its owner.

45

The Landing

At eleven o'clock in the morning the Scots Guards came back under command of 24th Guards Brigade and shortly afterwards the brigade commander, Brigadier A. S. P. Murray, drove to Anzio to see if he could make contact with the Rangers, who were reported to have taken the town. 'It was a most exciting journey,' he later wrote, 'as for some time we could not find anyone, and we did not as yet know if the Boche had gone or not. However, all was well, though we did meet a few Germans who ran like Hell when they saw us, leaving their equipment just as it was. I suppose they took us for the advance guard of the armoured division.' It all reminded him of what he had read about the Suvla landings at Gallipoli.

By then the beachhead had been visited by Generals Alexander and Clark, who departed having expressed satisfaction with the way things had gone. General Lucas was not so convinced.

The most up-to-date Intelligence available before embarking had indicated that there were no fresh defences or new pillboxes on or behind the beaches—although not even the most optimistic had ever expected that the existing ones would be all but unmanned. The crucial question was the whereabouts of the 29th and 90th Panzer Grenadier Divisions. 29th Panzer Grenadier Division had already been reported on the southern front—although there was no guarantee that it was all there. 90th Panzer Grenadier Division posed more of a mystery. Latest indications were that they were still in the Rome area, and it was from them that General Lucas anticipated the first intervention. Nine o'clock was the expected hour, but nine o'clock passed and no Germans came. Shortly afterwards, General Alexander told Lucas that the 90th Panzer Grenadier Division had also recently been identified on the main front, but Lucas still remained sceptical. At four o'clock that afternoon he approached General Penney, who with his headquarters had been forbidden to land and was continuing to provide a floating reserve should it be needed, and told him that he hoped his boys were ready as a German counter-attack was expected at four o'clock. As General Penney's 'boys' consisted of only two of his brigades, the other, the 3rd Infantry Brigade, was not due to land until the following morning, he fervently hoped that the commander of Sixth Corps was wrong. Four o'clock also passed with no change of tempo. The truth was that the Germans had nothing to attack with. Although their improvisation was masterly, it was long after four o'clock on D-Day before they were able to create a solid front, and some days after that before they were in a position to counter-attack in strength

As a very cold night fell on D-Day and the troops settled down to sleep, it was clear that complete surprise had been achieved. The impossible had happened, an unopposed landing had been made. There had been little enemy opposition except for some tiresome and

46

ineffective shelling from some 88 mm guns in the woods behind the beaches—those were dealt with swiftly and comprehensively by the cruisers and destroyers, who were beginning to feel rather left out of things. A more novel resistance but equally ineffective, was the random shelling by some colossal pieces, the famous German railway guns, which were christened Anzio Annie, or Anzio Express or Anzio Archie, collective nicknames for any artillery weapon over 170 mm. Their shells made a noise like passing express trains, and their rate of fire was very slow indeed. But they were out of range of any gun then landed or of the supporting ships, and although aircraft tried to spot where they were hiding, they failed to locate them and the shelling had to be endured. The only Germans seen were the 200-odd prisoners who had been captured during the day for the loss of 154 men.

There was a feeling of jubilation in the air, but there was also a brooding chilly sensation that perhaps it could not all be as good as it appeared. Inland lay the long high range of the snow-capped Lepini Hills. To the north stretched the equally formidable Alban Hills, so very close and seeming to enclose the Anzio plain. It was as though they were in an amphitheatre, and if anyone on that beautiful day thought of himself as a player before an audience looking down at him from the hills above, he was not far wrong. But there were few on shore that night who did not sleep confident that a determined thrust towards Rome would be made at dawn.

3

Advance

24–26 January

The wait seemed interminable. The initial elation at the unopposed landing had given way to a creeping disquiet that a wonderful opportunity was being lost. 'When are we going?' soldiers would ask; the usual reply that this was a period of consolidation and that 'we were building up our strength', was wearing thin. There was a feeling that precious hours were slipping by.

Throughout 22 and 23 January troops poured ashore. By the afternoon of D + 1 (23 January) the first of the cargo from the Liberty ships was being ferried to the beaches. By 0800 hours on D + 2 the original convoy had been completely unloaded and was on its way back to Naples for more.

Peter Beach was proving increasingly unsatisfactory, for the surf made things difficult for the DUKWs and the shelving shore and sand bars prevented the larger landing craft from reaching the beach. It was decided to divert the 3rd Infantry Brigade, to Anzio Port itself, which had been cleared of obstruction and had started to receive business by the evening of the first day. So, after much steaming about—and a confusion of orders and counter-orders—the LCIs carrying the Brigade started to approach the little port. The 1st Battalion the Duke of Wellington's Regiment were first to approach. 'As we edged towards the little harbour', the commanding officer, Lt.-Col. B. W. Webb-Carter DSO, afterwards wrote:

> . . . we saw a shell hit one of the LCTs which was discharging vehicles at the quay. In sharp contrast to the Naval view of the E-boat menace, these land-projected missiles filled the whole crew of our craft with a burning desire to get us on the beach as soon as possible, and get out of range. We joined a sort of queue and taking our turn at last breasted the small quay. The two gangways were shoved out, and encouraged by the exhortations of the sailors we doubled ashore.

There was little evidence of the fighting in the town, but already the military had made their mark. Signal wires festooned the place, bulldozers were clearing rubble, engineers were at work checking for booby-traps while the cabalistic signs without which no military operation is complete and which are known only to the initiated, were beginning to sprout on wall and door.

On Peter Beach everything was in ordered control. Gaps and paths had been signed and imperturbable military policemen were directing traffic. Sappers toiled with strips of corrugated roadway, while fifteen-hundred-weight trucks and scout cars were being laboriously winched out of the axle-deep sand. The only evidence of the enemy were neat piles of lifted mines and a number of impassive prisoners. Outside the sand bars, the car park of landing craft was beginning to diminish and the pontoons were doing a roaring trade. A captured German officer sat watching the scene; he was impressed. 'Every man knew his place and his job. There was no confusion, disorder or muddle.' And the sea remained calm.

Behind the beachhead, the scene was strangely peaceful. As the Dukes moved to their position, their commanding officer remembered that

. . . the road was lined on both sides with marching troops of the three battalions of the brigade. The environs of Anzio looked attractive. Handsome villas and bright little farms mingled with plentiful trees to vary the landscape. . . . Our positions were in a wood about half a mile from the main Anzio–Rome road on which we now stood. The Battalion streamed in and having arranged for all-round defence, as the best textbooks recommend, we sat down to await developments. The shelling seemed to have stopped.

The 1st Battalion Irish Guards made their way inland and past the little, neatly kept farms with the smell of freshly-baked bread in the crisp morning air.

They passed Italian farm labourers on their way to work and greeted them politely. The Italians showed singularly little interest. 'Dove Tedeschi?' asked the Guardsmen. 'Niente Tedeschi,' replied the Italians, and jerked a thumb vaguely north-westward. 'Roma.' 'Rome,' translated the scholars. 'We will give the Holy Father a holiday,' said one enthusiastic man, 'and make Father Brookes acting unpaid Pope.'

Indeed there seemed no reason why they were not already well on the way to Rome. Whatever were his orders and his interpretation of those orders by the corps commander, General Lucas, there is no doubt that those who landed in Anzio during those days in January believed that they were to take part in a dash to Rome. They were there, so they thought, to penetrate inland and cut the vital road communications to the troops opposing General Clark's 5th U.S. Army.

In half-hearted fashion the battalions dug in. There was no urgency in the air, it all seemed slightly irrelevant in the sunshine which had succeeded a misty dawn. Officers played cards, men wrote letters home, others slept. No one seemed to know what was happening, or more important why. And there, no more than ten miles away across a serene countryside of neat farms and farmsteads lay the Alban Hills, the Colli Laziali.

At this stage in affairs they were beckoning, enticing, tantalisingly near, and even to the most humble of military strategists on the beachhead clearly of fundamental importance. Later they assumed a sinister, brooding presence, a menace, an awesome and ever-present reminder of what might have been. Sometimes the hills were clear and even without binoculars it was possible to pick out individual farmhouses or the symmetrical lines of vineyards on the lower slopes and the neat clusters of white houses which were the town of Albano, Lanuvio or Velletri, names steeped in ancient Roman history. At other times the Alban Hills were merely misty purple shapes seemingly miles away.

In those early days of the beachhead it was all very puzzling, and rather unreal. On the first morning, and on many subsequent occasions, General Penney approached General Lucas seeking permission to probe forward and gain contact with the enemy as there appeared to be so little German opposition, but the request was turned down. Now all anyone could do was to wait, while commanding officers tried to satisfy their officers' insistent enquiries, and those same officers used up all the excuses they could think of answering their men's asked and unasked questions. A little desultory shelling showed that there were Germans about. The occasional, rather distant burst of small-arms fire in the distance told that someone was having a small private battle somewhere. But now the initial feeling of elation had been succeeded by bewilderment, anger and resignation. There seemed nothing to stop them being in Rome in no time at all.

There are rumours that some did indeed reach Rome during those early days. The water-truck driver of one battalion is alleged to have driven to Rome, filled his water tanks and then returned safely—and he now declines to ruin a good story. Certainly, on that first morning, Brigadier T. B. L. Churchill, commanding the Commandos, drove forward in his jeep as far as the railway bridge at Campoleone, fourteen miles up the Via Anziate, without seeing a single German.

When they woke on 23 January (D + 1) it was to the steady drip of rain. This was, for many, their first taste of the fickleness of Italian weather. Gone was the warmth and the sunshine of the day before; instead there was rain, a rain which they came to associate peculiarly with Anzio before long, and which to many is a lasting memory. It was a steady, driving, sleeting rain which permeated everywhere, which turned tracks into quagmires, and flat ground into a slimy, slithering mess of mud. And with the change in weather the Germans seemed to become more active.

As the afternoon of 23 January (D + 1) wore on, the German presence became more marked. With dusk came a brisk raid by torpedo bombers and radio-guided glider bombs on the assembled shipping. By then Anzio port and the beach area were ringed with anti-aircraft defences of all kinds, including barrage balloons to discourage low-flying attacks. As the first enemy aircraft appeared, the sky filled with puffs of smoke as the fleet woke up. Despite the hail of anti-aircraft fire, the destroyer *Janus* was sunk and *Jervis* hit, losing some feet of her bow. Not without loss, however, for the German plane was caught in a criss-cross of tracer and plunged into the ground a little behind the beach, to the huge delight of the many onlookers. So the long second day came to an end, and the sea began to rise.

The meteorological experts had forecast that they would be lucky to have two days in every week when the beaches could remain open. Now their augury was to come true. By midnight there was a slight swell. By four o'clock in the morning a Force Four wind was blowing and giving every indication of increasing. The small craft were sent scuttling to the shelter of Anzio harbour and the beach parties, gathered despondently to watch the wind rising, wondered how the pontoons would stand the buffeting they were now being subjected to.

By dawn the sea was positively rough, and rising. The pontoons were straining at their cables, and by eight o'clock both had broached to and the beach was abandoned as unusable. From then on the majority of stores, the mounting tonnage of ammunition, rations and all the paraphernalia of war, was to come through the port of Anzio.

At dusk on D + 2 the Luftwaffe tried again. Once more with success, for the American destroyer *Plunkett* was hit and all three hospital ships, despite being painted white, with full illumination and bearing prominent red crosses, found themselves targets for a particularly vicious attack. The *Saint David* was sunk with the loss of many lives, the *Leinster* damaged, and the *Saint Andrew* received a number of near misses.

By then the assault brigade of the 1st British Infantry Division had been ashore for nearly forty-eight hours; the follow-up brigade, 24th Guards Brigade, almost as long. The 3rd Infantry Brigade was becoming increasingly restive at the continued inaction. The leading elements had pushed on for eight miles up the Anzio–Rome road, the Via Anziate, to the Campo di Carne (the Field of Flesh) and to what the Americans called the First Overpass, but which to veterans of Anzio was always referred to as the 'Flyover'. They had met no opposition, but they were told to halt there and probe no further.

On the American flank there were ominous signs of greater German activity. On the first evening, enemy patrols had appeared in the area of the Mussolini Canal, which marked the right-hand edge of the beachhead, as a prelude to an attack on a number of the bridges over the canal. The attack was by an old adversary, the Hermann Goering Panzer Division, which had crossed swords with the 3rd U.S. Infantry Division at Salerno and before that in Sicily. The attack was successful and the Germans regained five of the bridges. During the course of the following day the crossings were wrested back, and by ten o'clock on 24 January (D + 2) the last had been retaken. Elsewhere on the eastern sector, General Truscott's division pushed forward to a mile or so beyond the hamlet of Le Ferriere, seven miles north-east of Nettuno, and there met substantial enemy opposition which at first slowed and then stopped altogether any further advance in that quarter. It was clear that here the Germans were going to have to be dug out of their positions one by one. By then the beachhead line was twenty-six miles long.

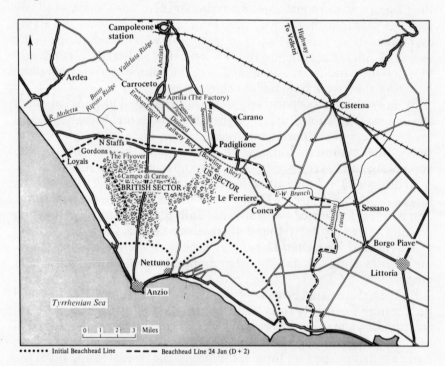

•••••• Initial Beachhead Line   — — — Beachhead Line 24 Jan (D + 2)

The Beachhead Line, 24 January

On the night of the landing, there had been only skeleton German forces in the area of Anzio. A battalion of 71st Panzer Grenadier Regiment, 129th Reconnaissance Battalion and some engineers, all of

29th Panzer Grenadier Division, were in the area between Terracina and Velletri, with elements forward near the coast. The battalion had recently been withdrawn from the Cassino front and sent to the seaside to recuperate. To keep their hand in they had been ordered to set about blowing up the harbour installations, such as they were, in Anzio port—fortunately they had hardly started.

The first intimation of the landing would appear to have come from a German corporal in a railway construction company who was in the area collecting timber. He immediately jumped on his motor-cycle and sped to Albano to give the alarm. By five o'clock in the morning other reports had been received, and aerial reconnaissance at dawn confirmed that an invasion was under way. Shortly after seven o'clock that morning Case Richard was activated.

Within hours of the landing seven more battalions had arrived, as well as other units, and the Headquarters of 1st Parachute Corps, hurriedly pulled back from the Garigliano front, were on the way. Most impressive was the assembly of anti-aircraft flak units of the Luftwaffe, whose weapons, converted to their anti-tank role, were to play a significant part in the battles that followed. By mid-morning on D-Day, a ring of anti-tank guns covered the lower slopes of the Alban Hills and had started to seal off the Via Anziate in the area of Campoleone. In the meantime Brigadier-General Schlemmer, who had recently been in Rome and was now commanding the rear echelons of 1st Parachute Corps, was given command of the landing area and ordered to hold as far forward as he could.

From then on the build-up of German forces gathered momentum. Nine more battalions arrived on 24 January (D + 2) and by 1800 hours on 25 January (D + 3) there were elements of no fewer than ten German divisions south of the Tiber under 1st Parachute Corps, and a further five on the way. But this was a medley of units, partly trained, for the most part inexperienced and unused to working together, least of all with a strange headquarters—indeed command and communications problems were two of the greatest headaches the Germans had to contend with. One of the most impressive features of the German reaction to the landing was the way this hotch-potch of units, arriving in any order and in any shape, were knitted into coherent fighting formations. It was a remarkable achievement of improvisation and pre-planning—Case Richard had proved its worth.

Each unit earmarked under this contingency plan knew precisely when and by what route it must come; where were positioned dumps of food, ammunition and fuel; who was assigned to protect the route from partisans or parachute drops; who was to ensure that the roads and bridges were in good repair and to make certain that the mountain passes were clear of snow. The timetable was meticulous. The troops

53

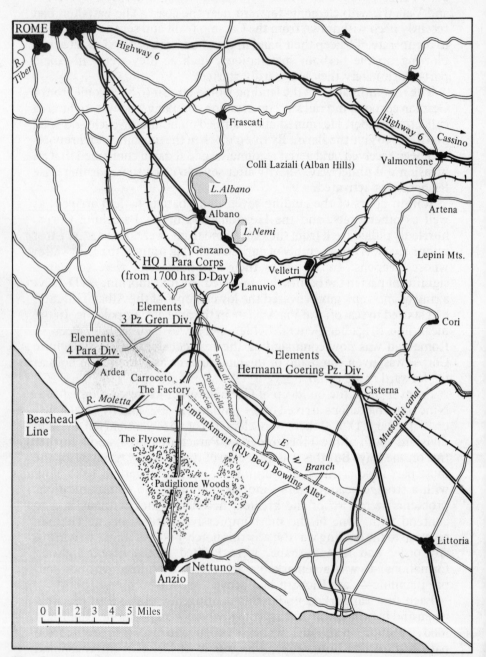

ROME
R. Tiber
Highway 6
Frascati
Colli Laziali (Alban Hills)
L.Albano
Albano
L.Nemi
Genzano
Highway 6 → Cassino
Valmontone
Artena
HQ 1 Para Corps
(from 1700 hrs D-Day)
Lanuvio
Velletri
Lepini Mts.
Elements
3 Pz Gren Div.
Cori
Elements
4 Para Div.
Elements
Hermann Goering Pz. Div.
Ardea
Carroceto
The Factory
R. Moletta
Fosso di Spaccasassi
Fosso della Ficoccia
Cisterna
Mussolini canal
Beachead
Line
The Flyover
Embankment (Rly Bed) Bowling Alley
E
W Branch
Padiglione Woods
Littoria
Anzio
Nettuno
0 1 2 3 4 5 Miles

The German build-up

assigned were at eight hours' notice to move. First off were the reconnaissance and other mobile units, long before the rest of their parent divisions. In the event most were well on their way before darkness fell on D-Day.

Of the greatest significance was the move of 3rd Panzer Grenadier Division. Its units were scattered over much of central Italy, although most were in the area of Valmontone some thirty miles from the coast and astride Highway Six to Rome. Ordered at 0725 hours to concentrate near Albano, by forced marches and despite repeated dive-bomber attacks on the road, in the late afternoon the forward elements of their 29th Panzer Grenadier Regiment were already astride the Via Anziate near Campoleone and impeding any advance towards the Alban Hills.

The reaction of the Hermann Goering Panzer Division was as swift. Within hours their headquarters, which had been in the area of Frosinone, was back operating on the Cisterna sector, and their widely scattered units were already beginning to return to the fold. In the evening there were enough troops on the ground for General Schlemmer—before, at 1700 hours on D-Day, he handed over command to General Schlemm of 1st Parachute Corps—to designate sectors to his fast assembling divisions. 3rd Panzer Grenadier Division was to be responsible for the central axis, the Via Anziate. The Hermann Goering Panzer Division was given the eastern flank opposing the 3rd U.S. Infantry Division. And 4th Parachute Division, which had been north of Rome, was ordered to block all southern exits from the city and to take over the western flank of the beachhead around Ardea and the Moletta River.

That afternoon Kesselring visited the beachhead front. He was considerably displeased that Schlemmer had disobeyed his specific command for the beachhead to be opposed as far forward as possible, and he was incensed that the Allies had been allowed to penetrate as far as they had. But as he watched the beachhead he became increasingly confident of his own position. He had taken a gamble that the Allies would not push on too vigorously and had resisted all the persuasions of his staff that this was the time to pull back from Cassino and the Garigliano front. He felt then, as some Germans still do, that the Allies had missed a uniquely favourable opportunity. The gloom, which had descended on the German headquarters staffs after they had first learned of the landing, had passed. As Kesselring put it in his memoirs, 'I was certain that time was our ally.'

To the Allied troops in the beachhead time appeared to be of no consequence. But at last, late on 23 January (D + 1) 'an armoured reconnaissance' was ordered for the morrow. Fifty hours after the first assault wave had set foot on Anzio soil there was at last to be a proper attempt to gain contact with the enemy defences.

It is one of the criticisms levelled at General Lucas that no reconnaissance in depth was undertaken before. That such an effort would have caused a considerable degree of disruption to the Germans is quite evident, and would have quite materially delayed their build-up. But no patrols were sent out; indeed the landing tables, had they been studied with care, would have revealed that no strong thrust had been intended at that early stage in the life of the beachhead. The 1st Reconnaissance Regiment indeed had a dozen armoured cars (Baker Force) which were scheduled to land at D + 90 minutes, but their next element, 'B' Squadron, was not ashore until 25 January (D + 3) and the whole regiment was not landed until the 28th. Nor was any appreciable force of armour available, as Combat Command 'A' of General Ernie Harmon's 1st U.S. Armoured Division was not complete in the beachhead until 28 January (D + 6).

As dawn was breaking on 24 January, a strong patrol of carriers with some anti-tank guns sped up the road towards Rome, motoring unmolested past neat farms and carefully cultivated fields. Three miles beyond the 'Flyover' the road takes a bend and the railway diverges slightly until both plunge under the raised bed of a disused railway—a place which became known as the 'Embankment' over the days that followed, and which stretched to the south-east—so straight that the Americans referred to it as the 'Bowling Alley'.

They negotiated this first obstacle without trouble and reached the outskirts of the little village of Carroceto and here they came under fire. It seemed to come from a large group of modern buildings beyond and to the right of the village. The patrol fanned out to investigate. As they proceeded from building to building they drew the fire of a number of 88 mm guns, but the place seemed sparsely occupied. By now the Germans were beginning to show resentment at their presence. Some shelling had started and there was the ominous sight of some 88 mm self-propelled (SP) guns and a tank heading towards them, as well as what appeared to be a force of infantry crossing the open ground to the rear and making for the road by which they had come up. With their mission accomplished, the time had come to get away. Without trouble the whole patrol withdrew; their casualties were five men missing.

The buildings occupied by the Germans posed something of a conundrum as they appeared on no map. The place was dominated by a huge chimney, very like a factory chimney from a distance, and ever afterwards the place, which was to be a focus for both sides on that part of the front until the eventual break-out, was known as the 'Factory'. It was in fact a large agricultural settlement established in early Fascist days and called Aprilia; and referred to by *The Times* as a 'typically Fascist collection of institutionalised buildings', but as the 'Factory' it rapidly gained notoriety. It stood like a fortress dominating the surrounding ground.

It was evident that the Germans were in and around the Factory in some force. The prisoners taken by the patrol turned out to be from 29th Panzer Grenadier Regiment, of 3rd Panzer Grenadier Division, confirmation of the identifications of the past few days. It was now apparent that there was to be no easy drive to Rome. The Via Anziate was the only practicable route on this side of the beachhead and 24th Guards Brigade was ordered to clear it next day.

Meanwhile, to the west, the 2nd Brigade had been creeping forward. It was closer, more wooded country on this side of the beachhead; it also held more Germans. The line of the Moletta River was the immediate objective and around mid-day on 24 January the three battalions of the brigade started to probe forward. By dusk the Gordons had established themselves with their battalion headquarters at La Cogna and their forward companies near the Moletta itself. To their right now, the North Staffords were well forward of the Lateral Road which ran due west from the Flyover. On the coast, however, the Loyals were having greater difficulty around the Torre San Lorenzo, later known as Stonk Corner. They had to fight their way forward against heavy artillery and mortar fire, as well as formidable strong-points manned by very active Germans. Not until dawn the following day were they established on their objectives east of the coast road, and the light then revealed that one of their companies was now exposed on a forward slope and in full view of a strong German position across a small valley. They were not extricated until well into the following morning.

A frosty dawn broke on 25 January to reveal a long line of transport formed up on the straight road back to Anzio. The plan was for No. 1 Company of the 5th Grenadiers to capture the Embankment as a springboard for a full-scale attack on the Factory. There was only enough transport to carry two companies of the battalion. The rest had to walk, and as there was only one road and it was considered impossible to get off it, although necessity soon proved that false, the order of march was a ticklish problem especially as the forming up had to take place in the pitch dark.

At dawn a barrage from a field and medium regiment opened on Carroceto and the Factory beyond. Shortly afterwards the leading company spread out on either side of the road and with carriers and tanks in close attendance moved off and up the road to the north. At a respectful distance, a huge column, some two miles long, stretched back towards Anzio creating a traffic jam of monumental proportions. In the woods on either side of the Via Anziate the men of the Scots and Irish Guards stood watching the Grenadiers as they filed past. Ahead lay a flat landscape of tilled fields. To the right stretched a vast area of farmland as far as the eye could see, and on the left appeared pasture land, for the wadis and deep ditches which infested the country to the west of the Via Anziate were invisible except from directly above. Dotting the landscape were the little white standardised farmhouses, the *podere*, single-storied, constructed of stout masonry, with a small shed attached, and set to one side the substantial dome-shaped outside ovens. Standing at their doors the Italian peasants, who had not yet been evacuated, waved handkerchiefs or clapped their hands as the troops passed. It was a beautiful day, the Alban Hills stood out clearly, the sharp frost of the night before gave a crispness to the proceedings, and after all they were now heading for Rome.

Without a sign or sound from the Germans, No. 1 Company walked northwards. All seemed to be going well. But soon came a report that the leading company had found mines in the road south of the Embankment and a slight delay occurred while these were cleared. Then, as the platoons deployed along the Embankment, they came under fire, at first from some houses below the slopes of a ridge on their left and then from Carroceto and the Factory. The Germans also commenced to mortar and shell the Via Anziate. About this time the commanding officer of the Dukes came forward:

> We parked our jeeps among the others [he recounts in their regimental history], and joined the distinguished company. Looking down the long straight road we could see air-bursts feathering the air over the trees. The long line of Guardsmen were still marching steadily in extended formation down each side, but from Carroceto itself could be heard the rattle of small-arms fire. Looking at the dark bulk of the Alban Hills, which formed a backcloth for the whole scene, we could now see the flashes of the two 88-mm guns which were firing the air-bursts. The General told me they were out of range of our guns, but had asked for fighter-bombers to engage them. It was maddening to see the exact position of the guns but yet be impotent. . . . For a quarter of an hour we watched the scene. It seems odd now that the Boche did not open up on the unique target offered him. One shell on the Flyover that morning would have gained a rich return. It was actually the only observation post in that sector of the beachhead, as the enemy soon realised, and that was the first and only day in all the long agony of the Anzio operation when it was possible to stand on the top of the Flyover in safety.

With the Embankment secure, the rest of the battalion could advance and deal with the Factory. At 1430 hours, with the sun full in the faces of the defending Germans, they were off. Under cover of smoke, No. 2 Company took on the east side, while No. 4 went for the west. The first unpleasant shock came with the discovery of how large the complex of buildings was and how solid the concrete masonry. The 'Factory' was the headquarters of the local Fascist settlement, the apple of Mussolini's eye. Its offices, church, school, cinema, garage and apartments were stout modern buildings two or three stories high, with thick reinforced concrete walls, a maze of corridors and interconnecting rooms. Each building was a miniature stronghold. The staircases were jammed with rubble and each landing and corridor a steeplechase course of barricades. The Factory was a town planner's paradise, but to troops asked to clear the area of a wily and stubborn enemy, it was a nightmare.

Fortunately there seemed to be few Germans about, and those that were present were only too happy to surrender. Many were Alsatians who eagerly give information, and from them it was discovered that 3rd Battalion, 29th Panzer Grenadier Regiment were in residence. A few showed resistance, but it was more a question of ferreting them out than dealing with a co-ordinated resistance. In fact for days afterwards Germans kept popping up out of houses or else suspicious movement was seen at upper windows. The presence of these military wraiths, apart from the even more compelling one that the Factory attracted far more than its share of artillery fire, was good enough reason for staying outside the main complex of buildings.

By late afternoon the Grenadiers were firm in the Factory, with one company in Carroceto village, two more positioned around the main buildings and another covering the high ground on the right flank to prevent an attack from the east. But the Grenadiers were strung out in one thin line. In order to give some substance to the brigade position the Scots Guards and Irish Guards were moved up across country, the latter along the Embankment and the Scots a mile or so behind.

It had been a successful day, but in killed and wounded the Grenadiers had lost nearly a company, although they had taken over 100 prisoners. The most depressing thing, though, was the apparent strength of the enemy. One of the first Germans captured was a young officer. As he was waiting by the side of the road he suddenly spied a supporting Sherman tank of the 46th Royal Tank Regiment. His mouth fell open and his eyes all but popped from their sockets, he pushed his cap to the back of his head and in an awestruck voice said, pointing to the tank, 'If I had that, I would be in Rome by now.' And three days before, they would have been.

That night the Germans displayed their skill at infiltrating widely strung out positions, a tactic which was to be a feature in the Anzio battles from then on. Shortly before a cold dawn and under cover of a heavy hailstorm, the enemy managed to move up to within 200 yards of the Grenadiers' positions, and even to occupy some huts not far from the north-east corner of the Factory. As light broke over the beachhead and the rain came pouring down, the Germans opened up with heavy machine guns at point-blank range into the Factory buildings. Not far behind, were a number of self-propelled guns and tanks. This was the start of what was to prove a day of bitter fighting as 24th Guards Brigade struggled to keep their gains of the day before.

The attack, and a companion one to the east down the line of a deep ditch called the Fosso della Ficoccia, was mounted by battle groups of 3rd Panzer Grenadier Division with support from a troop of Tiger tanks and a number of self-propelled guns. Three guns were wiped out almost immediately by the Grenadiers' anti-tank guns and those of a section from the Scots Guards which had been brought up in support; the remainder were abandoned by their crews who scuttled for cover among the huts. There were five of them, with wooden walls and roofs but with stone surrounds and concrete foundations. They were on slightly higher ground and behind them the Germans could form up with complete impunity and largely unobserved. The only people who could deal with them was the extreme right flank company of the Grenadiers, No. 3 Company. One platoon put in a spirited attack, killing or capturing twenty-five Germans in the process. They were not able to enjoy this success for long, for two Tiger tanks advanced directly on the huts. As they had no weapon to deal with the tanks, and as the platoon had already suffered heavy casualties, it was deemed expedient to withdraw. With the seven men that remained, the platoon commander regained their former position, while the Germans took off their prisoners mounted on the tanks—a tactic which effectively prevented the Grenadiers' anti-tank guns from firing. Once more the Germans held the huts.

The rest of No. 3 Company had been under what seemed almost continuous mortaring and shelling from a number of Germans who persisted in trying to work round their completely open right flank. The ground between the huts and their position was completely exposed, but if the Germans were to be allowed to become permanent masters of the hut area, then who knows what devilment might befall the rest of the battalion. So the company commander, Captain T. S. Hohler, decided that he must rout them out before they settled in for good.

The company crossed the open ground at the run and soon drove out the tanks. By this time they were extremely weak, and to add to their discomfiture the tanks sent a stream of tracer bullets through the flimsy walls of the huts as they pulled back. It caused a number of casualties and Captain Hohler himself was wounded. The remains of the company were now in an extremely precarious position, quite isolated from the battalion and with only a single PIAT (Projector Infantry Anti-Tank) to deal with the Tigers should they decide to return.

While the only other surviving officer took post at the door armed with the remaining PIAT, the company commander, feeling faint, went into a hut and sat down beside some meal sacks, to be joined by a Guardsman from one of the platoons, whose Bren gun had jammed. Then, as the regimental history describes:

. . . a voice from the door suddenly shouted, 'Fire, Fire, Fire' but no answering report came from the PIAT. A few seconds later the turret of a tank appeared a few feet away with its gun trained on the hut. Almost at the same time the company commander heard a gurgling sound and saw the Bren gunner being led away with a Schmeisser jammed into his ribs, having been caught with the gun in pieces. Captain Hohler rather carefully lay down, put his steel helmet over his face, turned up his toes, and lay as one dead. The wounded Guardsman was then led off as well, but the ruse worked and Captain Hohler was not disturbed by any more Germans.

He himself managed to make his way back to find his company headquarters all but wiped out by a heavy shell. Once again the huts belonged to the enemy.

While their company commander was having his private war, the remaining platoon of No. 3 Company had their own problems. Attacked by tanks, to which they had no reply, they had retired to the upper floor of a small farmhouse to the south-east of the Factory. There they lay flat on the floor and remained undiscovered until nightfall. In the darkness they managed to extricate themselves.

The right flank of the Factory now lay completely open to the enemy. But they seemed to make little use of the opportunity and in the early afternoon an attack by a platoon of another company retook the huts, with the assistance of some American tanks which had come up in support, and held them for the rest of the day. A small minefield was laid later that night to discourage further German adventures from that direction.

To the Grenadiers' left, the Irish Guards were having troubles enough of their own. With the Factory taken, they had moved up in the late afternoon to Carroceto and extended along the Embankment in a north-westerly direction. The commanding officer, Colonel Scott, wisely ignoring suggestions that his battalion headquarters should occupy the largest and most prominent house in the area, took up residence in his Humber staff car parked near the road bridge under the Embankment; and there remained intact for the next three days.

The battalion was in a rough semi-circle. No. 4 Company was on the right flank linked with the Grenadiers in the Factory area, No. 1 Company was in the village of Carroceto; No. 2 was behind the Embankment, while No. 3 Company was pushed out on a limb covering the approach between the inaptly named Buon Riposo Ridge to their south-west—a long bare hillock which dominated the surrounding area—and the Vallelata Ridge which in its turn overlooked the road and railway north of Carroceto itself. They were spread out across a wide area, covering the best part of 1,000 yards in a great semi-circle stretching from the station building of Carroceto on the right to an outlying farm building where one of the platoons took up residence alongside the placid white oxen, some chickens and a long, thin black sow, which they declared must have been on hunger strike since the day it was born. No one could satisfactorily explain what happened to that sow afterwards, although the smell of sizzling pork which emanated from the company position that evening was evidence enough.

The Irish Guards had reached their position as dusk was breaking, and they started to dig-in in the gathering gloom. And as they dug, so came the rain. Just before dawn a sharp hailstorm woke everybody up. It was bitterly cold and the Guardsmen shivered and waited in their slit trenches for what the morning would bring. The shelling, which had been only spasmodic during the night, increased with the daylight, but no attack came. The companies were just beginning to contemplate the thought of breakfast, and rumours were passing the rounds that the battalion was to stand ready to make an armoured reconnaissance in force up the main road towards Campoleone, when Captain D. M. Kennedy, commanding No. 3 Company, reported excitedly on the wireless that he could see nine enemy tanks silhouetted in the mist not a mile away. This was the prelude to what was ever afterwards remembered by the Irish Guards veterans of Anzio as the worst shelling they ever experienced.

Promptly at eight o'clock the German attack started. As the Irish Guards Regimental History records:

> During the last three days the Germans had been massing every gun they could lay their hands on, guns of every age, kind, calibre and nationality—German guns, Italian guns, Czech guns, French, Russian and Yugoslav guns—modern 105 mm and 220 mm, strange old field pieces and monster railway guns. The air was full of iron dug from every mine in Europe; the fragments were marked in every known language west of the Urals.

At first the shelling was indiscriminate, but heavy, and then it became clear that it was concentrating on the left hand of No. 3 Company's platoons. As the artillery fire started the German tanks began to move forward. One of their first shots neatly sliced a haystack in two and set it on fire; the next all but demolished the farmhouse. Two tanks came up the valley to the north-west and the company anti-tank guns waited until they were within 400 yards and then fired for the first and last time. Both tanks burst into flames and then the anti-tank guns themselves disintegrated under a storm of shot from supporting enemy armour. This was the signal for a full-scale tank attack on the beleaguered farmhouse. Shell after shell tore into what was rapidly becoming a ruin. Then it was the turn of the German infantry. Through glasses it was possible to see what Captain Kennedy referred to as a herd of them advancing towards the ruined farm. They approached down the broad valley along the line of the Embankment to within 1,000 yards of the company position. First the 3-in. mortars opened fire and they were quickly followed by a full battery of 19th Field Regiment who were in support. It was all over in a matter of minutes. Hidden for some time by the fall of shot and a cascade of earth and stones and mud, when the scene cleared, the German infantry seemed to have disappeared. All that was left were a few disconsolate survivors bearing their wounded away. As the last of what had been a full three companies of German infantry departed, the voice of the battery commander was heard on the wireless, 'Does that suit you?' 'Highly delighted,' replied Kennedy. 'So far we are in the win.'

The scene along the Embankment was like a 'Bank Holiday crowd lining the stands for Surrey versus Middlesex at the Oval,' declared the battalion second-in-command, Major D. M. L. Gordon-Watson MC. Others reckoned that it was more like a colony of dispossessed moles going to earth. For No. 2 Company, most of battalion headquarters and a number of tanks, together with a remarkable number of people who appeared to have business in the area, burrowed into the soft earth of the Embankment with an amazing collection of Italian farm implements.

Once again the Germans tried to bring infantry up the line of the Embankment. To start with they were lorry-borne, but very soon they too were in retreat as the field regiment plastered the valley. Then, at last, the battery commander of the 80th Medium Regiment (The Scottish Horse), who had been at the Irish Guards' headquarters for some time, beseeching those in authority to allow him to deal with the troublesome German tanks in the No. 3 Company area, was given permission to use his guns. A few ranging rounds and then the full might of the regiment came down in and amongst the German tanks around the ruined farm. One promptly blew up, the others prudently withdrew. It appeared that for the moment anyway the Irish Guards would no longer be menaced from that quarter.

It was now nearing noon. The Irish Guards had been closely engaged for four hours, though to many it had seemed a lifetime. As the German shelling decreased, and the mist on the hills was wafted away by a gentle breeze, it was possible to see the Alban Hills in all their glory. Then they realised, as all troops in the Anzio beachhead were very soon to appreciate, that as the Regimental History put it, 'The Germans could sit in comfort on the steps of an old monastery on Monte Caro above the Rocca di Papa with a cup of coffee in one hand and a telephone in the other, and direct their guns as if they were playing on a sand model.' The Alban Hills were no longer the beckoning feature they had seemed before, instead they were beginning to assume a sinister symbolism. They became a goal which was not to be reached until a great many men of many nations had lost their lives.

But for the Irish Guards there was nothing to do but sit and suffer and wait for whatever unpleasantness the Germans had in store. During one of the brief lulls in the almost continuous shelling, the Padre, Father Brookes, was to be seen walking slowly up and down the path behind the Embankment with a steel helmet perched on top of his cap and with his nose stuck deep in his breviary reading his offices. It was a very comforting sight and not only to the new men in the battalion.

As the Irish Guards' adjutant sat in the gathering dusk of this their first day's action in Anzio the full extent of the battalion losses began to become apparent: the Irish Guards had suffered 117 casualties, of whom twenty were dead. It was a bitter introduction to Anzio.

The Scots Guards in their positions down the main road had come under direct mortar and artillery fire for much of the day, apparently from the Buon Riposo Ridge on their left. And there was nothing they could do about it but bring down answering fire on known and suspected enemy positions. All day the steady attrition, the gnawing away of their strength persisted.

Things were getting livelier, too, on the line of the Moletta River where the Loyals, the Gordons and the North Staffords of 2nd Brigade were in close contact with the enemy, and where the bridge over the Moletta had been blown on the first morning to prevent any German incursion from that direction. The sappers deputed to the task had found that the Germans had obligingly placed their own explosive charges, so it was a simple matter to complete the demolition. For the watching Loyals, though, there was a rather sombre air of finality about it all. That afternoon the Loyal's battalion headquarters had received a series of direct hits, but fortunately they were able to take refuge in the capacious cellar of a house. After dark they discreetly withdrew to a less vulnerable spot, but not until they had the pleasure of calling down fraternal fire from HMS *Loyal* which was providing naval support.

On the eastern sector, during the afternoon of the Grenadiers' reconnaissance, the 3rd U.S. Infantry Division made a sortie towards Cisterna, but ran up against firm opposition from a mixed force under command of the Hermann Goering Panzer Division who managed to halt the advance. But already the Germans were expressing unpleasant surprise at the weight of Allied artillery fire and finding the maintenance of their forward units extremely difficult. Next day, while the Grenadiers were having their Factory battle, two full battalions of the 3rd Division pushed up the main approach roads to Cisterna. One thrust reached as far as two miles beyond the east–west branch of the Mussolini Canal, which ran across their front, before meeting strong German positions. Another thrust went nearly as far until it too ran into strong enemy forces who made skilful use of every building, converting them into formidable little strong-points and covering the gaps between these miniature fortresses with roving tanks and SP-guns. Each fortress required a full-scale attack to deal with it, and each imposed a considerable delay on troops who were anxious to push on as quickly as possible. Despite the intervention of the 504th Parachute Infantry Regiment and the guns of USS *Brooklyn*, 3rd Division was still three miles short of Cisterna as dusk fell. General Truscott called a halt, for it was clear that a full-scale, carefully mounted attack was going to be needed to dislodge the enemy.

Between the 3rd Division and the British, the Rangers, with the 509th Parachute Infantry Battalion in support, moved in concert with the Grenadiers' attack, up the line of the Spaccasassi Creek. They reached the point where the creek changed direction to run east–west but there were held up by severe enemy artillery fire. Next day they attacked north and gained some valuable ground, but once again were held up, like their comrades near Cisterna, by stubborn resistance on the part of small bodies of enemy who occupied a cluster of farm and dairy buildings. These had to be cleared one by one, room by room in bitter hand-to-hand fighting. But by noon on 26 January the Rangers were masters of the Spaccasassi Creek to a point rather north-east of the Factory. Ahead lay woods and a large number of the enemy who, so prisoners said, were receiving massive reinforcements. And here, preventing any German advance down the line of the Spaccasassi, the Rangers stayed until finally relieved by the 1st Reconnaissance Regiment on 28 January.

General Lucas's build-up had been badly delayed by the weather. Although one of the three regiments of the 45th U.S. Infantry Division was now ashore, the rest were not due for some days. More critically, Combat Command 'A' of General Harmon's 1st U.S. Armoured Division which had been held up by storms, would not arrive for at least two days. Thus Lucas determined to wait until his main striking force had collected; he then intended making a concerted attack with the 1st British Infantry Division and the armoured division towards Campoleone, while Truscott's 3rd U.S. Infantry Division attacked at the same time towards Cisterna.

4

Expanding the Beachhead

26–31 January

There seemed little doubt to those in close contact that the enemy were in position in some strength, but Intelligence was scanty and there was a reluctance in higher quarters to believe that the Germans could possibly have reinforced as quickly as they had. It was decided that a patrol should be sent up the road to see how far it could get and report on the enemy opposition. On 26 January a platoon of the Irish Guards with a section of carriers drove north. They reached Milestone 23, two-and-a-half miles north of Carroceto and the same distance short of Campoleone, before the Germans took exception to their presence. The patrol withdrew to some higher ground from where they could observe the surrounding countryside. But they had satisfied themselves that the area was strongly held by the Germans.

This information was more than confirmed the next day by a strong and highly successful patrol of the 1st Reconnaissance Regiment under Lieutenants R. G. A. Beale and P. M. Grinley which penetrated two miles across country, skirting the Vallelata Ridge, which flanked the west side of the Via Anziate beyond Carroceto, to the railway bridge west of Milestone 23. Here they found the Germans in secure occupation, and after accounting for forty of them, as well as successfully dealing with an engineer party who were intending to lay demolition charges under the bridge, they withdrew with a number of prisoners and a lot of information. It was clear that the Germans had brought up a large number of troops to seal off the beachhead.

By this time the German line had already been thickened by the arrival of a number of new formations from a variety of divisions, while tactical reconnaissance reports told of a lot of activity in the Rome marshalling yards and continual movement of lorries heading south. On the eve of the next Allied attacks, on 29 and 30 January, the bulk of 65th Infantry Division had come into position to the west of the Via Anziate between 3rd Panzer Grenadier Division and 4th Parachute Division. Elements of 71st Infantry Division, diverted on their way to Cassino, were also in the line to the right of the Hermann Goering Panzer Division opposite the Americans and, providentially for the Germans, 26th Panzer Division reached Cisterna just before the main

American attack on the town took place. In addition, the first units of 114th Jaeger Division had been identified in the area east of the Via Anziate. In all, it was a nightmare for Allied Intelligence officers as units kept turning up from strange divisions which should by rights have been in Yugoslavia or had last been heard of in France.

There was increasing confidence in the German camp that the immediate danger had passed. As early as 23 January (D + 1), planning for a counter-attack five days later had started, but a shortage of supplies due to the winter weather and, to a lesser extent, Allied air interdiction, had delayed the assembly of the Case Richard forces. The counter-offensive was postponed to 1 February, and in the event did not take place until the 3rd of that month. But all through the latter days of January, the German reinforcements poured in from North Italy and elsewhere. Those from Germany had already left and were due to cross the Brenner Pass on 26 or 27 January. By the time the Allies were ready for their first major push to break out of their beachhead there were elements of no less than twelve divisions opposing them.

There had been changes in the German command structure, too. On 25 January Colonel-General Eberhard von Mackensen, commanding 14th Army (AOK 14), took over the tactical command of the Rome area, which included Anzio, with his headquarters just north of the capital. Hitler also was taking an increasing interest in the beachhead. On 28 January it was announced that the 'Battle of Rome' was starting, a conflict which was to be 'hard and merciless . . . not only against the enemy,' which was fair enough, 'but against all officers and units who fail in this decisive hour'—a curious note of defeatism. The 'Abscess South of Rome', as he called it, was about to be lanced.

On 27 January, the Scots Guards were sent to occupy a large farm north of the Factory, later to become known as Dung Farm—Smelly Horse Farm to the Germans—from the overpowering smell of rank manure and dead livestock which pervaded the place. During the night the Scots Guards moved forward to the farm, and by dawn the companies were well dug in some 1,500 yards forward of the Factory, and almost without casualties, except for the tragic loss of two company commanders.

Throughout this time the Irish Guards patrol had remained on their small hill by Milestone 23 reporting on enemy activity, but the Germans made no move even to drive them from their point of vantage. The enemy seemed remarkably quiescent, except for frequent shelling.

The occupation of Dung Farm by the Scots Guards was a preliminary to the next move forward by the division. It was decided that later that day, 28 January, 24th Guards Brigade would secure the lateral track 2,000 yards forward of Dung Farm in the area of Milestone 23 as a start line for a full-scale attack by the 3rd Brigade, who were fresh and had so

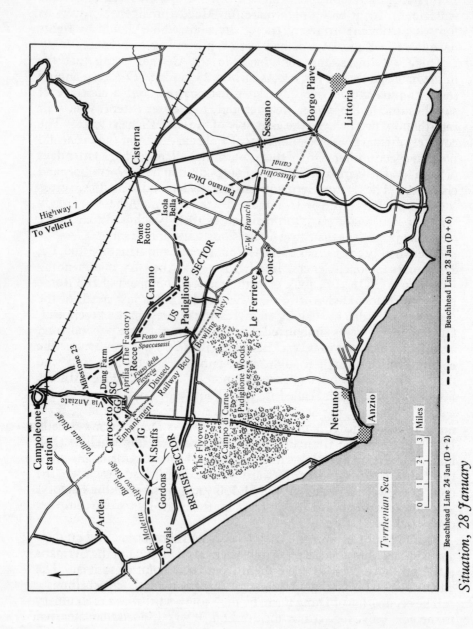

Situation, 28 January

Beachhead Line 24 Jan (D + 2)

Beachhead Line 28 Jan (D + 6)

far been uncommitted, to take the Campoleone area next day as a prelude to the promised break-out of the armour. The Irish Guards were to stay where they were in the area of Carroceto and the Embankment observing the left flank of what was beginning to appear a none-too-wide salient, while the Grenadiers moved up level with the Scots to attack in concert with them.

In the early afternoon Colonel Scott of the Irish Guards went forward to the Scots Guards' headquarters in Dung Farm from where the best view of the country ahead could be obtained from a window in a barn. Already there was the acting commanding officer of the Grenadiers, Major W. E. P. Miller, who had called forward his company commanders to brief them on the spot—the commanding officer, Lt.-Col. G. C. Gordon-Lennox DSO and the second-in-command, Major E. J. B. Nelson MC, having been wounded during the previous days. Shortly afterwards the brigade commander came up too.

They waited. They waited for some time, until a harassed officer burst in with the shattering news that the Grenadiers' Orders ('O') Group of company commanders had overshot the turning into Dung Farm, driven off towards Campoleone and been ambushed.

The way had appeared deceptively simple on the map—straight up the main road and then right down the turning to Dung Farm. The trouble was that the turn was almost indistinguishable from many other turns off the Via Anziate. There were eleven men in the party in three jeeps and they had driven north fully confident of their whereabouts. Suddenly everything became very quiet, there was no sign of anyone, and even the shelling seemed to have ceased. Their confidence was now tinged with the faintest tremor of apprehension. But the straight road ahead seemed clear, so they drove on. They came to a place where a huge crater had been blown in the road, but the jeeps negotiated that successfully; then, 100 yards further on, was another crater and, remarkably, a German walked round the corner of the road about eighty yards ahead and with the greatest unconcern watched them approach. Someone aimed to shoot him, but then lowered his rifle. It was too unsporting, especially as the German still showed no reaction to his enemies who were almost upon him. But now it was clear they must have overshot the turning. The drivers swung their jeeps across the narrow roadway and started to turn round, while the occupants of the jeeps jumped out and prepared to deal with any other Germans who might be about. Then an anti-tank gun opened up from a patch of scrub across a valley and this was followed by a hail of fire from spandaus and schmeissers with some grenades thrown in for good measure.

One of the jeeps was hit by the first shot and immediately burst into flames. The driver of another was wounded, his vehicle crashed into a bank across the road, and the third now drew down upon it all the weight of the German fire.

The incident was a tragic blow to the Grenadiers. Three officers and the three jeep drivers had been killed; another officer, it transpired, had been wounded and captured; only four escaped, rather shaken after the experience. It meant that of the thirteen officers in the four rifle companies who had arrived on the beachhead six days before only four survived, and the Grenadiers could only muster ten fit officers in all. The rest of the battalion were still in the Factory and dusk was not far off. To assemble and bring forward a new team of company commanders in time to see the ground and to organise what would by then have been a very late afternoon attack would not have been possible, so General Penney decided to postpone the attack of 1st British Infantry Division by twenty-four hours. It was a delay which in retrospect can be seen to have had the profoundest effect on subsequent events.

That evening the Sherwood Foresters of 3rd Brigade moved up to take over the Factory, while the Grenadiers pulled back to the Padiglione Woods to reorganise. That evening also the Rangers completed their hand-over of the area between the Factory and the Fosso di Spaccasassi to the 1st Reconnaissance Regiment and pulled back to an assembly area in the north-east corner of the beachhead.

Intelligence from higher formations was still scanty. Division and Corps headquarters persisted in maintaining that only a thin screen of Germans lay between the forward line and their objectives. They were quite unaware that already the Germans outnumbered those in the beachhead and that the adverse ratio was deteriorating daily. There was the greatest confidence that with vigorous pressure Campoleone could be taken without undue trouble, and that General Truscott's 3rd Infantry Division would soon be able to secure Cisterna. Those in the forward companies along the beachhead line were inclined to think otherwise. During a spell of active patrolling the Irish Guards had managed to take a couple of prisoners. One was a pioneer who was clearly delighted to have been taken prisoner: 'Nichts mehr Krieg, boom, boom,' he would say, grinning all over his face. The other was a different case. A hard-faced warrant officer, as the Irish Guards Intelligence Officer described him, who persisted in keeping his rat-trap mouth shut and refused to explain the parachute insignia on his jacket, the row of medal ribbons on his chest or the commendation for sterling work during the German airborne invasion of Crete. He could not be a parachutist, there were no parachutists on the front, the Intelligence experts explained, all but implying that the Irish Guards had invented the man, although earlier in the day one of the forward posts had reported three fresh German companies moving into position opposite them and expressed the conviction that these were parachute troops.

There were further frustrations for those at corps headquarters planning the break-through. For the last days Company Command 'A' of the 1st U.S. Armoured Division had been assembling in the beachhead. General Harmon's operational headquarters was ashore by 25 January (D + 3), but not until two days later, due to heavy storms on the Tyrrhenian Sea, did the rest of the combat group arrive at Anzio. On the afternoon of 29 January they made their first reconnaissance in force in preparation for the grand thrust the next day.

Three companies of the 1st Armoured Regiment drove up the Via Anziate from the Padiglione Woods to the Flyover. Here they turned left and soon were heading north-west towards the Buon Riposo Ridge. There were no enemy to be seen, it was all very quiet, until they were fired on by some 88-mm guns as they reached a house near the crossing of the Fosso di Carroceto. Swinging right-handed, the party then made their way below the Buon Riposo Ridge until the leading elements came on the railway Embankment north-west of Carroceto, where again they came under fire. Night was drawing in so they pulled in to some nearby fields and prepared to bivouac. The ground had appeared firm, but as the night wore on the vehicles sank deeper in the mud until they were thoroughly bogged. The troops spent the rest of the hours of darkness wearily winching them to higher and firmer ground. So much for the initial Intelligence Summary which had declared, 'The left flank of the bridgehead area consists of undulating country, thickly intersected by shallow streams which, even in wet weather, would exercise only a delaying influence on armour.'

General Lucas's grand design to break out of the beachhead involved a two-pronged thrust: to the west, along the line of the Via Anziate, Penney's 1st British Infantry Division was to take Campoleone and the road junction beyond. With that secure, 1st U.S. Armoured Division would pass through, swing to the left through the foothills and take the Alban Hills from the west. While this was happening, Truscott's 3rd Infantry Division, with the Rangers and the 504th Parachute Infantry Regiment in support, would capture Cisterna with a view to cutting Highway Seven and continuing the advance towards Velletri.

Opposing the 3rd Infantry Division were the Hermann Goering Panzer Division covering a huge front. But their line consisted of a series of strong-points, separated by huge gaps and not mutually supporting. All in all it was a situation which cried out for infiltration, one tailor-made for the Rangers.

These specially picked and trained men had been formed by Truscott when still a Brigadier-General and stationed in Northern Ireland.

Expanding the Beachhead

Modelled on the Commandos—the name Ranger was of Truscott's devising—he had been their inspiration in their formation and training. It was not surprising that he held a special affection for the élite formation now commanded by one of his own former officers, Colonel Bill Darby. The task now given to the Rangers was one peculiarly well suited to such a lightly armed special force, and it was intended that during darkness they would penetrate the German lines, enter Cisterna and hold it until the rest of the 3rd Division could reach them. It was a bold plan, and on 29 January it might have worked, but by the 30th when it was put into effect, the widely dispersed Hermann Goering Panzer Division had been substantially reinforced by units from 26th Panzer Division. The stage was set for the greatest of the many tragedies of Anzio.

The Rangers were far from fresh when they were relieved by the 1st Reconnaissance Regiment on 28 January. For five days they had been in the line, subject to frequent artillery fire and occasional air attacks. They pulled back to an assembly area behind the 3rd Division and happily slept the night through. Shortly after daybreak they learned of their new task. The plan was that at nine o'clock that evening they were to move to an area a few hundred yards north of the east–west branch of the Mussolini Canal on the road to Cisterna. At 0100 hours the following morning the 1st and 3rd Ranger Battalions were to approach Cisterna along a creek to the east of the road called the Fosso Pantano on the map. This seemed to run almost to Cisterna itself. Once clear of the ditch they were to enter Cisterna before dawn and occupy the town until relieved by the rest of the division. The division was to jump off at 0200 hours with the 4th Ranger Battalion driving up the main road behind the 1st and 3rd, while the 7th and 30th Infantry Regiments kept pace on either side. The opposition was not expected to be too heavy and the road appeared to be only held by outposts, nor had patrols reported many signs of enemy in the vicinity. As soon as it was daylight and the roads had been cleared of mines, the armour and tanks were then to drive through in one irresistible thrust to relieve the Rangers in Cisterna and push on towards Velletri.

Those officers who could get forward and see the country they were to attack over were reassured. It was good farming country, almost completely flat and with irrigation ditches interlacing the whole district, while here and there the white *podere* dotted the landscape. The country appeared unspoiled, but more important it also appeared to be empty of Gemans, except for a burned-out German tank a couple of miles up the dead straight road.

As night fell in the Rangers' assembly area, weapons were checked and then re-checked, bayonets and knives were sharpened, sticky grenades to deal with tanks were issued, tracer bullets removed from magazines—for there was no need to advertise their presence should they need to open fire during the dark—and extra grenades placed in any available pocket. Spirits were high, for a mail delivery was expected any moment—the first since landing. In the event it arrived too late. Promptly at 2100 hours the Rangers left the assembly area. In the lead were the 1st Battalion, then came the 3rd, while the 4th drew up the rear.

It was a dark, bitterly cold night, and quite silent, except for some heavy shelling far away to their left in the British sector. Promptly at 0100 hours the two leading battalions crossed their Line of Departure (as the Americans call what the British refer to as the Start Line) and swung to the right of the main road. Then working on a compass bearing, they headed due north along the Pantano Ditch.

One hour later the 4th Battalion of Rangers set off up the ditches on either side of the road to Cisterna. It was still very dark, it was still very quiet. Then, less than half a mile from their jumping-off point, the enemy seemed to come awake. First a lone spandau opened up and then what appeared to be a wall of tracer bullets criss-crossed their front. The leading companies stormed forward, but the German positions were very strong, and soon the following troops still sheltering in the ditches found themselves subject to savage and accurate mortar fire. No one had imagined that the Germans would be so securely entrenched. It was an unpleasant discovery, and the first inkling for Colonel Darby in his headquarters near the Rangers' assembly area that all was not as well as he had hoped.

Attempts to outflank the Germans met with little success, for as soon as the companies started to work their way to the right or left they found that the Germans were equally strong on the new sector. It was rapidly becoming apparent that the huge gaps they had hoped to find in the German line were no longer there. The Rangers lay low in the irrigation ditches in knee-deep, icy cold water firing at flashes which seemed to be all around them. Every approach appeared to be covered by strong enemy positions. Heavy artillery fire, to discourage any tank support, came down on the road behind them. It was a defence handled with masterly skill. Through the night the battle raged. Dawn revealed the 4th Rangers pinned down only a short distance from the point from which they had started, having suffered heavy casualties for no apparent appreciable territorial gain. At daybreak tanks and Tank Destroyers came forward to help. One by one the houses holding the enemy were torn apart, but then they were stopped by a minefield across the road covered by anti-tank gun fire and snipers.

Meanwhile the 1st and 3rd Rangers were working their way up their ditch in single file with the 1st Battalion in the lead. Their orders were to pass the 1st through to Cisterna come what may; if any opposition was met, then the 3rd was to deal with it. But there was no opposition, apart from a few isolated sentries who were killed silently and efficiently. Quietly the long column snaked its way up the almost dry ditch. There was a sinister silence, except for the sound of heavy firing to the left and then behind them. 'The 4th are having a bad time,' someone whispered. This was ominous, for the other Ranger battalion had started an hour later. At any moment they expected to be discovered and the alarm sounded, but, seemingly, the Germans were quite unaware of what was happening. Patrols went by on either side, but were allowed to pass. From time to time flares shot into the night, bathing the country in light, but the long line of men remained undetected. At one moment they found themselves behind a German battery and could clearly hear orders being passed to the enemy gunners, who were by that time heavily involved with the attack by the 4th Rangers. No one spotted the men passing right through their positions.

These incidents slowed their progress. Worse was to come, for when they reached the Cisterna road, a column of enemy vehicles was driving along it and the men had to cross one at a time. Around 0545 hours the 1st Battalion reached a position behind a German post. Major Jack Dobson, the commanding officer, realising that they were well behind time tried to make contact on the radio to report the situation. But the radio was dead and there was then nothing else to do than to follow orders and press on as fast as they could to reach Cisterna before daybreak.

When the sky started to lighten the forward elements of the 1st Battalion were still 800 yards short of their objective; between them and Cisterna lay level fields. The only chance now rested on a dash for the town. Springing from their ditch they rushed forward, and ran straight into Germans sleeping in a bivouac area. Most were bayoneted where they lay, but others gave the alarm. Beyond the bivouac area was a slight rise and here the Rangers were pinned down tantalisingly near their objective by heavy fire from troops south of Cisterna.

This was the signal for the Germans in the farmhouses along the Pantano ditch to come to life and start firing. In all, the Ranger battalions stretched back for over 1,000 yards, and only in a few places were they strong enough to undertake any but isolated actions against the Germans who poured in a withering fire at almost point-blank range on the trapped men below. Some Rangers charged the farmhouses and killed the occupants; others dug in to the banks of the ditch and challenged the Germans to come and get them. Then German mortars and artillery, up to then engaging targets to the south, were turned about and started to fire on the almost unprotected Rangers, irrespective of the risk to their own troops.

Reacting swiftly, the Germans started to press in on all sides. An armoured column of seventeen tanks began to work their way methodically up the ditch—shooting Rangers as they went—quite probably it was the one the Rangers had passed in the night. At first, as the column had come from the rear, they were thought to be American tanks, but when it was discovered they were not, the Rangers rose wrathfully from their ditch and despite heavy casualties planted sticky bombs on the tanks and the SP guns accompanying them. Fifteen were destroyed, two were captured and their crews eliminated. The Rangers manned the surviving tanks, but they were destroyed by their comrades, unaware who was in them.

By then one of the battalion commanders had been killed, the other wounded. The Rangers were very weak, their ammunition low and with all the Bazooka bombs expended. Towards noon other enemy columns started to converge on the Rangers from the Cisterna direction. Skilfully the Germans divided the remaining men into small groups and set about methodically rounding them up. Whenever opposition was met they pushed ahead a number of captured Rangers and threatened to shoot them unless their comrades surrendered.

At 1215 hours those around Colonel Darby heard a last poignant radio conversation with his old sergeant-major who manned the only set still working. Although disjointed it tells in anguished terms of the agony the Rangers were suffering:

> Shoot them if they come any closer . . . Issue some orders but don't let the boys give up! Get the officers to shoot! Don't let them do it! Get the old men together and lam for it . . . we're coming through. Hang on to this radio until the last minute. Stick together . . . use your head and do what is best. You're there, and I'm here, unfortunately, and I can't help you, but whatever happens, God bless you.*

At 1230 hours communications with the 1st and 3rd Ranger Battalions ceased. Of a strength of 767 Rangers who went in, six came out. Of the remainder, over half were either killed or wounded.

It was a propaganda success of mammoth proportions for the Germans. With much huffing and puffing the captured Rangers, the 'Prize Catch', were led through Rome as prisoners by their captors in a triumphal march. 'The Rangers have at last entered Rome, but they have come not as conquerors, but as our prisoners,' trumpeted the Germans. Curiously, when heads were counted later, they found that there were fewer Rangers than they had started out with! The escapees were the founder members of what became known as the Ranger Houdini Club, which was to include a good few of these magnificent

History of the Third Division in World War II, Infantry Journal Press, Washington, 1947.

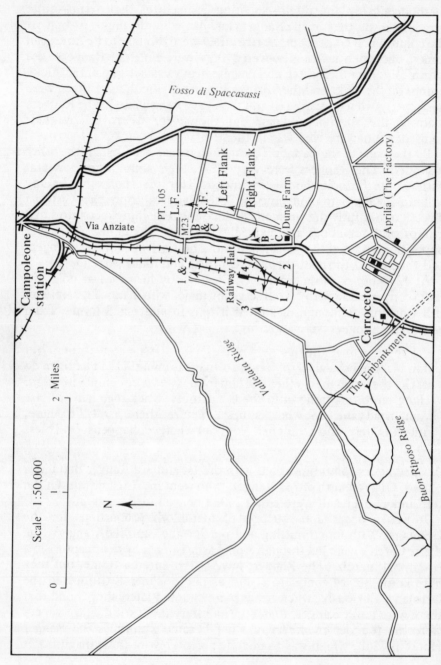

The night attack, 29/30 January (Scots Guards right, Irish Guards left of the Via Anziate)

fighting men before the war was over.

During the next thirty-six hours the men of the 3rd Division tried valiantly to fight through to where they hoped some Rangers might still be holding out, but in vain. On 31 January a company of the 4th Rangers managed to work their way round the Germans blocking the Cisterna Road and attack them from the rear. In record time 100 of the enemy surrendered, and the Rangers with tank support pushed on to Isola Bella two miles south of Cisterna. On their left, men of the 1st Battalion 30th Infantry Regiment, despite heavy resistance from the Germans, were able to get within 1,500 yards of the town. They did not know it, but they were nearly through. Their enemy was reeling. A final push would have made a huge hole in the German lines, but the 3rd Division had shot their bolt. Hurriedly a battalion of 26th Panzer Division was brought to fill the gap. Further to the left, around the small hamlet of Ponte Rotto, a tank versus tank action took place which left the Americans in possession of the place.

In three days the 3rd Infantry Division had suffered nearly 3,000 battle casualties and lost more than one-third of their tanks and Tank Destroyers. There were no more reserves. Reluctantly, Truscott called a halt to the advance. All his division could do now was to consolidate their hard-won gains and prepare for the German counter-attack which they knew was mounting. The right hand of General Lucas's two-pronged attack had come to a halt.

The task of the 24th Guards Brigade was easy, so they were told. All it entailed for the Irish Guards was a gentle walk until they were level with the Scots Guards in Dung Farm. Then the two battalions had to walk forward to their objective, only a couple of thousand yards ahead. Both battalion commanders had insisted on an early start so that there would be plenty of time for the companies to dig in and for their anti-tank guns to be well forward before dawn to deal with any enemy tanks which might then appear—although this was a possibility largely discounted by those above. However, a number of American Tank Destroyers were attached. These were virtually open tanks mounted with a 3-in. naval gun, a very potent piece of armament. The tank-busters, as they were known, on many occasions were able to wrest success from inevitable defeat as infantry unit after infantry unit had been attacked by German armour. They were to prove of the utmost value in the days that lay ahead.

During the night of 28 January the Sherwood Foresters in the Factory had heard the sound of considerable numbers of tracked vehicles to the north and east. It seemed clear that the Germans were bringing up more troops and armour, and at first light the forward positions of the Foresters and the Scots Guards around Dung Farm were subjected to heavy artillery fire. In the area of the Vallelata Ridge a number of snipers started to make things unpleasant for the Scots Guards, so a patrol was sent out which managed to deal with the nuisance. But it all boded rather ill for the attack that evening. Towards dusk the German shelling died down and an uneasy peace descended on the Carroceto area.

The start was intended for eleven o'clock that night, but because the Dukes, who were to relieve the Irish Guards for the attack, were held up behind a welter of transport on the Via Anziate, Colonel Scott decided to postpone zero-hour for forty-five minutes.

The German guns had fallen still on the western sector of the beachhead, and like their comrades of the Rangers ten miles to the east, the Irish Guards filed forward up the railway line beyond Carroceto in silence and total darkness. Only the careful tread of marching men disturbed the stillness of the night. Under such conditions, with everyone's nerves strung taut, the slightest sound is exaggerated in people's memories. Some remember the frogs which never ceased their croaking, or the noise when the telegraph lines hanging in festoons over the railway caught unsuspecting feet and twanged into the night like monstrous harps; others the steady crunch of boots on the cinders between the sleepers on the railway or the muffled oaths as someone met an unexpected obstacle.

Without incident, the companies reached the Start Line; they were now level with the Scots Guards. The plan was for Nos. 1 and 2 Companies to advance on either side of the railway line for some 2,000 yards to a point where a side road from the Vallelata Ridge reaches the Via Anziate around Milestone 23. No.3 Company operating on the left flank was to clear this road and as much of the ridge as they could, while No. 4 Company remained in reserve around a railway halt halfway to the objective. With such a dispersed force, it seemed sense for battalion headquarters to keep dissociated from the immediate company battles but where the battalion commander could co-ordinate affairs with the Scots Guards, so Colonel Scott moved to join Colonel Wedderburn in Dung Farm. Dung Farm was no haven but here the small party settled down to wait. The whole place, minute by minute, was beginning to lose its neat appearance as shell after shell crashed in and around the farm and the vehicles parked in a small dip behind it.

The Scots Guards, for their part, were to advance with two companies forward. Left Flank was to take the lead on the right up a ridge which conveniently ran north–south. Their objective was Point 105, a prominent feature some 2,000 yards ahead. Behind them would follow Right Flank. On the left 'B' Company, with 'C' following, would head up the Via Anziate clearing any enemy or obstruction until they too reached the general area of Milestone 23. It was their vital task to clear the way so that before dawn the support weapons, the anti-tank guns, and perhaps tanks could get up to the companies before daylight.

Just before the Irish Guards reached their Start Line the tremendous barrage which was to support them on to their objective broke on the ground ahead. Few on that attack thought that the Germans, if there were any, could live through such a holocaust. As the guns gradually shifted their fire northwards, so the Irish Guards Companies stepped off. Direction-finding was easy for the railway ran straight between the assault companies. But the way was much more difficult than air photographs had suggested and was criss-crossed by tiresome irrigation ditches which were deep and muddy and many of them too wide to jump.

Colonel Scott and his forward headquarters had moved out of Dung Farm into a convenient slit trench from where he could better hear how the battle was progressing. All seemed well. Almost monotonously Nos. 1 and 2 Companies regularly reported steady progress and no enemy. No. 3 Company way to the left had gone off the air soon after setting out, but as there was no sound of firing from the Vallelata Ridge, it appeared that all was going well there too. On the Scots Guards' front the leading companies reported excellent progress. Both battalions must be nearly halfway to their objectives, they reckoned.

The Irish Guards reached the railway halt without trouble and were beginning to congratulate themselves that all was well, when ahead of them the night was suddenly illuminated by a verey light and a stream of machine gun bullets swept across them from both sides. Almost immediately the Germans fired their artillery and mortar Defensive Fire tasks (DFs) and it was obvious that the railway halt was one of their targets.

Across the front of No. 2 Company on the right of the railway halt lay what appeared to be a wall of machine gun fire. In a matter of moments the right-hand platoon was completely wiped out by hidden machine guns. Some days later the company commander saw them as they had died, in perfect formation. Now, to make matters worse, the area they had just passed through seemed to have come alive with Germans, who had been passed in the darkness and were threatening to cut them off. Major G. P. M. FitzGerald, commanding No. 2 Company, decided that there was no future in continuing the way they had been going. To their left, where No. 1 Company had vanished into the night, all appeared to be quiet, so he switched direction and took No. 2 Company also up the left side of the railway.

It was a wise decision, for No. 1 Company had found the way considerably easier. Not only were Germans scarcer here but also the drainage ditches, instead of running across their front, ran in a north–south direction and provided fair cover. They reached their objective with only a single casualty and shortly afterwards they were joined by No. 2 Company.

A similar situation existed on the Scots Guards' front. Left Flank Company, closely followed by Right Flank, made excellent progress through the olive groves along the ridge north-east of Dung Farm. Apart from some troublesome Germans in a collection of outbuildings, their way appeared unimpeded and they continued without hindrance. The condition of the inner companies was not so happy. 'B' Company, in the lead, made their way without trouble for several hundred yards, but when ten yards short of the vital road a verey light soared up to reveal a thick line of wire along the main road. Then a storm of machine gun fire shattered the night. From battalion headquarters it sounded as though a major battle was raging. The two companies quickly suffered quite heavy casualties. There seemed no way to eliminate the firmly entrenched Germans in the dark, nor did there appear any way round, so Colonel Wedderburn, who was close behind the leading company, decided to switch his left attack. He ordered 'B' and 'C' Companies to return the way they had come and also make their way up by the ridge reported clear of enemy by Left Flank.

It was now shortly after midnight. The Scots Guards could report that all four of their companies were on or nearing their objectives. The two forward companies of the Irish Guards were now firm on theirs, while No. 3 Company appeared, from the amount of tracer and flares flying around, to be having some excitement in the area of Vallelata Ridge. But neither battalion had been able to clear the road, and there was no other way for the vital support weapons to get forward. Nor did the Germans along the Via Anziate itself and dug in along either side of the road show any inclination to pull back, despite the presence of the best part of two battalions behind them.

In fact the plan of attack for the 24th Guards Brigade was no secret, for an officer from another regiment had driven forward and repeated the mistake which the Grenadiers' 'O' Group had made. He had run into an ambush. He and his driver had been killed, and on him the Germans had found the orders for the night attack. The Germans had known precisely when and in which direction the attack was to come: the Irish Guards, in particular, had walked into a trap. The 'sleepy' Germans—as the Irish Guards described later—which they had passed through on their way forward to the railway halt, had lain doggo, waiting to attack the Guardsmen from the rear. It would appear to have been the intention of the Germans to allow the two battalions to pass on either side of them, but to hold strongly the centre road up which supporting anti-tank guns and armour must come. Their plan had worked to perfection.

The forward companies of both battalions felt well pleased with themselves though, for they had secured their objectives, and without heavy loss. Only the two commanding officers and the brigadier, who by this time had also come up to Dung Farm, appreciated the predicament they were really in. For with the Irish Guards having done a left hook and the Scots Guards a right hook, the area in between was not clear. Unless by daylight the anti-tank guns, and some armour and tank-busters could be taken forward, then the two battalions would be annihilated piecemeal by the German tanks which were known to be in the area. Although no one at the time realised it, a similar situation to that which befell the Rangers was about to occur on the Carroceto front.

Indeed, German tanks had already made their unwelcome appearance near the Irish Guards' position near a bridge. Here the two companies had set up a joint headquarters, partly from the lack of space, partly because there was only one wireless set working—the other had early on become unusable and the signaller, Lance-Corporal Holwell of the Royal Corps of Signals, was even now trying to mend it under the combined light of the moon and a small pencil torch. The moon was now high in the sky, it was almost as clear as daylight except when darkness descended as a friendly cloud passed over. For some time they had heard the ominous sound of tracks heading in their direction and soon enough, to their horror, two German tanks started trundling carefully towards them. It could only be a matter of time before the men lying in the open ground were spotted. To distract these unwelcome visitors two Guardsmen ran off to one side and opened a steady hail of bren fire at the tanks. Bren fire on tanks can be nothing more than an irritant, but it did force their commanders to close their visors and so all but blind the lumbering monsters. It also kept the tanks occupied for the next three-quarters of an hour as they tried to eliminate the troublesome fire. Eventually, wearying of the unsatisfactory sport, they made off the way they had come. The two companies who had been watching the proceedings, alternately digging like men possessed whenever a cloud crossed the moon, or lying as though dead and not daring to move when moonlight lit up the area, breathed collective sighs of relief. But their predicament was becoming obvious to all and there was no sign of their own support weapons.

Off to the west, No. 3 Company had been trudging across country towards Vallelata Ridge. The map indicated an easy route; the trouble was that the map bore little resemblance to the ground. At last they came on the gravel road which ran below Vallelata Ridge and almost simultaneously stirred up a nest of Germans. The whole ridge was dotted with farmhouses each holding their quota of very active Germans. It was clear that without armoured support any advance along that way was out of the question. In sour humour Captain Kennedy led his company back the way they had come to try a route more to the east. They came on a section of No. 4 Company in the area of the railway halt, where they found a message from the commanding officer to the effect that if anyone saw Kennedy they were to tell him to report immediately to Dung Farm. To Colonel Scott he made his way. It was now nearly four o'clock; there were one-and-a-half, perhaps two, hours of darkness left. The position was rapidly becoming desperate. Kennedy was given his orders. Collecting the carrier platoon, all the tank-busters he could find, and his own company, he set out once again for the Vallelata Ridge determined to fight up the Vallelata Road to Nos. 1 and 2 Companies, or perish in the attempt. He had little enough time to do it.

Colonel Wedderburn, from a position near his forward companies, had been urging the Guards' Brigade Headquarters to find some armour. 'We must have tanks if the job is to be successful,' he had repeatedly stressed. 'Something must be done.' In his turn, the brigadier had been bullying General Penney to release some of the precious tanks to come to the aid of his all-but-beleaguered battalions. At last, with some reluctance, five were spared; they were said to be on the way. What to do with them? Splitting them between the two battalions would give neither enough for the job. The Scots Guards had all four of their companies firmly on the objectives; further, they had found a way to get their anti-tank guns up the road along the ridge to the north-east of Dung Farm. With little hesitation the five precious tanks, all that was left of a complete squadron of the 46th Royal Tank Regiment, were allocated to the Scots Guards. It was now getting on for five o'clock.

The chance of Kennedy reaching the forward companies in time had always been a forlorn hope; by five o'clock, at most forty minutes before dawn, it was clear from the sound of battle away to the left that he never would. There was thus no other recourse but to order Nos. 1 and 2 Companies to withdraw while there was still a little darkness left. The only trouble was that they were out of communication.

A direct hit from a German mortar shell had demolished the remaining wireless set some time before; now the safety of the two Irish Guards companies depended on the skill and courage of one man, Lance-Corporal Holwell. For some hours now Corporal Holwell had been methodically taking his set to pieces. He had found that even the occasional flashes of his pencil torch drew down fire on his comrades, and so he moved off where only he would be the target, and worked away by himself. Shortly after five o'clock he managed to get the set working again. 'Number Two Company is on the air again, Sir,' the wireless operator at Irish Guards' Battalion Headquarters sang out. The word for the two companies to withdraw was passed and then the set went dead again as Lance-Corporal Holwell was killed by a burst of machine gun fire which also wrecked his radio. As the Irish Guards Regimental History records, 'If ever one man saved his comrades, it was Lance-Corporal Holwell.'

It was a bloody return. The route back down the railway turned out to be pitted with trenches full of Germans, and as soon as the smoke —which Colonel Scott had called for from the guns—came down it was swept away by a stiff breeze. The companies split into platoons, and the platoons into sections and tried to fight their way back. Two of the platoon commanders were killed in the first fifty yards, but the remainder struggled on with bayonets fixed. Indiscriminate German mortar fire and air-bursts from some tiresome 88-mm guns took toll of Germans and Guardsmen alike. Over the bodies of their friends who had been killed the night before, the Guardsmen attacked post after post, driving the Germans before them into the waiting muzzles of No. 4 Company who were trying to work their way forward from the railway halt to relieve pressure on the two forward companies. Slightly less than half Nos. 1 and 2 companies answered roll call that morning after the night attack. The rest lay dead or wounded or were captured along the line of Carroceto railway, which not so long before had been reported 'clear of the enemy'.

Meanwhile the irrepressible Captain Kennedy and his company were continuing their foray up the Vallelata Road. Around noon he came back to Dung Farm with fifty-five prisoners and was ordered to continue his activities by the divisional commander. By mid-afternoon he had more or less cleared the way along the entire length of the Vallelata Road and was able to rescue a party of wounded Irish Guardsmen who had been left in the lee of a railway bridge under a medical sergeant when the two companies had fought their way back.

Behind Dung Farm the Irish Guards set about reorganising and recovering from their experience of the night. They were not able to rest for long as the Scots Guards were reported as being under heavy attack from the east and north-east. So the weary Irish Guards companies moved forward once again and took over Dung Farm. The most forward platoon were in the flower garden where the Scotsmen had started to dig some graves. They were soon occupied by living Guardsmen, who found them 'most commodious', and prepared for what might happen next, particularly from the east, for they were beginning to realise that they were on the flanks and the Scots Guards were at the head of what was rapidly becoming a long, thin salient into enemy territory.

With the prospect of the tanks arriving now little more than a slim hope, the Scots Guards set about doing what they could to help themselves from the adversity they found themselves in. Every man who could be spared was collected as escort for a column of supporting arms which they were determined to fight through to the forward companies. The column was just setting off when an 88-mm gun started to shell the area. It was still quite dark, and thus it was the sheerest bad luck that the first shell landed in one of the anti-tank portees carrying ammunition which immediately burst into flames and set fire to the next vehicle. The whole column would have been destroyed, had it not been for the prompt action of the transport officer, Lieutenant F. McL. Hayward, who drove the next vehicle in line to safety thus making a break in the column. Despite this set-back, six anti-tank guns and a large column of ammunition were brought up to the forward companies along a track along the ridge. Not a moment too soon.

As dawn broke the first German attack began on the most forward Scots Guards' company, Left Flank. During the night advance Left Flank had overshot their objective and daylight revealed that their position was on a very vulnerable forward slope in full view of the enemy. It was now too late to pull back, and they could get no support from their neighbours who were too far away, so the only thing they could do was to continue digging in to the distressingly hard ground and to stick it out, hoping that tank support could come to their aid before it was too late. They managed to drive off two more strong enemy attacks, and at 0715 hours at Scots Guards' Battalion Headquarters they heard the excited voice of Major R. H. Bull MC, the company commander, jubilantly report that the enemy were in retreat and a tank had been destroyed. Ten minutes later came news that the company was surrounded and looked like being over-run, then . . . silence. The company commander must have been killed shortly afterwards. Only one wounded officer, who had been left for dead by the Germans for twenty-four hours, returned from Left Flank.

Elsewhere along the east flank of the salient things were becoming confused as the Germans probed forward. Dung Farm was by now rapidly being reduced to rubble by German shelling, and to make matters worse some SP guns had crept forward and were subjecting the remains of the farm to direct gunfire. The Scots Guards' support-company commander managed to commandeer a tank-buster, which succeeded in knocking out a couple. The rest trundled off, and the situation eased. But during the night attack and in resisting the German counter-attacks the following day the Scots Guards had lost three officers and forty-two other ranks killed, as well as many times that total wounded. These were the heaviest casualties ever sustained by any Scots Guards' battalion during the war.

But what neither the Scots nor the Irish Guards ever realised was how close they had been to breaking through. Their night attack had punched a huge hole nearly three kilometres wide between 3rd Panzer Grenadier Division and 65th Infantry Division in the Vallelata area. By their own admission the German line was no longer intact, and their artillery, due to the Allied counter-fire, was in complete disarray. All that lay between the forward companies of the two battalions of 24th Guards Brigade and Campoleone were twenty-odd men, two SP-guns and a Hornet (an SP tank destroyer) situated on a small hill, Point 93, under the command of a Lieutenant Semrau. It had been Semrau who had captured the divisional operation order the previous day which had warned of their attack, and he was to be awarded the Knight's Cross for his work that day.

While the Scots Guards were repelling German counter-attacks from the east of the Via Anziate, the 1st Armoured Division attempted to find reasonable tank-going to the west. With the area of Buon Riposo Ridge and the Moletta valley evidently quite unsuitable for tanks, General Harmon's attention was attracted by the railway embankment running north-west from Carroceto and which seemed to cross most of the troublesome ditches which had so impeded the reconnaissance the previous day. At dawn a strong force of the 1st Armoured Regiment with two battalions of the 6th Armoured Infantry Regiment struck up the railway embankment. They got as far as the Vallelata Road but there were held up by heavy German opposition. The promised air support was grounded due to low clouds. Further, a number of tanks became bogged and at the crucial moment reports of a German tank concentration north-west of Carroceto which threatened the west flank of the divisional thrust diverted a part of the force to deal with the new threat—which proved to be illusory. The advance up the Embankment ground to a halt. It had been a frustrating day for the armour and had convinced General Harmon that this was not tank country. His eyes now turned towards the Via Anziate itself and he was convinced that given a bit of room to manoeuvre and some reasonably firm ground to deploy he could force his way through.

On the morning of 30 January, as part of the policy to bring up all available troops for the main attack next day, the battalions of the 2nd Infantry Brigade on the Moletta River were relieved by the American 36th Combat Engineer Regiment who thus found themselves fighting in the unaccustomed role of infantry. Accordingly, two battalions of 2nd Brigade moved to the area of the Padiglione Woods, while the Loyals went forward to fill a gap between the 509th Parachute Infantry Battalion, who had taken over from the Rangers, and the 1st Reconnaissance Regiment to the immediate right of the Factory. On that day too the 3rd Division made another attempt on Cisterna, but once more had to be content with fractional gains for heavy losses which left them still two miles short of the town. However, by now all attention was concentrated on 1st Division's front where the 3rd Infantry Brigade were preparing to mount their attack.

Expanding the Beachhead

Zero-hour had been originally scheduled to be at 0930 hours that morning, but as the Scots and Irish Guards were still reorganising from the aftermath of the night attack, the time was put back. Waiting all along the main road to Anzio was the 1st Armoured Division ready to spring forward the moment Campoleone Station was taken and the way lay clear for the armour to 'go through'—words which to those at Anzio were to assume a tragic irony as the weeks passed. Their objective was the heights west of Castelgandolfo, the Pope's summer home in the Alban Hills, eight miles away. It was a grandiose design. For the Alban Hills, which had looked so close and so seductive a few days before were now beginning to appear a remote jade.

When eventually they were captured four months later, officers who went up and looked back towards Anzio could see their battlefield like a chessboard beneath them. It was possible to pick out the features which they had come to know so well, the Flyover, the line of the Lateral Road, the Wadis or Gullies which appeared so deceptively flat from a distance, the line of the Railway Embankment, the twin towns of Anzio and Nettuno in the distance, and the more broken area of the Campagna close to the hills and around Albano where the Germans had their concentration areas and their tank parks. How different Campoleone, Carroceto and the 'Factory' looked from this side. How narrow was the strip of bloody country which they had held for so long at the cost of so many thousand lives. And they saw how vulnerable they had been from enemy observers in the hills who could pin-point each gun flash, could note and notice every movement in the beachhead. Then they realised what Anzio had meant to them all. Several months later, when the victorious Allied armies were advancing towards the north of Italy and the early spring of 1944 had become an unpleasant memory, a visitor was surprised to see a note under the talc on a Gunner officer's desk. It read, 'Remember, it can never be as bad as it was at Anzio.'

Since midnight the assault companies of the two battalions of 3rd Brigade which were to make the attack, the Dukes on the left and the KSLI on the right, had been waiting uncomfortably in the general area of Carroceto and the Factory, taking what cover they could find. With foreboding they heard the sound of heavy gunfire to their left and to their front. Shivering in their hurriedly dug slit-trenches they could hear furious fighting, the almost continuous noise of schmeisser and spandau, the less frequent chatter of the bren, and the sharp crack of the German 88-mm guns. A web of tracer seemed to hang like a veil over the whole area. Of more immediate concern were a number of shells which, clearly aimed at Dung Farm to the front, landed amongst the waiting men causing a number of casualties. It was not a happy omen.

The morning passed and then the afternoon wore on. It was a drowsy day, quite warm and sunny. From time to time messages found their

86

way to the companies that zero-hour had been postponed, then that it had been postponed again, this time to 1300 hours. The men of 3rd Brigade were beginning to wonder if a night attack might not in the end be necessary. At last zero-hour was fixed for 1510 hours.

But the Start Line was still not secure. Although the Scots Guards dominated it from their positions, the area behind them on the Via Anziate was still strongly held by the Germans. In their prepared positions they had caused irritation and casualties all day, and showed not the slightest inclination to move. They would have to be winkled out one by one before the 3rd Brigade attack could go in. It was out of the question to leave them where they were, for anti-tank weapons would be needed in Campoleone Station as soon as possible as there were a good few enemy tanks around.

'C' Company of the KSLI was deputed for the task of eliminating the troublesome enemy of the Via Anziate. With a full squadron of tanks the company, under Major I. G. Mansell, set to the task with a will and soon was reported as 'going well'. By noon the Germans had been routed out of the houses and barns along the way; many were killed and over eighty captured. It had been a classic little piece of infantry/tank co-operation. The way now lay clear for the 3rd Brigade attack.

On the right, the KSLI crossed their Start Line, a dirt road, without trouble and started to thread their way through a maze of olive groves and close cultivation. As they advanced with great steadiness and precision, closely supported by tanks, the shelling became heavier and heavier; despite being well spread out, casualties began to mount. To their left could be heard the sound of heavy fighting, for the left-hand assault company of the Dukes, 'B' Company, was having considerable trouble from a group of houses near the main road. The Dukes seemed to be attracting a greater proportion of mortar and shell fire. One shell hit a burned-out American tank on the road, and it started to burn, filling the air with filthy fumes. Dourly the Dukes pushed on.

By five o'clock the KSLI had reached their objective just short of the railway line in the area of Point 131, much helped by their supporting tanks whenever opposition looked like getting out of hand.

Now, as the light began to fade and with his forward companies reported on their objectives, the commanding officer of the KSLI, Lt.-Col. W. P. Careless, went to see them, accompanied by his runner. Together they made their way forward to where the companies had been reported. They walked for some time. It was strangely quiet; the shelling appeared concentrated on the Dukes off to the west, and the ground was closer than he had expected. There was no sign of the companies, but ahead lay a large red barn. This, too, appeared to be unoccupied so Colonel Careless went to investigate and found that it was a messroom with tables laid for a meal. Near-by was a house, and to

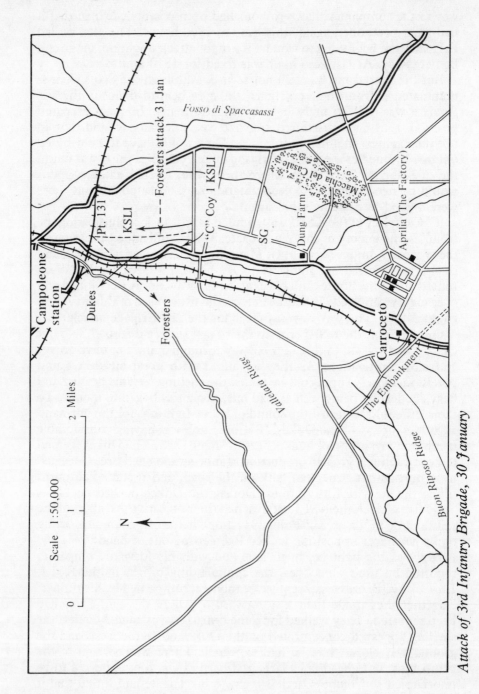

Fosso di Spaccasassi

Foresters attack 31 Jan

Pt. 131

KSLI

"C" Coy 1 KSLI

SG

Macchia del Casale

Dung Farm

Aprilia (The Factory)

Campoleone station

Dukes

Foresters

Valletta Ridge

Carroceto

The Embankment

Buon Riposo Ridge

Scale 1:50,000

N

2 Miles

1

0

Attack of 3rd Infantry Brigade, 30 January

his horror he found that the back had been knocked out and sitting in the front room was an SP gun with some Germans clustered around it. Backing away, he beat a hasty retreat and lay low in some vines until darkness started to fall and he reckoned that it was safe to return. By great good fortune, the first person he met was his runner, and then within minutes a voice came from the depth of a bush, 'Don't shoot, Tommy, don't shoot.' And to the colonel's utter astonishment three Germans emerged with their hands up. They were only too happy to surrender, their sole concern being the safety of their girl friends in Florence and Genoa, which they had heard had been heavily bombed the day before. Together with his trophies the commanding officer returned to his headquarters, more than a little relieved.

Almost as dramatic were the adventures of Captain H. Ripley, anti-tank officer of the KSLI. As dusk was settling on the battlefield he made his way forward to site his guns. Ahead lay the railway line, so he crept up to it until he could see railway waggons on the track and hear German voices from behind them. Then he too made his way back. It was clear that here was no place for anti-tank guns.

Although the KSLI were now firm, the Dukes were still behind, for their 'B' Company was having considerable trouble in farms and houses along the main road and had also been heavily mortared for their pains. Theirs was a tedious, but utterly essential job which caused considerable casualties. To their right, the other companies, according to plan, had passed round and taken up the lead. At dusk 'C' and 'D' companies were firm on some higher ground south of the railway and had already started to dig in. Just as the light was fading, the company commander of 'C' Company, Major P. P. Benson, spied an enemy armoured car pull up to a small rise, and on going to investigate discovered a German officer and his batman calmly loading some kit into the car. With his 0.38 revolver Benson shot the officer—a remarkable feat at any time—and then with his own batman shouldering the German's camp bed, calmly returned to his company position. Here there was intensive digging under way, and with the main road at last clear of enemy it was possible to bring forward the battalion anti-tank guns. Their role now superseded, the tanks, which had done sterling work all day, withdrew to the comparative safety of their harbour areas behind Carroceto. Between them the Dukes and KSLI had taken 278 prisoners.

Far off to the east covering the right flank of the attack, 'A' squadron of the 1st Reconnaissance Regiment was pushing up the Spaccasassi Road, but could get no further than the woods of the Macchia del Casale before they were held up by some well-sited 88-mm guns and a cluster of farmhouses, some of whose windows inconveniently possessed shutters of steel.

Expanding the Beachhead

It had been a successful day except that precious time had been lost; for although they did not realise it, time was the one commodity which was very scarce: German reinforcements were pouring in. Nevertheless, 6th Corps began to breathe easier and start to look longingly once again towards Rome. The first stage of the capture of Campoleone had been achieved and there were many who regretted that Campoleone and Cisterna—the two vital road and rail centres in the area—had not been captured immediately after the landing when they were theirs for the taking.

Now it was the turn of the Foresters. In the afternoon of the previous day they had handed over the Factory and followed in the wake of the Dukes and KSLI ready to pass through when the line of the railway had been reached. By the time this was accomplished daylight had faded and it was decided to postpone their attack until the following day. Throughout the night the Dukes and KSLI reported a lot of enemy patrol activity. This was beaten off without much trouble, but what boded ill for the morrow was the great deal of enemy vehicle movement reported north of the Campoleone Station. Nor was the report from the survivors of a fighting patrol of the Foresters, which made its way across the railway line and was then caught by heavy machine gun fire, any more encouraging. Campoleone Station and the area beyond was obviously occupied by a strong German force.

In training in Britain, and all through the North African campaign, at the landing at Pantellaria and later in Italy, the three battalions of the 3rd Infantry Brigade, the 1st Duke of Wellington's Regiment, the 1st King's Shropshire Light Infantry and the 2nd Battalion the Sherwood Foresters had served together, fought together and played together. Casualties in one were almost looked on as casualties in their own regimental families; thus it was with a sense of sorrow and apprehension that the forward battalions of the brigade looked on the morrow.

The Foresters spent an uneasy night in limbo between Dung Farm and Campoleone Station. They had to dig their slit-trenches in hard and rocky ground, and to add to their discomfiture they were intermittently shelled, which meant very little sleep for anyone. Shortly after daybreak, the commanding officer, Lt.-Col. G. R. G. Bird, gave out his orders for the attack. Of necessity they were brief. There was no information as to what lay behind the railway line, for the report of the fighting patrol had been imprecise, except to say that the enemy seemed to be very thick on the ground. The plan was for 'A' and 'C' Companies, left and right respectively, to take the line of the railway and then 'D' and 'B' were to pass through and secure Campoleone Station itself. Way back, somewhere near the Padiglione Woods and forward in the area of Carroceto, lurked the tanks of the 1st U.S. Armoured Division, ready for the armoured breakthrough which would follow the Foresters' success, although there was beginning to creep into a good many minds the awful presentiment that this might never take place. Those who had come in contact with the enemy had no illusions about their strength and their ability, and if they had forgotten, near a burned-out Sherman tank on the side of the road there was for all to see, the gruesome remains of an American tank officer who had been driving a jeep. He was lolling forward, a cigar still clamped firmly between his teeth.

The attack was to take place at 1030 hours, in broad daylight and with support from a squadron of the 46th Royal Tank Regiment. Under cover of a heavy barrage the two leading companies of the Foresters, in extended line and with bayonets fixed, started to walk forward. Morale in the battalion had been of the highest, there was no anxiety in the ranks, to the stolid British infantry this was just another job. To those in the KSLI who watched them walking forward, though, it all smacked unpleasantly of pictures they had seen of infantry advancing in the last war. But with their officers leading, the Foresters trudged unemotionally on. From the moment they rose from their slit-trenches they were under fire, accurate and heavy fire, and the casualties began to mount. Through the vineyards the two leading companies pressed on while a gathering storm of enemy shell-fire fell around them. At last they reached the comparative shelter of the embankment by the railway line and there took stock.

The platoons had been seriously weakened by casualties, but the two companies were still strong enough to try to take the embankment and the houses immediately beyond it. Opposite 'C' Company, the company commander, Major R. A. Rubens, saw a culvert under the railway line and through this he made his way with the leading platoons. The culvert was mined with anti-tank mines, but otherwise seemed clear. Beyond lay some houses and a very strong German position, for he could see tanks and SP guns moving around. As soon as the company emerged from the culvert they came under immediate and very heavy fire. To one side lay a small railwayman's hut. One platoon doubled forward to occupy it hoping to find some cover, but before they reached it a direct hit from a German tank demolished the flimsy building. With casualties mounting steadily, with his company little more than a remnant and he himself wounded in the leg, there seemed no hope of pushing through without tank support. So Major Rubens ordered his platoons to return through the culvert the way they had come. There were very few left to do so. He himself was crippled and lay in the open while his runner and batman put a splint on his leg in full view of the enemy who never shot at them. Then, more or less patched up, he was carried back through the culvert. Once again the Germans never disturbed the small party.

The experiences of the other forward company, 'A' Company, were similar. With great bravery a few men managed to cross the railway line, but they were soon enough driven back again. Others tried and were shot down by enfilading fire from the machine guns mounted in the railway waggons which Captain Ripley had seen on his foray the evening before and which swept the raised railway bed with an impenetrable sheet of fire. 'A' Company, too, recoiled, having suffered crippling losses.

The attacking companies were pulled back 300 yards and a fierce bombardment with field and medium guns was brought down on the defenders of Campoleone. Almost before the dust had settled, the Foresters' reserve companies made their attack. They too reached the railway line without much trouble, but like their comrades, when they tried to cross it they were greeted with the same heavy German fire, which seemed not one jot the less after the heavy shelling. Tanks of the armoured division came to their support and drove right up to the railway, but even with their aid the Foresters could not cross the embankment, and casualties mounted alarmingly. It was just not possible, against the skilfully-sited German defences, to pass infantry across the railway line.

In the middle of these frustrations General Harmon came forward to see for himself what was the hold-up. He wrote later:

> I came up in a tank—a jeep wouldn't have lived long there—to watch my tanks, spread on the level ground to the right and left, trade fire with the Germans. I decided I would plow up the steep slope where the Foresters were entrenched. My tank climbed the hill, and then I called a halt and got out to walk. There were dead bodies everywhere. I had never seen so many dead men in one place. They lay so close together that I had to step with care. I shouted for the commanding officer.
>
> From a foxhole there arose a mud-covered sergeant with a handle-bar moustache. He was the highest-ranking officer still alive. He stood stiffly to attention.
>
> 'How is it going?' I asked. The answer was all around me.
>
> 'Well, Sir,' the sergeant said, 'there were 116 of us when we first came up, and there are sixteen of us left. We're ordered to hold out until sundown, and I think, with a little good fortune we can manage to do so.'*

Brigadier J. G. James DSO, commander of 3rd Infantry Brigade, decided to call off the attack. The tanks retired out of range of the German gun-fire and wearily the 2nd Battalion the Sherwood Foresters began to pull back. They reorganised on the left of the main road

*Saturday Evening Post.

behind the Dukes. It was a heart-breaking reunion. The strongest rifle company could muster only forty men and the weakest numbered less than twenty. All the company commanders were casualties; 'A' Company was commanded by the sergeant. All that Colonel Bird had left under his command were eight officers and around 250 men, and he himself had been twice wounded, and was soon afterwards to be evacuated. Two-thirds of the battalion had been wiped out.

All the carriers of the brigade which could move were mobilised to rescue the wounded. Under any form of makeshift white flag, they drove forward to the edge of the railway embankment itself on their mercy missions, and the Germans left them alone. Further back, and not all far back at that, many of the wounded were introduced for the first time to a remarkable body of men, the American Field Service, a band of intrepid ambulance volunteers. They considered themselves civilians in battledress. For the most part they had been rejected for military service on medical grounds. They received no pay, although Uncle Sam was good enough to pay their expenses and provide uniforms. They had a number of particular characteristics: they never took time off and were always volunteering for hazardous jobs, and they took a special delight in driving heavily-scarred ambulances—this despite the earnest entreaties of the doctors that casualties did not like being reminded of where they were by seeing daylight through the bodywork. But many a man wounded in the Anzio beachhead owed his life to their courage, skill and above all to their imperturbability.

That night, a reinforcement of four officers, who had been waiting restlessly in the rear areas to join their battalion while rumours of the virtual annihilation of the Foresters were rife, came up. And wearily, still half-stunned by the hammering they had received, the rest of the battalion dug their new positions, waiting for what the morrow would bring. The attack of 1st British Infantry Division had come to a halt.

The morrow brought nothing but more and almost continuous shelling. This was all an unpleasant new experience for most of the troops. Throughout the campaign in North Africa and during the advance up Italy they had been more used to giving than receiving artillery fire. Now the Germans appeared to have a distressingly abundant supply of ammunition and guns to fire it. It seemed as though the Germans were biding their time and building up their forces for one horrendous test of strength. Indeed the sound of heavy traffic behind Campoleone and on both the left and right flanks told that something big was brewing.

A simple glance at the battle map showed how vulnerable the Allies in the beachhead now were. For the left flank of the perimeter had assumed a remarkable and alarming shape. A salient some four miles long had been plunged towards the Alban Hills. At the head of this was the 3rd Infantry Brigade on a front of less than 3,000 yards. To their rear the salient narrowed, until in places it was only a matter of a few hundred yards across, with the main road, the Via Anziate, and the parallel railway line pointing in one direction to Campoleone, the Alban Hills and, derisively, to Rome; in the other direction to Carroceto, the Flyover, to Anzio—the very heart of the beachhead—and the sea.

The Germans were fully aware how vulnerable their enemy's position was. The salient 'positively demanded' taking out, a German general afterwards declared, and it was as sure as anything in war, that they would attack the shoulders of the excrescence—the 'Thumb' as it came to be known throughout the world—rather than make a headlong assault on the tip and the positions of the 3rd Infantry Brigade.

That was not to say that the brigade was left in peace. Through the days succeeding the attack the enemy probed at the three battalions, but all the time at higher headquarters there was a feeling that the enemy were trying to discover where and in what strength the position was held, not for immediate use, but rather as essential information which would sooner or later become of inestimable value. The question was, how soon or how late.

5

Counter-stroke

1–4 February

The initiative was now with the Germans. 6th Corps was on the defensive. Indeed, early on the morning of 2 February, General Lucas had told Truscott that his Intelligence staff had discovered the Germans were in far greater strength than they had originally thought, and were preparing to launch a counter-offensive to drive them into the sea; in consequence their new Corps mission was to hold the existing beachhead line. It was an unaccustomed, uncomfortable experience, and morale at higher headquarters dropped almost visibly. The euphoria of the early days had been now succeeded by a tingle of apprehension. Observers found that the further back from the front line they went the more pronounced became the depressing air of gloom.

German counter-attack plans had by now crystallised. Their attack, only a preliminary to the main assault which was designed to crush the beachhead altogether, was in three stages. First, it was intended to eliminate the salient north of the Factory; then Carroceto and the Factory itself were to be captured to provide the spring-board for the final drive down the Via Anziate. And a third element was introduced, namely to capture a bridge over the Fosso di Feminamorta—the Ditch of the Dead Woman, soon to gain notoriety as the Ditch of the Dead Men—south-west of Ponte Rotto on the Cisterna front, to provide a foothold for a subsequent attack in that quarter.

The first attacks were scheduled for the night of 2/3 February, but Allied shells had knocked out the German artillery communications, so, in the event, the German attack was postponed for twenty-four hours. Meanwhile, on 1 February, the sore-tried 29th Panzer Grenadier Regiment, which had withstood the brunt of the attacks by 24th Guards Brigade and 3rd Brigade, was pulled back to reform for the coming attack. They were relieved by a regiment of 715th Infantry Division who moved in west of Campoleone Station. They started to probe forward vigorously at the Duke's positions.

There was dissatisfaction in German circles with their organisation, and with some headquarters. 'Schlemm's staff will not do,' it was declared, 'they sit around all day smoking cigars,' although Kesselring

The Salient, 1–3 February

Scale 1:50,000

Miles

N

0   1   2

Campoleone station

Fosso di Spaccasassi

Fosso della Ficoccia

1st Reconnaissance Regiment

Loyals

KSLI

Dukes

Foresters

Milestone 23

Pt. 105

A

C

D

B

Gordons

Dung Farm

Aprilia (The Factory)

Irish Guards

1

2

3

4

Milestone 24

Scots Guards

Vallelata Ridge

Grenadiers

Carroceto

The Embankment

(Disused Railway Bed)

THE CAVES

Pantoni

Buon Riposo Ridge

North Staffords

THE WADIS

R. Moletta

157th US Infantry Regiment

had great confidence in Schlemm himself. There was also the problem that the beachhead front had now become too large for one corps headquarters to handle, thus the very experienced General Herr with 76th Panzer Corps Headquarters was brought in from the Adriatic front. He was given the whole sector from the Mussolini Canal to the Via Anziate, while the sector west of the Anziate to the mouth of the Moletta River was made the responsibility of Schlemm's 1st Parachute Corps.

The attack to eliminate the salient was to be mounted by a battle group comprising 3rd Panzer Grenadier and 715th Infantry Divisions with elements of 26th Panzer Division in support, striking from the north and the east—this was known as Battle Group Gräser, after the commander of 3rd Panzer Grenadier Division; while a regiment of 65th Infantry Division and units of 4th Parachute Division attacked from the west—this was known as Battle Group Pfeiffer. Initially, the attack was to be mounted by two main bodies, the 'Western Group' comprising three infantry battalions and two light artillery battalions of Battle Group Pfeiffer, the 'Eastern Group' of three infantry battalions and two light artillery battalions of Battle Group Gräser. The two groups were intended to converge on the Via Anziate near Milestone 23, and with a line secured behind the 3rd Infantry Brigade, they would proceed to roll them upwards. It was a simple plan, and it was very nearly successful.

2 February was quiet on the front of the 1st British Infantry Division, apart from spasmodic shelling and frequent tales from forward positions of the sound of enemy movement. Wherever it was spotted, concentrations of artillery fire were brought down, and thus many a potential German probing attack was still-born.

As the day progressed, reports of German build-up increased. At 1225 hours 'A' Squadron of the 1st Reconnaissance Regiment east of Dung Farm reported Germans forming up in the woods to their front. Twenty minutes later, an observation post of 19th Field Regiment spotted what they estimated to be two enemy companies below Vallelata Ridge and shortly afterwards a convoy, 1,500 yards long, was sighted along the Embankment. As these enemy sightings were marked on the battle maps at divisional headquarters the picture was becoming ominously clear.

At the tip of the salient the Dukes were subjected to heavy shelling all day, and it became increasingly evident that the enemy were creeping around the left flank of their position. Sure enough, in the early afternoon of 3 February, the Dukes were attacked from the west and the south-west. At first the enemy made inroads into the left forward company position, but in the evening a brisk counter-attack with the help of some tanks of the 46th Royal Tanks had restored the situation.

Counter-stroke

The Germans pulled back to a ridge some 300 yards to the west, and from there watched and waited.

That afternoon No. 3 Company of the Irish Guards, on the extreme left of the battalion position, among the farms and barns along the Vallelata Road, were involved in a curious incident. Without warning, the company was charged by what they reckoned was about 1,000 sheep. At the time it was considered a piece of light relief, but with hindsight it was seen as a German ploy to test the defences and discover what wire and mines lay before the company position.

The evening passed peacefully enough. Food was brought up from the rear echelons by the quartermasters. The meal was passed out in platoon or section areas. Weapons were checked in the few remaining moments of daylight, and ammunition for the night distributed. Wireless and telephone lines were tested and then tested again, and the defensive fire tasks on the map compared with likely lines of attack on the ground. This done, the 1st British Infantry Division settled down to wait for what the night would bring.

At eleven o'clock precisely a heavy barrage came down on the Irish Guards' positions. It lasted for five minutes and then lifted. A silence descended on the battlefield. Eyes probed the darkness all along the fringes of the salient. Keen ears listened to every sound which might betray an infiltrating German patrol, for by now no one held any illusions about the almost uncanny skill of the enemy at working their way between widely-spaced positions, and those of the Irish Guards were 700 to 800 yards apart.

But no one was left guessing what was to happen for long, as an even fiercer bombardment of shells and mortars came down about their ears. It appeared to be concentrated on the hapless No. 3 Company below the ridge, and soon enough it was clear what it portended. Urgently, the company commander called for immediate DF tasks to his front and flanks. Those in 3rd Brigade at the tip of the salient listened with some apprehension to what was happening behind them. Their apprehension was to increase as the night wore on.

German mortar bombs had set fire to some haystacks near the centre of the No. 3 Company position and these burned with a nice steady glow illuminating the country around and giving the machine gunners all the light they needed. The Germans 'came on in mass very thick and fast', a survivor described later. One machine gun fired over 8,000 rounds at almost point-blank range, but nothing seemed to stop the German infantry who swarmed on, over and into the position shouting and gesticulating. For some minutes the company wireless operator kept up a running commentary and then the company commander came on the air: 'My headquarters is in a critical position, the Germans are at the door;' then . . . silence. After a while, too, the shooting became spasmodic below the Vallelata Ridge, and then it ceased altogether.

Meanwhile reports had been coming in of considerable German infiltration behind the Irish Guards and between the Irish and the Scots Guards further down the Vallelata Ridge towards Carroceto. Almost at the same time, the Gordons on the right shoulder of the salient reported that the enemy were trying to work their way between their forward companies. Elsewhere the Germans seemed active too. On the Buon Riposo Ridge, the North Staffords reported heavy mortar fire and considerable patrol activity. The Grenadiers to their north along the Embankment behind the Scots Guards found more Germans trying to make their way down the line of the Embankment towards Carroceto. While 3rd Brigade in their uneasy position at the tip of the Salient, had their own share of worries.

Shortly after 2100 hours the forward companies of the KSLI reported a lot of enemy activity south of the Campoleone railway line, and called for immediate fire on their front. This fell with superb accuracy on the enemy as they were forming up for an attack. Elsewhere, the Germans were creeping up using what cover there was, and around midnight they managed to capture a building between the two forward companies, but a prompt counter-attack soon dislodged them. By dawn, the three battalions of 3rd Brigade had restored their positions and were full of confidence that they could stay there for ever. However, although the tip of the salient was holding, the situation on the shoulders behind them was far from happy.

Close behind the Foresters, in the area around the railway bridge, Nos. 1 and 2 Companies of the Irish Guards and their Battalion Headquarters were rapidly becoming isolated. 1,200 yards to their rear, at the railway halt, lay No. 4 Company, acting as longstop. But with the elimination of No. 3 Company below Vallelata Ridge, a huge hole had been driven between the Irish Guards and the Scots Guards to the south.

As the night progressed it became quite clear that the enemy had infiltrated behind the forward companies of the Irish Guards and were now either on or very near the main road. The battalion was commanded by Major D. M. L. Gordon-Watson MC, while Colonel Scott and the company commanders were back in 'B' Echelon recouping their strength. So it was what the commanding officer referred to as his 'second eleven' who took the agony of the next hours, for the situation of the Irish Guards was now acute. However, provided they stayed where they were, Major Gordon-Watson was confident, come the dawn, that the situation could be restored with the aid of a few tanks. From time to time the enemy fired red or white verey lights, varied by occasional pillars of greenish smoke. What these indicated, no one knew, but to confuse the proceedings the Irish Guards repeated or varied the signals, with gratifying results as the Germans, who were now clearly in some force between the forward companies and the longstop company, repeatedly shelled what were clearly their own positions.

At battalion headquarters, they were busy planning how to deal with the enemy around them as soon as the promised tanks arrived. Some could be seen far down the road beyond Dung Farm where Colonel Scott was by now installed. A few hours before, he had been roused in 'B' Echelon with the shattering news that the Irish Guards were surrounded, with one company destroyed and the remainder hanging on but isolated, and now he was trying to organise the rescue of the remains of his stricken battalion. Gladly he passed on the message that our 'heavy friends', the 'beetle-crushers' were on the way.

The 'heavy friends', though, were having problems of their own. A troop of tanks which had been near the railway bridge near the Irish Guards' headquarters, found themselves in the unpleasant situation of having Germans sitting on a bank above them energetically trying to drop grenades down their turrets. They therefore prudently withdrew down the main road, the last to do so for some hours, for the Germans who had by now reached it let them pass, thankful to be rid of such troublesome creatures. On the way the retreating tanks passed two derelict Shermans which had broken down, but still had their crews abroad, although the Germans were not aware of it. One of these crews made their way back safely during the hours of darkness; the other sat it out, giving an admirable running commentary on what was happening around them, and were then able to support a subsequent counter-attack with their machine guns.

At 0430 hours 'B' Squadron of the 46th Royal Tank Regiment was earmarked to go to the aid of The Irish Guards. As the main road was clearly unusable and under observation, if not in actual possession by the enemy, they were ordered to strike through the Gordons' position to the east of the Via Anziate and then come in to join the Irish Guards from the right. They duly set forth, and to their horror discovered that not only were their flanks quite exposed, both from the main road and from German anti-tank guns sitting on a ridge to the east, but that the country through which they had to pass was no longer in Allied hands.

On the Gordons' front the situation at dusk had seemed to be satisfactory, despite the great distance the battalion covered and the perils of having their forward companies strung well out with huge gaps between them (see map page 96). 'C' Company was near the main road and behind the lateral road which was the Start Line of the 3rd Brigade attack; 'A' Company was forward of them, in and around Point 105 where four days before Left Flank Company of the Scots Guards had been overrun; 'D' Company was to the right of 'A'; and 'B' Company rather forward and to the north-east of Dung Farm. There was no substance and less depth to their position, nor were the companies in a position to give any mutual support to each other. Further, the ground sloped gently to the east and thus the whole position was under observation, particularly from the woods to the east and south-east. Any movement at all in 'A' Company's area drew immediate and very accurate fire. There were few places on their whole front of close on two miles where the Germans could not see what was happening, but one of these was the area just north of Dung Farm—which was ever afterwards known by the Gordons as Horror Farm—and with good reason. Here Lt.-Col. J. Peddie DSO set up his headquarters. Hardly had they arrived when a patrol from the 1st Reconnaissance Regiment sent to investigate some suspicious-looking farmhouses found they were occupied by what looked like two companies of Germans. Thereupon Colonel Peddie set about making his own headquarters into a strong-point, although at that stage in the beachhead battle mines and wire were scarce commodities.

Precisely at eleven o'clock a huge explosion took place behind the headquarters as a heavy gun ranged in on their position. It was the prelude to a bombardment the like of which none of them had ever experienced before. 'B' Company, meanwhile, had gone off the air, and a patrol sent forward to find out what was afoot returned at midnight with the news that all the sheep on the plain seemed to be on the move. Indeed in battalion headquarters it was possible to hear their bells as they scampered across the plain. Then, at 0100 hours while the rain poured down without mercy and visibility became minimal, a vicious barrage came down on the area of Horror Farm, and small-arms' fire could be heard from the direction of the forward companies. Some time later 'B' Company came back on the air with the unpleasant news that large numbers of enemy had come between them and 'D' Company on their left, and that the mortar platoon who were dug in behind them had been overrun by the enemy. A counter-attack restored the situation somewhat. By 0200 hours all seemed well and a patrol sent down the main road reported the way clear. A jeep and ambulance were sent forward to collect wounded and both failed to return. It was the first inkling that all might not be as secure as they had supposed.

Some hours before dawn, an officer from 'B' Company heard a German officer talking in front of the position and saying: 'There are two companies behind the two companies in front.' At first it was thought that the German had been referring to the Gordons' layout, but as the night wore on, they began to wonder. Indeed, it was later discovered that two complete German companies had penetrated between 'D' and 'B' Companies of the Gordons and were holding the slightly higher ground behind their position, while two more were in front of their lines and hidden beyond a ridge. Meanwhile, there were ominous sounds of digging somewhere inside the battalion area. It was a pitch dark night and nothing could be done until morning, but if Germans really were in force between and behind the forward companies the situation was extremely grave.

For much of the night 'C' Company too had been off the air and all messages were passed through their neighbours to the front, 'A' Company. Shortly before first light, 'A' Company reported that Tiger tanks were deploying to the east to attack. Then communications suddenly ceased. Anxiously, the little band at battalion headquarters waited for the dawn; it seemed an unconscionable time in coming.

At last, with a faint lightening of the sky it was possible to see enough to try to find out what was happening. The providential arrival of 'B' Squadron of the 46th Royal Tanks, thwarted on their way forward to relieve the Irish Guards, gave the battalion commander a force with which to start tidying up the position. Together with 'B' Company and supported by fire from the Reconnaissance Regiment to the south-east, they swept forward, rounding up the best part of 200 prisoners. 'D' Company reported, 'tanks are doing a grand job of work'; then, anxiously, they said that they could see the forward companies withdrawing, and asked why. This was a shattering turn of events, and to this day has never been satisfactorily explained as the company commander of 'A' Company was killed soon afterwards. Had the two forward companies stayed where they were they might have survived until the supporting tanks came forward, but once out of the shelter of their slit-trenches they were vulnerable to attacks from the front, and on their way back duly ran into the Germans who were in force behind them, while heavy machine gun fire from across the main road where the Germans had managed to split the Irish Guards' position caused further casualties. Worse was to follow, for 'D' Company, assuming that a general withdrawal had been ordered, also announced that they were pulling back. They suffered the same fate as their comrades of 'A' and 'C' Companies.

The Gordons were not the only unit in trouble. At 0015 hours, the KSLI reported that they were being attacked from both north and east and that the enemy were within 100 yards of their battalion headquarters. In the early hours of the morning 3rd Brigade Head-quarters, who were on the main road 400 yards north of Carroceto, to their disgust and dismay found themselves the object of intensive small-arms fire, apparently from all directions and particularly from the right rear, which was highly disturbing. They beat a hasty retreat to safer pastures but it was now unpleasantly obvious that the 3rd Brigade were well and truly cut off from the rest of the division.

With the forward companies of the Gordons overrun, the situation of the Irish Guards was now critical, for with Germans all around them, the only place out of direct observation from the enemy had been in the bed of the lateral road, but now this was enfiladed by tanks and machine guns from the east and the Gordons' old position. It was clear that with the Germans behind them in strength and blocking the main road it was not likely that armour could get up in time to effect a rescue. The only answer was to start pulling back, and in broad daylight. Major Gordon-Watson informed brigade that his position was untenable and unless something was done about it within five minutes, he would have to start bringing back the remnants of his companies. At the same time he ordered the long-stop company at the railway halt to start fighting their way forward to clear a way for his withdrawal.

At 1100 hours, Nos. 1 and 2 Companies of the Irish Guards with their battalion headquarters started withdrawing, together with the invaluable platoon of the 2nd/7th Middlesex Regiment who had fought courageously throughout the night and broken up infantry attack after infantry attack on their positions, accounting for, so they calculated, the best part of 200 enemy. The platoon was only nine strong by that time, but they still managed to bring out their own guns and a number of wounded Guardsmen. By now the forward positions were completely surrounded, so leaving their carriers around the railway bridge, the Irish Guards split into small parties and started to work their way to the south.

At their battalion headquarters they mustered all who were unwounded and plunged into the ditches and wadis which lay between them and No. 4 Company. In a matter of minutes the party had become widely separated, as one group pushed on and another tried a different route. The latter, trudging through the bewildering collection of winding gullies, suddenly found themselves overlooked by the grinning faces of Germans armed with spandaus. The gist of their remarks was apparent to even the non-German speakers, and the column halted with ill-grace and a lot of muttering. The Germans slid down the bank, removed the weapon and reversed the order to march. With a guard to each man, the column marched back the way they had come. Captain S. H. Combe, Headquarter Company commander, at the head of the column, spoke to his particular guard in a polite voice, 'I am going to do you in when I get a chance.' He did not have long to wait. The party emerged from the gully into the sunken road by the railway bridge, climbed the bank and continued northwards. As they came into the open, a hail of bullets halted and disconcerted the Germans. Captain Combe walked on and picked up a rifle from the bank and shot his guard. This was the signal for a general slaughter of the escort. Every Irish Guardsman picked up something—a rifle, a spade, or even a petrol tin—and laid about him. Of the thirty Germans who had formed the escort twenty were killed, nine taken prisoner and one was officially recorded as 'missing'. They then reversed the order of march and this time returned without further incident.

The Regimental Sergeant-Major and a Guardsman had drawn up the rear of the battalion headquarters party but became separated from the main batch. Soon enough they too were captured and two Germans placed as guards. But as the captors were hungry and the sergeant-major was carrying a plentiful supply of sandwiches, the roles were soon reversed and in due time the two Irishmen returned with their trophies. To be greeted by the acting Commanding Officer who tersely enquired why they were so late!

The roll call that night showed the Irish Guards to be 140 strong—outnumbered even by the prisoners they had brought back with them. Through the hours of darkness, individuals, and small groups of men dribbled back, some through the Scots Guards, some through the Grenadiers, some through the huge gaps between the other battalions and companies of the 1st British Division. By dawn the following day they could muster 260 men, and with the welcome reinforcement of 80 more it was possible to put three rifle companies into the field.

Elsewhere, throughout the morning, there had been ominous reports of enemy armour. Some to the north-west of the salient, some due west in the area of the railway embankment. There was even talk of the reconnaissance unit of an armoured division being sighted on the coast road beyond the Moletta River where the 36th U.S. Engineer Regiment held a huge frontage on what up to then had been considered a peaceful part of real estate. Then, shortly after one o'clock, the squadron commander of 'B' Squadron of the 1st Reconnaissance Regiment, Major J. A. Acland, who was on the eastern side of the salient, to his amazement, saw a number of tanks moving leisurely into a large field. As he watched more and more moved in; it was a target beyond price. Within minutes nearly every gun on the sector was engaging the enemy. Even as the ranging rounds came down, the tanks continued into the field until there were upwards of a dozen of them. More tanks appeared and yet more and then the concentration fell. Some disappeared in the mud and soil and rock thrown up by the shells, others continued to come forward into the centre of the field in a detached sort of way, like blundering animals, and regardless of the shot which was coming down all around them. A number received direct hits and blew up, the others beat a hasty retreat, the stragglers were caught by the anti-tank guns of the Reconnaissance squadron.

The 3rd Infantry Brigade viewed the collapsing situation to their rear with increasing apprehension. For some hours now there had been no land communication to the rear and it was certain that they were now cut off. But their day had been enlivened by an incident which was to become a talking point for long afterwards. For in the middle of the murky morning, through the accumulated haze and smoke around them, the Foresters saw a party of troops making their unhurried way up the railway line from Carroceto. At first they were taken for Germans but suddenly it dawned that these were British prisoners being herded back by German guards. The mixed bag of prisoners from many regiments had been marched along with their hands at their sides, but approaching the Foresters' position the guards told them to raise them above their heads and drove their captives towards the Foresters. The intention was obvious. Unable to fire for fear of hitting their comrades, a number of Foresters in the rear positions were forced to surrender and join the party. This was too much. To shoot would have been to imperil their own troops, so the Foresters' Battalion Headquarters mounted a quick attack. Some of the group had already gone by, but the remainder were rescued, their guards shot, or in turn captured. Those who had passed the Foresters were seen by the KSLI.

A rescue party then was quickly organised. Major Mansell with a couple of carriers charged down on the column of prisoners, cheered away like hounds to cover by those at the KSLI battalion headquarters. The German guards tried to fire a ragged volley but then turned and ran, and the prisoners, for the most part, were rescued.

The fate of the 3rd Infantry Brigade now rested on the resistance being put up by those left on the shoulders of the salient. The Germans were in tenuous occupation of the Via Anziate between Milestones 23 and 24. It could be only a question of time before those at the tip of the 'Thumb' were consumed piecemeal by the enemy who were closing in from all sides, regardless of the very heavy casualties they were suffering from the Allied artillery fire. German prisoners complained of the attack being hurriedly mounted without adequate reconnaissance, and some units moved up during the night by forced marches being thrown directly into battle. Throughout the long day of 4 February the Irish Guards and the survivors of the 6th Gordons with assistance from the tanks of the 46th Royal Tank Regiment, who were subjected to tiresome sniper fire, fought stubbornly in the area of Dung Farm and to the west of the main road and kept the enemy at bay, while to the south, the Scots Guards and Grenadiers beat off attack after attack. And the defence held.

But help was at hand, for the 168th Brigade of the 56th (London) Infantry Division—the Black Cats, as they were referred to from their divisional sign—had arrived in the beachhead. This brigade—the International Brigade they liked to call themselves—consisted of the 1st

Battalion the London Irish Rifles, the 1st Battalion the London Scottish and the 10th Battalion the Royal Berkshire Regiment; their arrival was providential, but they were far from fresh.

Since the New Year the brigade had been closely involved in the efforts to secure Mount Damiano, a prominent feature north of the Garigliano River. During these hard-fought battles, in miserable weather against a stubborn enemy, all three regiments had suffered heavy casualties. They were in desperate need of a rest and refit when they were withdrawn; it had never occurred to them that this was not what was in store. To their surprise they motored to near Naples. Here their numbers were made good and at the end of January the three battalions embarked for Anzio. They knew little about the Anzio landing. Early reports had spoken of negligible opposition and a few sleepy Germans. By now, surely, they assumed 6th Corps must be well inland. They dreamed of a few sunny days in corps reserve and then a triumphal entry into Rome—in anticipation the London Scottish started to polish their belts.

Brigadier K. C. Davidson, commanding the Brigade, expecting to hear that this was indeed to be their role, reported to 1st Divisional Headquarters on arrival, and there met the corps commander. General Lucas placed his hand on Brigadier Davidson's shoulder, 'Say, Brigadier,' he said, 'I am mighty glad to see you. You're the last pea in my pod.'

On the journey up, the ships' crews painted a gloomy picture of constant shell-fire and told harrowing tales of unloading their ship under vicious air and artillery attack. But when the brigade arrived all was peaceful, it was a lovely spring morning, herald of a beautiful Italian day. In the distance the Alban Hills looked very close, so close that it never occurred to them that they might still be held by the enemy. In the rest area a few desultory shells had come whining over and one or two fell near. Nor did they relish the unpleasant novelty of an air raid, for the Luftwaffe had been rare visitors in their experience. From their arrival they had been at thirty minutes' notice to move—in any of several directions. Then, early on the morning of 4 February they had gone up to exiguous reserve positions around the Flyover. But there were no specific orders and no news of what was happening to the front, although the sound of heavy artillery fire, from both sides, showed that a full-scale battle was raging. Thus the summons that came to the London Scottish on the morning of 4 February, shortly after they reached their Flyover positions, was something of a shock.

The first part of the journey was in lorries but the last miles were on foot over the open fields. Behind The Factory, which was gradually disintegrating under artillery fire, they shook out into extended line and at four o'clock started to walk forward. The Gordon Highlanders were the Regular Army foster regiment to the London Scottish, so it was a happy choice that the latter were chosen for this attack. The interchange of officers and non-commissioned officers between the two regiments was extensive. Colonel Peddie of the Gordons had himself been a member of the 'Scottish' at one time, so the reunion of the two regiments was warm, if brief.

Ahead lay an indeterminate number of Germans who had enjoyed all morning to dig in. A hasty barrage had been called for and behind a massive artillery concentration the two leading companies of the London Scottish with the support of all the remaining tanks of the 46th Royal Tank Regiment passed through the remnants of the Gordons and pushed northwards through the olive groves beyond Dung Farm. At first there was little opposition, but as they neared the Gordons' former positions, they found the Germans in determined possession. All around were trenches full of the enemy, while to the east and to the west along the main road heavy flanking fire poured down on the Scottish. They pressed dourly on, winkling Germans out of the trenches as they went and packing some off to the rear to surrender to those less occupied. On the right, 'D' Company, under Major H. R. R. Attwooll MC, found the opposition stiffening as they approached the lateral road which had been the start of the 3rd Brigade attack so long ago. But fighting forward with great gallantry they secured their objective. Of the seventy-eight men Major Attwooll had started with, ten remained.

To his left, along the general line of the main road, Major J. A. Findlay with 'A' Company was having an even tougher time. All along the Via Anziate and in the farmhouses by the road the Germans had established themselves in strength. One by one the farmhouses were dealt with by the tanks, and then, while the defenders were still dazed, the Scottish went in with the bayonet. It was slow work it was expensive work, but it was succeeding. At last 'A' Company too reached their objective, but there were only five men with Major Findlay left to enjoy their victory. Now, to their delight, they could see the Germans in front of them pulling out to the east. The little party with General Penney and the 3rd Brigade Commander around Dung Farm at last could see the satisfying sight of fourteen Shermans on the objective. By five o'clock the route back for the 3rd Brigade was clear.

The previous hours had been anxious ones for the beleaguered battalions of the 3rd Infantry Brigade. After the incident of the prisoners, the brigade sat back to see what other unpleasantness the day would bring. It was not long in coming, for it became abundantly clear that a noose was gradually tightening around their highly exposed position. To the east, the KSLI became uncomfortably aware that a lot of enemy were gathering, for the noise of tracked vehicles could be clearly heard, ominously rather to their rear. Sure enough, over the brow of a ridge three enemy tanks appeared and drove slowly across the front, seemingly as bewildered about the exact location of the 3rd Brigade as they were about the enemy. They disappeared in a fold of the ground and then reappeared again and all three were wiped out in quick succession by Captain H. Ripley, KSLI anti-tank platoon commander. Shortly afterwards a further four tanks crossed the ridge in the same place—these were accounted for by the gunners of 81st Anti-Tank Regiment attached to the battalion. The sight of seven smoking hulks was a most heartening one.

On the other side of the tip of the salient, the Dukes were beginning to find themselves heavily occupied. Colonel Webb-Carter and two of his company commanders were in the rear resting, while the battalion was commanded by the second-in-command, Major M. M. Davie. Before leaving, Colonel Webb-Carter had sought permission to pull back his very exposed forward companies, but this was refused. Thus Major Davie could only watch sadly, and largely impotently, while they were gradually nibbled away as the day wore on.

Communications were at best scanty; at other times non-existent. To make matters worse, whenever German planes flew over the Dukes' headquarters they jammed the frequency and all that could be heard over the wireless were the German pilots commenting on the presence of 'Englischen Truppen'. Around mid-day it became clear that 'D' Company, in a horribly exposed position to the right, must have been overrun, and it seemed that battalion headquarters itself might be next to go when two German tanks moved to the top of a ridge above the gully where they had withdrawn for safety.

Here, through a haze of static, and in an old code, for theirs was long since out-of-date, they deciphered enough to learn that the 3rd Infantry Brigade was to disengage and pull back; the Dukes at 1715 hours, the KSLI at 1800 hours, and the Foresters thirty minutes later.

Darkness fell early on the evening of 4 February and in teeming rain the KSLI started to withdraw. 'C' Company moved back first to a covering position to the rear and to the east, and immediately ran into a force of enemy tanks and infantry which barred the way back. The tanks they left burning, the infantry were driven off. Then, using a couple of carriers as rearguard and under a fierce bombardment of all known and suspected enemy positions, the forward companies of the KSLI fought their way back. By 1830 hours they had broken contact. By midnight the whole battalion with all their support weapons and vehicles were behind Carroceto.

The Foresters followed in the wake of the KSLI, but their vehicles had all been cut off by the Germans who had gradually been encroaching on their positions, as if they knew that the battalion opposing them was perilously weak. Thus their anti-tank guns had to be left in the hands of the enemy, but the machine gunners brought their weapons out on their backs—it was a long carry. The route they chose was straight down the main road which was being criss-crossed with fire, but most of it was high. Around one o'clock in the morning they too had reached Carroceto.

The Dukes, though, were in a more parlous situation. One company was already overrun, and the others were in very close contact with the enemy. The only way back would be through 'A' Company who rather tentatively were holding the most southerly point of the battalion front, although that 'front' was by now a series of thin and quite unsupporting segments. The message to break contact was passed.

As dusk was settling on 4 February, the 1st Battalion the Duke of Wellington's Regiment started their long way back. Smoke had been asked for to cover the withdrawal, but it was not forthcoming; they could now only rely on the gathering darkness and their own wits to evade their enemy who was all around them and closing in fast. In the event 'C' Company, the remains of 'B' Company, and battalion headquarters all arrived about the same time in 'A' Company's area: so too did some German tanks. These troublesome creatures had been in evidence for some time, nor were they alone, for a platoon of German infantry kept them close company throughout the long afternoon. They sat quietly on a ridge between 'B' Company and 'A' Company dominating both positions as well as battalion headquarters, unhappily sited between the two, and at dusk must have moved closer to 'A' Company as though anticipating the Dukes' next move. Thus to Major Davie's horror his party ran straight into them on the way back. As he wrote later himself:

It was now everyone for himself. Some managed to gain 'A' Coy's slit trenches. I remember lying in a rut made by a tank. By now it was 1730 hours, and we were taking cover just where we could . . . During the next three-quarters of an hour, most of us were literally pinned to the ground, trying to make ourselves as invisible as possible. It was obviously impossible to continue our withdrawal until it was dark. However, we were faced with another problem—there was a full moon. The enemy tanks had withdrawn as the day closed, with the exception of one which was burning well after a direct hit from one of our anti-tank guns, manned by private soldiers slap in the open. It was a magnificent feat. At about 1800 hours it was evident that an enormous black cloud would soon cover the moon for at least twenty minutes. I gave the order to continue the withdrawal as soon as the cloud passed over the moon.

In small groups, the Dukes made their way back towards Anzio. One flank was illuminated by the pinkish glow of a burning tank, the other by a haystack which had been set on fire, but the trip back was comparatively uneventful. In the olive groves, no more than fifty yards away, they could hear Germans talking. Clearly the enemy were as confused about the situation as everyone else. The battalion, but without any carriers or support weapons, were behind Carroceto by the early hours of the morning of 5 February. There were eleven officers and 250 men missing.

The impossible had been achieved. 3rd Infantry Brigade had broken from close contact with the enemy and escaped from their salient. It was a remarkable feat. And with the rescue of the three battalions, the Irish Guards and Gordons were now free to pull back themselves and reorganise, leaving the London Scottish who by their gallantry and fortitude in clearing the way had made it all possible.

For much of the night Colonel Peddie of the Gordons had been waiting at Horror Farm for the battalions of the 3rd Brigade to pass back through his position, as had been the intention. He waited in vain, and at length he decided to go to the main road to find out if any had passed. To his amazement he discovered that by then almost the whole brigade had come by quietly, safely and in good order down the Via Anziate. He returned to Horror Farm where the Gordons were assembling in a setting, the veterans recall, like a scene from Dante's Inferno.

The whole place was under heavy shell-fire, and all around the flash of bursting shells lit up the scene in horrifying detail to a backcloth of tracer arcs crossing the sky. From time to time there was the sharp crack of a rifle from some sniper or other who had lain up while the London Scottish had passed, and a tank which had moved up from the east and started to fire directly at the farm added to the general bedlam. One of the barns had been set on fire and in the steady glow it was possible to see that it had started to snow. Waiting stoically, while Horror Farm disintegrated around them, were the wounded, some on stretchers waiting to be carried to the rear, while limping in was a long column of walking wounded, making their own painful way for help, or on the arms of their comrades. A good few were Gordons, but most of the rest were from the London Scottish who had lost 120 men that day.

The Gordons collected into small groups before making wearily to the rear. There were very few left. Of 'A' Company only twenty men found their way back; from 'D' Company, two; from 'C' Company not a single man; while 'B' Company throughout their magnificent defence and counter-attack had suffered severely. Altogether ten officers and 319 men were missing.

Around midnight, the remains of the London Scottish, their task now completed, pulled back to behind the Factory. Horror Farm, or what was left of it, was abandoned to the Germans.

6

The Closing Noose

5–8 February

The salient now successfully dealt with, the Germans' next task was to pinch out the British positions holding forward of the Flyover as a prelude to breaking through down the Albano-Anzio axis towards the sea. Before doing so, however, two battalions of 26th Panzer Division, with elements of two other divisions, attacked Ponte Rotto south-west of Cisterna. It was a preliminary to the main attack on the Campoleone sector, and described as a 'noisy affair' by General Truscott. By first light on 6 February the Germans had withdrawn before the Americans could put in a counter-attack.

5 and 6 February passed peacefully on the front of the 1st British Division. Peacefully that is except for ceaseless patrol activity and the clear indication that the Germans were building up their strength for a major attack. Throughout the previous two days there had been increasing enemy air activity and continual reports of tank movement in the areas around and forward of Campoleone Station as well as to the north-west beyond the Buon Riposo and Vallelata Ridges, and, more ominously, towards the east and north-east which was the better tank country and where the battalions of the 168th Brigade were spread out in front of and to the east of the Factory. All across the Front, there was the awesome feeling that the moment of truth was upon them.

The German attack on Carroceto was to be mounted by Battle Group Gräser from the north and north-east, and 65th Infantry Division from the west. The brunt of Gräser's attack was to be undertaken by 29th Panzer Grenadier Regiment of 3rd Panzer Grenadier Division, now returned to the fray, whose objective was initially the Fosso della Ficoccia and then the cemetery north of the Factory and the bridge at Guardapassi over the Fosso. Another battle group comprising 735th Grenadier Regiment was to strike south from the Macchia del Casale, while a third element of Gräser's force, consisting principally of 725th Grenadier Regiment, pushed down the Via Anziate from the north. While this attack was in progress, Battle Group Pfeiffer, of 65th Infantry Division and 11th Parachute Regiment, continued their attacks from the west, their objectives the Embankment towards Carroceto and the Buon Riposo Ridge as an avenue to attack the

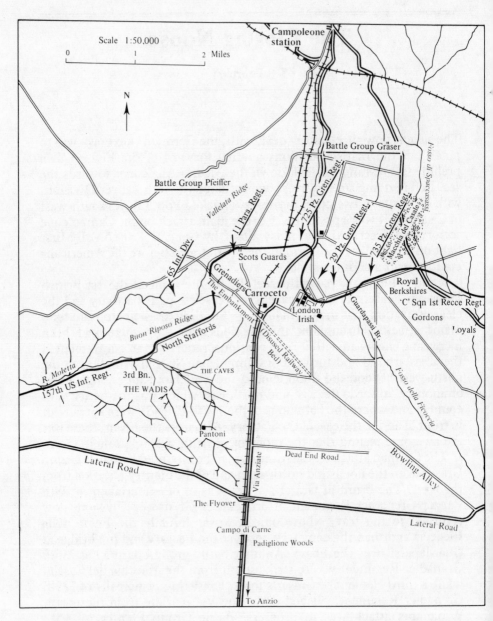

The Salient, 5 February

Flyover from the west. The main attack was synchronised to start at 2130 hours on 7 February; the preliminaries were earlier.

During the night of 6 February a message of the highest authenticity came through that a German attack was confidently expected at four o'clock the following morning. The battalions stood to. Gun and mortar crews waited by their weapons ready to bring down immediate fire should it be called for. Listening posts lying far out in front of their platoons scanned the familiar landscape ahead for any suspicious movement. The moon was nearly full and the whole plain was illuminated with a ghostly light. In section and platoon positions not a word was spoken. Telephone messages saying that all was well and that there was nothing to report were passed on in whispers.

The divisional forecast was one hour out. Promptly at 0500 hours, under cover of smoke and very heavy artillery fire, the Germans attacked the Factory area in their first efforts to fight through to the vital Carroceto bridges.

Like the other battalions of the 168th Brigade, the 1st Battalion the London Irish Rifles holding the Factory, had been hurriedly withdrawn from Mount Damiano. No one was sorry to leave, but by then they were down to three weak companies, and all were very tired. A reinforcement of ten officers and 250 men brought them up to strength, but few of the new arrivals had ever seen action before. Thus it was an almost new battalion who were pitchforked into the Anzio battle. The draft had been distributed among the existing companies, but there was no time to train; no time for men to get to know their officers or each other; and there was no time to engender that vital regimental spirit which comes of shared endeavours and shared hardships. The 'Irish' they were, and as the 'Irish' they fought and many died. Yet there were few Irishmen among them, fewer still of the 'Ballymena Boys' who had made up the regiment in distant 1941. Instead there was a mixture of any and every regiment in the British Army, including a large number of gunners—for the most part from disbanded light anti-aircraft units, no longer needed in their original role as the Luftwaffe was so rarely in the sky—who proved to be fine infantry, despite their lack of infantry training.

During the night of 4/5 February the London Irish took over the Factory sector from the ubiquitous 1st Reconnaissance Regiment. The next day was quiet which gave them a chance to know the country around them. Mud seemed to be the prevailing surface, glutinous sticky mud which rendered progress off the roads impossible even for tracked vehicles and was made worse by the rain which poured down in unceasing torrents. All across the land to the north and to the east of the Factory lay shallow irrigation ditches which were mostly full of water.

Their slit-trenches were soon awash and they lived perpetually wet with their feet in water. The complaint known as trench foot, which had been such a scourge in Flanders during the First World War, made its unpleasant reappearance, although the canny ones stood in tins in the bottom of their slits. And another phenomenon of that last War—battle exhaustion it was now called—started seriously to concern the medical staffs for the first time. But grumble at the weather and conditions though they did, the Germans were in a like case and the boggy state of the ground was one of the principal factors which saved the beachhead.

The Irish, though, were too preoccupied on their own account to concern themselves overmuch with the welfare of the Germans. Their task was likely to be a formidable one, and they knew it as they worked hard through the day of 6 February preparing their positions with the paltry quantity of mines and wire that could be spared. Their front covered some 1,500 yards. To the west, linking with the Scots Guards in the general area of Carroceto, lay their 'A' Company. To the right, some 500 yards forward of the Factory and covering the approach from the north was 'D' Company. And far away to the east, out of touch and out of mutual support, covering the menacing Fosso della Ficoccia which thrust like an arrow into the Allied lines, lay 'B' Company. It was the usual pattern of too large a front for too few men and with no depth, which was to become painfully familiar during the Anzio battles. With such a weak battalion Lt.-Col. I. R. Good DSO, the commanding officer, had no alternative. To the right of the Irish across the Fosso lay the 10th Royal Berkshires, while between the two battalions and to their rear lay the remnants of the London Scottish.

The Factory itself was too unhealthy to stay in and seemed to attract an inordinate amount of German fire. The only defenders were a number of observation posts who lived an unpleasant life in the higher buildings and for the most part had to stay where they were through the daylight hours as the only staircases to these eyries were outside the buildings and, tiresomely, in full view of the enemy.

It was 'D' Company in their highly exposed position north of the Factory who took the first onslaught of the enemy, while the 10th Royal Berkshires beyond the Fosso della Ficoccia also came under heavy and accurate artillery fire. These were probing attacks by the Germans. Insidious activity by groups of about platoon strength who tried to see where were the forward positions and sound the mettle of the defenders. Of the layout they soon enough found out all they needed to know, of their mettle they were left in no doubt long before the day was ended.

There were tales of enemy concentrations of both tanks and infantry to the north and east and it was clear that a major effort could be expected soon. From the way the Factory dominated the surrounding

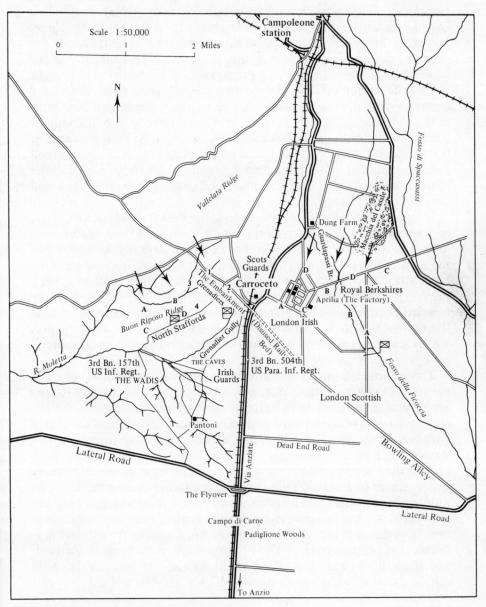

The fight for Carroceto, 7–9 February

countryside, it was only too apparent that this would be in the forefront of the enemy's ambitions. Throughout the day the Germans probed ceaselessly. This was close-quarter fighting at its worst with rifles, bayonets and grenades. At first the Germans tried using infantry alone, but when this proved unsuccessful they brought up some tanks. By the evening, despite fighting grimly, the position of 'D' Company of the London Irish was to say the least precarious. 'B' Company to their right were little better off, for the Germans established themselves in a cemetery opposite their position and managing to mount machine guns in the stout though low walls of the graveyard were able to fire without hindrance not only on 'B' Company, but also on the exposed flank of 'D' Company. With 'D' Company now all but cut off, Colonel Good asked permission to bring them back to a more secure position, but the request was refused. There was no ground to give, they must fight, and die, where they stood.

It soon became clear that the attack on the Factory was but a foretaste of what was to happen across the whole divisional front before very long. The dawn of 7 February broke to reveal a clear sky, some sun and the Alban Hills in all their glory. The troops who had stood to for some time, stood down and set about the more mundane matter of getting breakfast. There was a deathly stillness throughout the morning. In the forward positions, if one listened hard enough, it was possible to hear the ominous crunch of tracks, while the dearth of the artillery fire, which had menaced their lives almost continuously and so accurately, gave portent of something terrible about to happen.

Throughout the long, silent afternoon, reports came in from all along the front of concentrations of enemy troops. Then the shelling started again, and intensified as the afternoon wore on, particularly on the approach roads to the forward positions. Another dimension was added with the unpleasant appearance of a number of enemy aircraft, which strafed the forward positions, particularly those of the London Irish around the Factory, while Anzio and Nettuno were subjected to three heavy attacks by Focke Wulffs and Messerschmitts during the day. The number of prisoners taken suddenly increased also, and many eagerly foretold of stirring things to come—it was evident that they had crossed over in order to avoid taking part in the great attack. At last darkness fell on that portentous day. The evening meals were brought forward, and then the forward battalions of the British 1st Infantry Division settled down to what was to prove a highly disturbed night.

Lying like a great whaleback on the surrounding plain, the Buon Riposo Ridge dominated the country to the north and west of the Flyover. Here, on a front of scarcely one mile, were situated the 2nd Battalion the North Staffordshire Regiment. The top and southern side of the ridge bore neatly cultivated fields, while towards the Vallelata Ridge to the north and to the north-west, lay an indeterminate scrubby sort of country which in places came right up to and, more important, between the positions held by the North Staffords' forward companies, 'A' and 'B'. A little to the rear, to provide some substance to an overlong position, were 'C' and 'D' companies. Battalion headquarters was under the brow of the hill approachable either from the north where the 5th Grenadiers were along the Embankment, or by using the road which ran along the top of the ridge and then dipped down.

Ever since moving to the Buon Riposo Ridge on 1 February, the North Staffords had felt rather than seen the enemy building up in front of them. At night the rumbling of large convoys of lorries could be heard to the north-west as the Germans started to collect supplies for the coming attack. And as the days passed, so the German activity increased in tempo and the artillery and mortar fire in intensity. Then, on 5 February, the whole front before them went completely quiet for two days. They had experienced it before in North Africa and the veterans among them had no illusions about what this sudden cessation of activity meant. The only question remaining was when and in what form the German attack would come. When the occasional shell passed overhead and enemy patrols were active they knew that whatever the Hun was hatching up was not imminent, but now, when a frozen silence covered their sector, it was unnerving and sinister. The whole of 7 February passed in peace, but it left them wondering.

Shortly after dark there was the sound of fighting to their left, where Germans started to probe forward vigorously at the 3rd Battalion of the 157th U.S. Regiment who covered the northern part of the Moletta front. Then, without warning, a fusillade rang out to the front of 'B' Company of the North Staffords. A sniper and bren post had been suddenly charged and overwhelmed. A brisk counter-attack quickly regained it and there was a moment or two to relax. Soon however, dire reports of Germans trying to work their way between the companies started to come in, and even more ominous ones that in places it was feared that there were Germans actually behind the forward positions. And there was very little that could be done about it, for great scrub-covered gullies cut into the positions of the forward companies all along the front inviting infiltration; it was clear that the Germans had made excellent use of them. The moon was high in the sky, it was bright as daylight; when the Germans attacked they were clearly visible.

At 2130 hours three companies were attacked, more or less simultaneously. At first the North Staffords appeared to be holding firm and Lt.-Col. A. J. Snodgrass, the commanding officer, announced confidently to brigade headquarters over his wireless 'everything all right, we'll just sit here till morning and then sort things out.' But then the full gravity of the situation became only too apparent. 'C' Company had thought themselves immune from direct attack, but having passed between the forward two companies, the Germans suddenly swooped from the flank and in a matter of moments their situation was critical. To their rear lay the mortar platoon. They fired mortar bombs as fast as any team in history, then found themselves attacked by overwhelming numbers of Germans who swarmed down into the mortar pits. Here a bloody hand-to-hand battle developed as the mortar men fixed bayonets and drove off their attackers. Then, when running low on ammunition, they pulled back towards battalion headquarters, bringing their mortar sights with them.

On the 'A' and 'B' Company fronts everything appeared to happen at once. One moment there were no Germans, and the next the place appeared to be swarming with fanatically shouting enemy as two or three battalions surged on to Buon Riposo Ridge, supported by tanks and SP guns making skilful use of the moonlight.

'B' Company gradually contracted and pulled in towards their company headquarters. Their strength was down to around thirty by then, and they were totally isolated with Germans behind them and to either flank. The remnants tried to work their way back towards battalion headquarters but found their way barred.

'A' Company too was almost isolated, and more enemy could be seen in the clear moonlight working their way from 'B' Company's former position to cut them off completely. As silently as he could, the company commander, Major J. E. Mason, gathered in the remnants of his company, barely twenty strong by this time, and waited for the enemy to come. Unsuspectingly the Germans approached. When they were only twenty-five yards away Major Mason gave the order to fire. The shattering volley completely broke the enemy, but as this volley used nearly the last of their ammunition and they were out of touch with their battalion headquarters, there was no recourse but to withdraw. Major Mason brought back the few survivors of his company to their right through a company of Grenadiers, from where he was able to contact a highly relieved Colonel Snodgrass, who had assumed that the entire company had been lost. Only the remnents of 'C' Company now remained, having pulled back to a slightly firmer position, but their situation continued critical. Curiously, the Germans seemed intent on by-passing them so they were able to warn battalion headquarters that the enemy were heading fast in their direction.

Since the first German attacks the Irish Guards, now resting in an area 2,000 yards north of the Flyover known as the Caves, had been listening with increasing consternation to reports of mounting German pressure on the North Staffords' position, for the Irish Guards were the only remaining body of troops between the ridge and the main road.

Around midnight they heard that all the North Staffords companies were off the air and that their battalion headquarters was surrounded. Then their commanding officer was called to the set. With great reluctance Colonel Scott agreed to send a company to the North Staffords. The promised reinforcement was none too soon.

Since the first attack on the North Staffords the situation had become increasingly confused and critical, and if Colonel Snodgrass had any doubts about their own fate they were soon confirmed when Germans started coming down the slope straight towards his battalion headquarters and through the positions formerly occupied by his forward companies. Hearing of the Irish Guards company heading their way the response, 'O.K. It had better keep the double up' seemed wise advice, for it appeared probable that very soon there would be nothing left for the reinforcement to reinforce. Back in the North Staffords' headquarters the commanding officer with his adjutant, Regimental Sergeant Major and Provost Sergeant, all armed with rifles, prepared to make the enemy pay heavily before their small stronghold fell, and set about engaging the Germans who were crossing a field to their flank. Through the next hours, stragglers from all companies joined battalion headquarters and helped drive off the enemy.

Meanwhile, back in the Irish Guards' headquarters, as their Regimental History put it:

Colonel Scott remained by the wireless for a few minutes after his conversation with the Brigadier. He sat in silence slowly tearing up an old letter, before saying to the Adjutant, "Tell David (O'Cock) to take out Number One Company", and then went back to the fire and emptied his pockets into it. The Adjutant tried to make his voice sound non-committal, but the effort only made him croak. 'We will be ready in about twenty minutes,' replied Captain O'Cock. 'Try and keep in touch with me.' They talked at intervals after Number One had set out, Captain O'Cock giving a commentary on his progress and what he could see, the Adjutant guiding him by the map and explaining the various sounds of battle. 'I think this must be them. Yes, it's their left-hand company.' After an interval, Captain O'Cock's voice came up again. 'Their Battalion headquarters are clamouring for us to join them. Do we go?' The Adjutant had to reply, 'Yes. You must get through to them.' Another crackling silence and then Captain O'Cock came up for the last time. 'We've hit the Germans.' Nothing more was heard from or of Number One Company until Rome Radio gave the names of a few prisoners.

At dawn twenty bedraggled men of one of the platoons filed down the gully into the Caves, but they knew nothing of the rest of the company. They had been held up at a stream soon after setting out, and by the time they had crossed it the rest of the company had disappeared. They had tried to catch up, but at each gully junction had to guess which way to turn and became thoroughly lost until they came on some Americans with whom they stayed until daylight.

Around three o'clock in the morning Colonel Snodgrass and the remnants of the 2nd Battalion the North Staffordshire Regiment pulled back towards the main road, while individual men breaking off from the action worked their way back towards the Flyover. As the depleted ranks were being mustered a sudden German artillery concentration landed in the middle of them adding twenty-six more names to the casualty lists. The next day the North Staffords could muster only two weak rifle companies; they had lost nearly three-quarters of their strength.

All the reserves Brigadier Murray had available were already committed, nor could the Brigadier extract any more help from divisional headquarters who refused to consider the threat from Buon Riposo anything more than a local attack. Whereas the 3rd Brigade had been brought forward to a stop-gap position for the promised German onslaught the previous day, on this night of nights, when the fate of the beachhead balanced on a knife-edge and depended on the dogged courage of a handful of men in half a dozen different and quite isolated positions, General Penney remained adamant—although, in truth, he had little enough to spare.

Under command of 24th Guards Brigade was the 3rd Battalion 504th U.S. Parachute Infantry under their inimitable commander Lt.-Col. Leslie G. Freeman, a tall Virginian whose calm assurance and great charm was to prove a godsend to all who came in contact with him. As the Irish Guards' history recalled, he endeared himself to them all with his first words, 'Those Krauts, I sure hate their guts.' And each morning as he strode into the Guards' position he would be greeted by Colonel Scott with the words, 'Hi'ya, Colonel, what d'ya know?' to which he always replied, 'Morning, Colonel, not a Goddam thing!' Already Colonel Freeman had committed his companies one by one to fill gaps wherever they appeared, and he agreed strongly with Colonel Scott who expressed the opinion that he didn't like 'being a little Dutch boy, running up and down plugging holes in the dyke.' The trouble was that the dyke looked like being breached in half a dozen different places at any time.

Those listening in on the brigade wireless set had been regaled a few minutes after eleven o'clock that night by a conversation between Brigadier Murray and Colonel Scott: 'Do you realise that I have sent all that I have got away now,' the colonel explained. 'Well, draw in your horns, recall the interception unit'—which was patrolling up the Via Anziate, a task which was to become more and more important as the night wore on. 'I will draw in my horns, as you politely call it, and I will leave the carrier patrol out.' 'O.K.,' replied the brigadier, 'this will leave you a little something.' 'Then thank God for a little something,' came back the withering reply, 'there are fifty very unpleasant gentlemen down this road somewhere.' But the Irish Guards had very few men left. With one company lost without trace on the way to the North Staffords, and another sent up to help the Scots Guards at Carroceto, even including all the drivers, cooks and miscellaneous Guardsmen they could collect, the battalion totalled less than 200 men. Now, towards morning on 8 February, they stood by to go to the aid of the Grenadiers who were in all sorts of trouble.

7 February had passed peacefully on the Grenadiers' front, ominously peaceful the veterans of those days recall. Even when dusk fell and night crept over the battlefield there was no visible activity on the German side, just, in the distance, the rumble of transport and tracked vehicles on the move, and the awesome feeling that something was about to happen. The early part of the night was peaceful too. They were unaware that since the first hours of darkness the enemy had been quietly working their way up the gullies and ditches which penetrated their wide front.

Shortly after last light, a patrol under Lieutenant M. J. Hussey went forward from No. 1 Company towards the Vallelata Ridge to scout around the area to the north-west. Their route took them up the Embankment where there had been no sight nor sound of Germans all day. The moon had risen and the whole plain was bathed in a soft light when distances can be very deceptive. There was no deception about what the patrol commander saw, though, for a bare 500 yards away and moving fast towards the company positions were three columns of men. They were marching in close formation as though on the road and each was about one battalion strong. He hurried back to report what he had seen.

No. 3 Company, in an isolated position west of the Embankment, had experienced an uneasy night; there was a feeling that something was happening, or about to happen, but it was difficult to tell just what. The first real intimation that all was not as well as it might be was the sound of heavy firing from the North Staffords' position. Some time later came the mysterious and disturbing noise of troops digging in on the ground behind them. They weren't left wondering for long, for two of the forward platoons reported German columns advancing rapidly towards them. Then, without any further warning, the Guardsmen suddenly found themselves involved in a close-quarter fight with an enemy who appeared to come on them from all sides.

Each of the Grenadier companies was in the shape of a parallelogram and each some 500 yards from the other. Even within their company areas, the ground dictated that their platoons had to be too far apart to help each other. Thus each small body of men must fight on its own, as happened so often at Anzio, without the benefit of mutual support and usually without fully realising what was happening either to flank or rear. It was impossible for battalion headquarters to gain a coherent picture of what was happening to their companies, and nearly so for company commanders even inside their own perimeters, especially when opposed by such masters of infiltration as the Germans. Thus, in a matter of moments, No. 3 Company found that there were Germans behind them, in front of them and even among them. Surrounded and swamped, and despite fighting heroic individual section and slit-trench battles, No.3 Company all but ceased to exist within half an hour. Urgently, Captain N. D. M. Johnstone, the company commander, reported that there seemed to be Germans all around him and then he went off the air. After smashing his wireless set, Captain Johnstone collected the remnants of his company—only nine men by this time—and made his way to the No. 1 Company position.

Here, too, things were far from comfortable. Without warning the Guardsmen found themselves involved in a bitter fight. 'I was suddenly aware,' wrote a platoon commander afterwards, 'that a lot of Germans had materialised, as it seemed, out of the air.' The position centred on a cluster of farm buildings, and this proved the focus of their defence. Time and again it was taken and lost, and then retaken again. For nearly an hour the company held out. By now their link with battalion headquarters had been broken and it was becoming evident that there were Germans working their way behind, threatening to cut them off from the rest of the battalion and in particular from No. 2 Company who were firmly entrenched further down the Embankment. By then the combined Nos. 1 and 3 Companies totalled a bare fifty men and they were also running out of ammunition, so the two company commanders decided to withdraw towards No. 2 Company so as to make a smaller, tighter perimeter nearer the vital road and rail junction at Carroceto.

They started to make their way down the Embankment, a jeep towing an anti-tank gun leading the way. It soon became clear that the way was no longer open when it ran into an ambush. There was no escape that way, so splitting up into small parties each led by an officer or non-commissioned officer they scattered, making use of whatever cover there was. Some were captured almost immediately, some managed to lie up until moonset and then in the blessed darkness make a stealthy return. Others, in the peculiar way that was possible in such broken ground, managed to find their way back without incident.

With another officer, Lieutenant Hussey spent a number of dramatic hours crouching in a ditch while the Germans patrolled above urging them to come out. A German officer, speaking in faultless English, pointed out, 'We know you are down there, if you do not come out before I count three, we'll grenade the ditch and you will be killed.' The two officers hugged the ground. The grenades duly exploded all around them, but they were untouched. After crouching, hardly daring to breathe, let alone move, for half an hour, they gingerly left their ditch and started to walk back towards their own lines. Just before dawn they came on a German position from the rear and discarding their helmets and equipment, armed only with revolvers and grenades, they calmly started to walk through the middle of the enemy. No one paid any attention to the two strange figures in their midst, saying a few 'Offizier' in a more or less gutteral accent, or the occasional 'Gudt Nacht' when circumstances seemed to require it, and they almost got through. Ahead lay a ditch lined with German troops—their front line. Beyond was open country. Starting to run, the two officers leaped the German ditch from behind to the astonishment of the occupants and throwing grenades as they ran, sprinted for the fields beyond. Hit by a schmeisser bullet as he slipped on jumping the ditch, Lieutenant Hussey was wounded and captured.

Within little less than two hours nearly half the Grenadiers had vanished from the scene. To the anxious listeners at battalion headquarters there seemed no end to the calamities of the night, for, almost immediately after the combined Nos. 1 and 3 Companies went off the air, No. 4 Company reported that they were being heavily attacked from the rear by some Germans, who, having passed through the North Staffords' position, had worked their way round behind Buon Riposo Ridge in their drive for the main road. There was no help forthcoming and Lt.-Col. A. C. Huntington MVO, who was killed shortly before daybreak the next day—the third commanding officer the Grenadiers had lost in twelve days—could only listen helplessly while the inevitable happened to the hapless No. 4 Company. After a while the company commander came through on the wireless to say that with the few surviving men of his company he was pulling back towards battalion headquarters, and then there was silence. Some hours later a few men returned from No. 4 Company and told graphically of the last stand of one of the platoon commanders, Lieutenant E. D. Collie, a huge man of six feet five inches who covered their withdrawal and was last seen vigorously bayoneting Germans.

At 0346 hours battalion headquarters sent a message to brigade headquarters, 'Situation Report. Nothing heard of Number One for forty-five minutes. Numbers Three and Four believed over-run. Ourselves surrounded and there is a bloody German on the ridge above us throwing grenades.' Thus within four hours of the first German attack the 5th Grenadiers were in a tight perimeter around the Carroceto bridges—they were to lose over 300 officers and men in three days—with No. 2 Company still along the Embankment, linking, more or less, with the Scots Guards on their right, while a mixed collection of any Guardsmen who could bear arms, those from Headquarters Company, Support Company, and men from the echelons who had brought up rations or ammunition and then stayed, occupied a gully no more than 300 yards from the main road. In the vital gap between No. 2 Company of the Grenadiers and their battalion headquarters was Company 'H' of the 504th Parachute Infantry commanded by an outstanding officer, Captain Dick La Riviere. And that was all between the Germans and the main road. To the south, far away out of sight, and nearly out of sound, was the Irish Guards trying to fill the huge gap which had been created behind the North Staffords' former position.

The Germans had suffered severely, not only from the withering small-arms fire from the infantry companies before they were overrun, but also by the packed mass of the guns of the divisional and corps artillery. Earlier in the night the Germans had made an attack on the 3rd U.S. Division in the area around Ponte Rotto but this was soon identified as a feint; thus all the guns on the beachhead were concentrated on the area of Via Anziate, and their support was sorely needed.

A quick glance at the battle map at headquarters of the 1st British Division was enough to show that what they were facing was a full-scale attempt on the main road and in particular on the Carroceto bridges. Already tanks and lorried infantry had been reported on and beyond Buon Riposo Ridge. This could mean only that the Germans were standing ready to exploit the break to the road; indeed the road was already under small-arms fire.

The significance of the western approach was as clear to the enemy as it was to those who gloomily studied the battle maps at 1st Division Headquarters. For the next three weeks the Germans tried in vain to clear the troublesome resistance which was holding them up to the west of the main road. There was no single factor which saved the beachhead, and any attempt to find one must inevitably become an invidious exercise, but without the courage and sacrifice of those who fought on that flank, in particular the survivors of the 5th Grenadiers with the men of the 3rd Battalion 504th Parachute Infantry Regiment in what became known as Grenadier Gully; the 2nd Battalion 157th Infantry Regiment and later the 2nd/7th Queens Regiment in the Caves; and the other battalions and regiments, both British and American, who found themselves fighting the bitter and confusing war of the Wadis, the beachhead would undoubtedly have been lost.

Thus history had ordained that the Carroceto bridges were to be the crucial spot on the front. If the Germans could have captured them they would have been all but through. The Scots Guards and the remains of

1 'A war to which there was no quick solution.' A mule on the main Italian front, January 1944

2 The architects of the Peter Beach landing: (from left) Rear-Admiral R. H. Troubridge; Major-General John P. Lucas, commanding Sixth Corps; and Major-General W. R. C. Penney, commander of the British 1st Infantry Division

3 By 5 o'clock on the first evening the port of Anzio was beginning to take customers. American LSTs moored at the hard; in the background the ruins of the seaside resort, and the first German prisoners bound for captivity

4 Congestion on Peter Beach, and out to sea was a 'car park' of ever increasing dimensions

5 On X-Ray Beach all was serene. Units of the US 3rd Infantry Division landing without let or hindrance on the morning of D-Day

6 The road to Rome!

7 The Via Anziate: five days after the landing and Rome just 30 miles away! A view looking north from the Flyover – behind the house on the right can be seen Aprilia (the Factory), beyond lie the Alban Hills and between is the dead flat plain of the Campo di Carne (the Field of Flesh)

8 Looking north-east towards the Alban Hills. Across the front is the Embankment; through the ruins of Carroceto runs the Via Anziate, past Milestone 25 and on; right of Milestone 25 is the Factory; beyond lies Dung Farm (Smell[y] Farm) in this aerial view); further on, where road and railway start to converge, is Campoleone Station

9 The Pantano Ditch and Cisterna, scene of the greatest of Anzio's many tragedies, the annihilation of the Rangers. In the foreground is what remains of Isola Bella

10 Anzio in February: although unpleasant in the extreme for the Allies, these conditions rendered the German armour almost useless

11 The famous Flyover looking north-west. To the left is the Wadi Country, seemingly flat and innocuous but in reality a tortuous maze of deep ditches. Beyond can be seen the low whaleback of the Buon Riposo Ridge

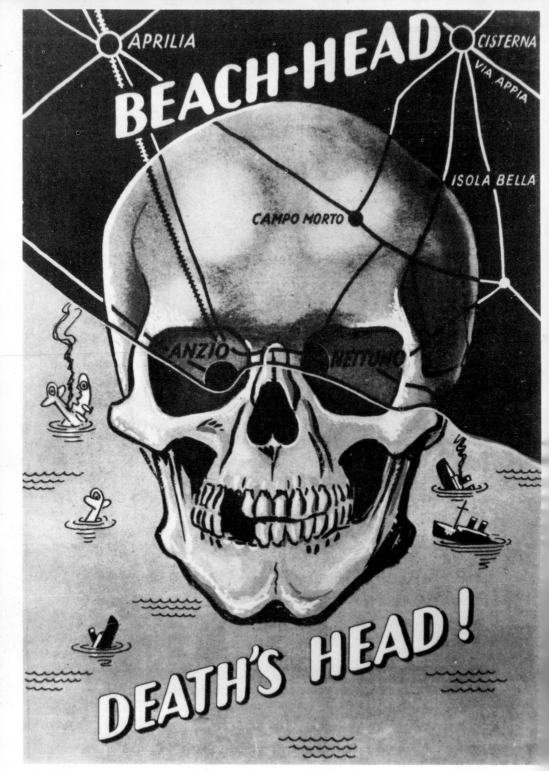

12   A German propaganda leaflet

13 On 3 March the German attacks came to a halt – beaten by the determination and courage of the British and American soldiery, the weight of the Allied artillery and naval gunfire which could be brought to bear anywhere on that constricted front, and . . . the weather

14 In the ruins of Nettuno: General Sir Harold Alexander and Major-General Lucian K. Truscott, shortly after the latter took command of the Sixth Corps

15 Wadi Country: one of the shallower ditches, now dry, in the part of the beachhead which epitomized for many all that was most terrible at Anzio

16 A forward slit-trench of the infamous Fortress, an outpost in Wadi Country: flat fields intersected by deep ditches full of impenetrable bramble and scrub ... and under observation by day

17 The Mussolini Canal on the eastern flank of the beachhead, home and hunting ground of the 1st Special Service Force – the Black Devils of Anzio – an élite American/Canadian special brigade

18 In the catacombs of Nettuno lived Sixth Corps Headquarters

19 Others had to make do with what they could build themselves

20 German weapons: a miniature tank (B IV) filled with explosives and radio-controlled. Likened by its handlers to a 'rather dangerous toy'

21 'Anzio Annie' derailed: a massive German 280mm railway gun. Guns such as these, and slightly smaller brethren, used to pound the beachhead and port area

22 Hell's Half Acre. There was no 'safe' area at Anzio; even hospitals and casualty stations had to take their chance with the rest

23 'A camaraderie never closer in the Second World War': British beer being put to the test

24 Operation Diadem: at 2300 hours on 11 May a massive barrage from guns of all calibres broke on the main Italian front. For the first time for four months the troops at Anzio could feel themselves part of larger events. In a fortnight junction was effected; the beachhead was no more

25 On 25 May Cisterna fell

26 Meanwhile, at Borgo Grappa at 8 o'clock on the morning of 25 May, reconnaissance units advancing from the south met the men from the beachhead. It was a wonderful morning

27 Victors: General Mark Clark, commander US Fifth Army, accompanied by Major-General Geoffrey Keyes and Major-General Lucian K. Truscott commanding the Six Corps, mounts the steps of the Capitol in Rome

the Grenadiers would have been engulfed, the London Irish, still grimly hanging on to the Factory area, would have been taken from the flank and rear, and the 10th Royal Berkshires who were to show courage and self-sacrifice not exceeded anywhere during that long, hard night would have found themselves isolated. The way would have been clear for the Germans to drive to the sea.

The front door to the bridges was in fairly firm hands, with the Scots Guards and No. 2 Company of the Grenadiers in prepared positions, in touch with each other and able to provide a degree of mutual support. To the right there was a gap between the Scots Guards and the London Irish; indeed Germans had already worked their way into the west and rear of the Factory, but they were in small numbers, and as long as the Irish remained firm, and there was every indication that they would, then that approach too was as solid as it was ever likely to be. But the back door, the approach from the west from the Buon Riposo Ridge was a different matter. All that lay between the Germans and the road was a long slope, a gully and a couple of open fields.

In the bottom of the gully Colonel Huntingdon had established his headquarters. The Intelligence Officer of the Grenadiers later described the scene:

> A track leading south-west from the Embankment dipped into the Gully, the walls of which rose higher as the track went further in. The stretch which concerned Battalion Headquarters was shaped like a question-mark, with the loop to the south. At the stalk of the question-mark, the Gully became deep and narrow, just deep enough and wide enough to accommodate a wireless truck and a couple of tents. Fifty yards south of the headquarters the Gully flattened out and here was the one and only crossing place over a deep ditch with slippery sheer sides covered with a tangle of brambles and containing knee-deep water. On the near side was a small rise of volcanic earth and a dry, shallow gully. To the west rose 300 yards of grassy slope to the crest of a foothill of the Buon Riposo Ridge.

From this vantage point the Grenadiers were to discover only too soon that their position was completely overlooked from above as the Germans attacked in the full moonlight.

And there is no doubt that the little party of Grenadiers and the American parachutists would have been overwhelmed in a matter of minutes until, as the Regimental History relates,

> They were brought up short by an obstacle which they had not expected—the Ditch . . . For some time the Germans ran uncertainly up and down the far side, losing heavily in the concentrated fire of the Grenadiers and the Americans. Then they found the crossing place. It was no more than a rough track hewn

through the brambles by some Italian peasant long ago, but once through it they were immediately opposite the shelving entrance to the Gully, and unless halted in time they would be in a position to roll up the whole Headquarters from the south.

It so happened that the crucial part of the Gully opposite the Ditch crossing was held by Major W. P. Sidney, commander of Support Company, with a handful of men. Hearing the splashing as the Germans came through the water, he advanced to the edge of the Ditch, stood upright in the face of intense fire, and held off the Germans with his tommy-gun. The gun jammed, Major Sidney withdrew to the edge of the steep ramp leading down into the Gully, and, though one or two Germans had now succeeded in crossing the Ditch, he prevented them getting any further by throwing grenades at any who showed themselves. The grenades were handed up to him by two Guardsmen who were priming them as fast as they could. In their eagerness, one grenade was detonated prematurely, killing one of the Guardsmen and wounding Major Sidney in the back. He remained for some minutes more at his post, blocking single-handed, and completely without cover, the crossing over the Ditch. Major Sidney was awarded the Victoria Cross.

And by the strange alchemy of war that was the end; the Germans had had enough for the moment. The few who had struggled across the Ditch were methodically eliminated by the Grenadiers, and Major Sidney, who had been wounded again in the face, this time by a German stick grenade, was able to have his wounds dressed. Suddenly there was no one left to shoot at.

The respite was brief. Promptly at 0330 hours the Germans attacked again. Perhaps the defenders had found a new confidence; perhaps the Germans themselves had lost heart; in any case the second attack was broken by small arms and artillery fire. Very few of the enemy managed to reach the Ditch this time. As dawn approached the attacks diminished and the Grenadiers with their American comrades began to breathe more easily. Just before daylight came the news which everyone had been expecting hourly, that the Germans had cut the Via Anziate between Carroceto and the Flyover. Fortunately it was not true.

Almost at the same time as the North Staffords had been attacked on Buon Riposo Ridge (see map 11 page 115), the 10th Battalion the Royal Berkshire Regiment also found themselves the object of German attentions. The country in which their positions lay was almost completely flat with no cover. There was the occasional building, derelict farmhouses for the most part, a barn or two and a number of huts. Their front was a mile wide bounded on either side by a stream with a deep

126

ditch; the Fosso di Spaccasassi on the right, and the Fosso della Ficoccia on the left, beyond which lay the London Irish around the Factory. To their front, a bare 350 yards away, lay a wood which was firmly in the possession of the Germans. To their right, the 1st Reconnaissance Regiment covered a front of nearly 4,000 yards and called themselves, with some justification, the 'Thin Red Line' of Anzio, and further to the east were the Loyals of the 2nd Infantry Brigade.

On the evening of 5 February the Berkshires had moved into this undesirable position. With no protection of any sort, they dug where they could. Ammunition and equipment had to be man-carried as no vehicles, not even a jeep, could struggle through the mud to their forward positions. Feverishly they set about establishing their defence; minefields were laid before their rapidly developing positions; wire placed to impede any advance. A house which became known as House 'Z' and was uncomfortably close to their lines, was found to be holding some Germans. These were routed out and the dismaying intelligence gathered that there were no less than four separate German battalions in the area, and that they intended to mount a two-pronged attack, one towards their own positions and those of the London Irish down the line of the Fosso della Ficoccia, and the other from the north-east.

They waited all through the long morning and afternoon of 7 February. There was no movement in the area, for everyone was pinned down by heavy and accurate shelling. Casualties began to mount, despite the protection of their slit-trenches which were deep at the beginning of the day and with the spur of enemy shelling became deeper still. Nevertheless, the monotonous cry of 'Stretcher-bearer' became an all too frequent reminder that their numbers were dwindling steadily.

The evening came and went and then just before ten o'clock that evening the German attack started in earnest. Throughout the past two days 'C' Company on the right of the battalion position had been receiving the heaviest casualties. It became imperative to relieve them by one of the less committed companies. But when? The time chosen was unhappily at 9.30 that evening. While the difficult and complicated process of a relief in the line was in progress, when slit-trenches were occupied by men of the new company and men of the old, when others, their relief complete, were hurrying over open ground without protection to their collecting points, the German attack fell.

Although the Berkshires were not to know it, their adversary had been having severe troubles of his own. While the attack down the Fosso della Ficoccia went off on schedule under one battle group of 3rd Panzer Grenadier Division, that through the woods to their front by the other prong of General Gräser's forces had been badly delayed by the boggy ground which they had to cross. Thus the first attack fell on the London Irish to the left and on their own 'D' Company. This enabled some of the relieved 'C' Company to get back—it was as well they did, for those few survivors were to prove of inestimable value before the agony of the 10th Royal Berkshires was over.

With 'D' Company taking the brunt of the early German attack, Lt.-Col. I. R. Baird DSO, MC, the commanding officer, sent forward his reserve company, 'A', to help, and then, when things were at their worst, played his last stroke. In the bright moonlight and along routes which had been studied and examined in daylight, his carriers drove forward firing at point-blank range. By midnight the situation was restored.

At about the same time that the carriers were sweeping all before them, the long-expected attack broke on the right of the battalion. The relief had been badly held up by the German shelling and the nightmare feared by those relieving each other came to pass with a vengeance. 'C' Company still held the right flank positions which were in full view of the enemy, the rest were held by the incoming 'B' Company. Milling about behind was a mixture of both companies making use of whatever cover they could find and suffering heavily from the heavy German mortar and artillery fire. 'C' Company commander had already been wounded, so the combined companies were under command of Major H. Greenaway. At midnight he reported that they were more or less surrounded, to which Colonel Baird replied, 'You have got the men and ammunition, fight it out.' For the next hours they did. A platoon of 'A' Company was switched to go to their aid, and every man capable of carrying an ammunition box was sent forward. Clerks, drivers, even the cook-sergeant, a former 'B' Company man, brought forward his quota of ammunition and stayed with his old company to fight.

By two o'clock in the morning 'B' Company had been all but overrun, but a counter-attack restored the situation. At 0230 hours there was a brief lull, but only while the Germans gathered their strength for one more effort. An hour later another attack broke on the hard-pressed companies, this time of an even greater intensity than before. In a matter of moments they were all but swamped, but managed to hold on, just. The whole of the right flank of the battalion position was now in enemy hands, although so confused was the situation that this unpalatable fact did not become clear until dawn. At eight o'clock that morning 'B' Company reported that there were enemy on three sides and that tanks were approaching from the woods to their front. The medium artillery dealt with the tanks, and the 10th Royal Berkshires breathed again.

The morning of 8 February thus found the 1st British Division hanging on grimly. The Buon Riposo Ridge was now firmly in enemy hands. The few survivors of the North Staffords were for the most part behind the Flyover, although a good number of individuals were fighting with the Irish Guards, the Grenadiers and the American parachutists. They too started to return to their unit at daybreak but there were not many. The North Staffords had lost a staggering twenty-three officers and over 300 men in a matter of eight hours.

Blocking the exits from the Buon Riposo Valley towards the Via Anziate were the last remnants of the Irish Guards and the 3rd Battalion 504th Parachute Infantry. The Grenadiers, or rather their battalion headquarters, were still in the Gully and No. 2 Company on the Embankment. The Scots Guards, who had spent the night being heavily shelled and wondering at the apparent dissolution all around them, were in and around Carroceto. The London Irish were in their positions on the outskirts of the Factory, with the London Scottish a thousand or so yards behind in reserve, while the 10th Royal Berkshires had a precarious hold on the country to the east.

The most parlous situation, though, which threatened the very existence of all the troops forward of the Flyover, was in the Buon Riposo area. If reports were correct about enemy lorried infantry and tanks massing behind the Ridge, then it was clear that this was the most threatened quarter. Should the enemy punch their way through to the

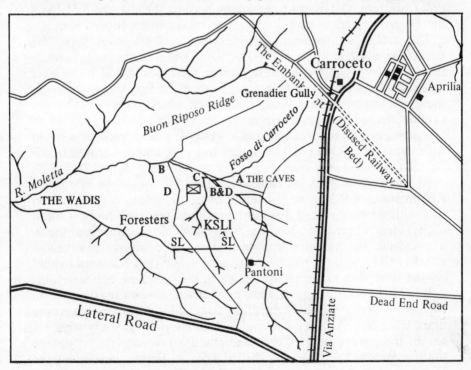

Positions after 3rd Infantry Brigade attack, 8 February

Via Anziate, then the whole house of cards which represented the state of the British 1st Infantry Division would collapse. General Penney therefore decided that a counter-attack must be put in by the only reserve he still possessed, the 3rd Infantry Brigade, to try to regain the North Staffords' lost positions.

The night of 7/8 February had been one of continual disturbance and alarms for the 3rd Infantry Brigade. They were then in a reserve position south of the Flyover under orders to counter-attack 'anywhere', and as the night progressed and the situation deteriorated on the 1st Division's front a counter-attack before dawn became increasingly likely. During the previous day, the Foresters had moved up and dug positions in the boggy ground north of the Lateral Road east of the Flyover and having dug them were ordered to march back to their echelon area in Padiglione Woods, a distance of five miles. No sooner there, than they were told to march back the way they had come and occupy the positions they had just dug, and there, to everyone's relief they were allowed to stay. The experiences of the other battalions of the brigade were as frustrating. Thus there was no rest for even the reserve brigade for forty-eight hours, and during the last night no less than three different 'O' Groups were summoned. At the last, the KSLI and the Foresters learned that they were to retake Buon Riposo Ridge.

The attack was ordered for 1130 hours. This would give the Foresters, who had only a short distance to travel, ample time to reach their Start Line on time, but little enough time for the KSLI who were then manning a position on the eastern side of the Flyover. In the event the attack was postponed, firstly to 1230 hours and finally to 1330 hours to allow the KSLI to get through. But the artillery barrage, which had been designed to support the attack, could not be altered. It went in with devastating effect at 1230 hours and gave ample warning to the Germans of what was afoot.

At five o'clock that morning a troop of 'B' Squadron of the 1st Reconnaissance Regiment was sent forward to join their 'A' Squadron who with the survivors of the North Staffords, were still holding south of the ridge. Three hours later the whole of 'B' Squadron joined them. Throughout the morning the small force were subject to repeated attacks and had a lot of trouble with snipers, but they managed to hold on and were in position to help shoot in the attacking battalions.

By 1330 hours the Foresters had been on their Start Line for close on two hours, under continuous artillery fire, and were suffering a steady drain of casualties. They had also had ample time to study what lay ahead, and it was a far from inviting sight. To their right they could see the Via Anziate being steadily shelled along its length; beyond lay the Factory, its great mass menacing the flat landscape. At the head of the Via Anziate could be seen the few houses which comprised Carroceto and between the hamlet and themselves lay a depressing expanse of indeterminate country, some fields, some scrubby land intersected by what appeared to be thin lines twisting on the surface of the fields—the wadis or gullies. But all eyes were focused on the ridge itself 2,000 yards ahead. It was no more than 300 feet at its highest point, yet it dominated the surrounding countryside. The master of the Buon Riposo Ridge was master of the road to Anzio—or would have been were it not for the wadis. These features were to become synonymous with all the horror of Anzio for those who fought west of the main road, but at that stage, for the Foresters and for the KSLI in their turn, they were ominous and uninviting ditches on either side of the approach road to the Start Line stretching off to goodness knows where. Across the line of their attack, below the crest of the ridge itself lay the Fosso Di Carroceto, a broad, deep wadi. To the west it ultimately flowed into the Moletta River, to the north-east it wound its way at the foot of the Buon Riposo Ridge until it finally petered out in Grenadier Gully short of Carroceto village.

The KSLI had nearly 5,000 yards to cover to reach their Start Line, over half of this in full view of the enemy. The company commanders had been called forward by the commanding officer, and had a chance to see the ground they were to attack over. The rest of the battalion were being brought forward by the adjutant at what was described as a 'racing pace'. With minutes to spare, the battalion reached the Start Line, but there was no time to stop and they lined up directly. Platoon commanders were told the ridge 'over there' was their objective, and that had to suffice. The formation of companies envisaged by the commanding officer, with 'B' Company on the right and 'C' on the left, with the other two in reserve was no longer practicable as German shelling had disrupted the order of march. Thus 'B' Company duly attacked on the right, but it was a combined 'C' and 'D' companies, hurriedly amalgamated, who were deputed to take on the left. They formed up in dead ground to the enemy, but within 100 yards of the Start Line the two battalions emerged into the open. For a few agonising minutes the companies were subjected to a violent bombardment, until with relief they plunged into the wadis across the path. The only trouble was that the wadis did not run straight, in fact it was difficult to keep direction at all in that tangle of bramble and scrub. With the sides of each wadi more sheer and slippery than the last, it was remarkable that any formed body of men reached the Fosso di Carroceto at all. That they did was almost wholly due to the courage and skill of the non-commissioned officers of the 1st Battalion the King's Shropshire Light Infantry, for within minutes of the start both company commanders of the leading companies had become casualties, and by the time they reached the Fosso there were no officers still on their feet in either 'B' or 'C' Companies.

The companies arrived in a disordered state and very weak. Ahead of them lay 400 yards of gradually rising ground to the top of the tantalizing ridge. As soon as they came from the shelter of the Fosso they were greeted with withering flanking fire from German machine guns firing down the side of the ridge from the east. Even with the help of the Squadrons of the Reconnaissance Regiment and of the tanks of the 46th Royal Tank Regiment, who could do little more in that impossible country than engage the enemy from static positions, the KSLI could not push on.

To their left, the Foresters, depleted so heavily in the Campoleone battle, were now to be depleted again. Their approach to the ridge was less wadi-bound than that of the KSLI, but although there were fewer gullies to confuse their advance, so there were fewer gullies to give cover. They advanced across what was virtually open ground in extended order with all the support that could be mustered. And as they walked forward their ranks visibly began to thin.

This was no death or glory charge, nor a darting from cover to cover in the time-honoured fashion of field tactics, but a steady trudge forward. The officers in the lead, feeling naked and horribly exposed, were aware, with a consciousness rather than certain knowledge, that those with them were becoming fewer all the time, but they also knew that if they stopped or hesitated, others would stop too, and might not start again.

Soon communications with the three forward companies ceased altogether, but it was possible to read the flow of battle by the chatter of small arms as the gallant Foresters fought their way forward against increasingly heavy opposition. Soon, though, the wireless log at battalion headquarters could only record 'Position obscure.' And obscure it was to remain until in the middle of the afternoon, when 'A' Company of the Foresters reported themselves on their objective, with a strength of thirty-five men; while 'B' Company were in firm occupation of a hillock to their rear. But they also had to say that there was no sign of 'C' Company—it later transpired that every officer and man had been either killed or wounded or was missing.

'On the objective, but too weak to hold it': how often was the frustrating pattern to be repeated before the Battle of Anzio was over. But it was clear that the Foresters could not stay where they were, for the KSLI were still caught up in the Fosso di Carroceto, could not go forward and were most reluctant to go back. Nor was it possible to bring up the support weapons, for German tanks which were now on the ridge would have annihilated them as soon as they broke cover and long before they had reached the forward companies. It was essential to be firm in some sort of defensive position before darkness fell, or they would be consumed piecemeal before the night was out. Thus the

Foresters fell back to secure a small perimeter around a farmhouse, and the KSLI withdrew to conform. But both battalions had an isolated company. It was not ideal, but it had to suffice. However, by their sacrifice, the two battalions of 3rd Brigade had secured for the moment the vital left flank of the divisional position, but at heavy cost.

As night fell on 8 February, so fell the rain. Freezing, icy rain, and those nestling in the wadis, believing that here was a secure haven from the shelling, found that soon they were standing in knee-deep and rising water. Food was brought up, a remarkable achievement by the quartermasters under the circumstances, including the first issue of bread in the beachhead. The two battalion headquarters were sharing a house by this time, and the Regimental History of the KSLI paints a vivid picture of the scene:

A gunner OP was by the house and was in process of relief by another OP. There were vehicles from the Reconnaissance Regiment hoping to tuck themselves in for the night under the shelter of the house. There was a 'Quad' towing an anti-tank gun (part of 81st Anti-Tank Regiment who were to play an invaluable part in the battle for the beachhead) trying to get into some position by the house. There were three vehicles of the administrative vehicles, brought up by our Quartermaster close behind them. There were four large three-tonners carrying wire. It was pouring with rain. The ground already a sea of mud, was turning into a quagmire, and the area of the house was being heavily shelled. In the failing light, it was not surprising that the position was 'not absolutely clear'.

7

The Battle for Carroceto

8–10 February

It was now the turn of those to the east of the Factory (see map 11 page 115). The daylight hours of 8 February had been comparatively quiet ones for the 10th Royal Berkshires, trying hard to restore their positions after the disasters of the previous night. The forward companies had suffered severely and Colonel Baird would dearly have liked to pull them back from the east–west road which they straddled, to more secure positions to the rear. But it was not to be. The order from division was that all ground was to be held to the last. How much longer it could be held, though, was more doubtful for it was clear to all ranks of the 10th Royal Berkshire Regiment that there were not likely to be many men alive and still fighting after the next German attack. The strength return showed a total of only 340 all ranks, but morale was high and Brigadier Davidson commanding the 168th Brigade wrote to the commanding officer that evening asking that all soldiers be told of his appreciation of their gallantry and steadfast courage.

In fact the stubborn resistance of the battalions of the 1st Infantry Division had severely hampered German plans. Carroceto was to have been taken during the night of 7/8 February and the main attack on the Factory, a double effort designed to eliminate the London Irish and the Berkshires at the same time, had been intended for the morning of 8 February. But mounting casualties particularly from the very heavy Allied artillery fire rendered that impossible. It was postponed to midnight.

The first part of the night was quiet, although there were disturbing indications of German infiltration around the outside of the two forward companies of the Berkshires as well as between them. Irritating small parties of the enemy crept into the many little outbuildings which abounded around the larger farmhouses and from there opened up at short range. Each incursion was dealt with as it occurred. It was a wearying business and an expensive one, but it must be done, for the Germans were adept at exploiting any foothold within the widely spread positions.

At midnight precisely, during a heavy thunderstorm, the Germans attacked the two forward companies. By making use of the Fosso della

Ficoccia, they were able to infiltrate round the left flank of 'D' Company and invest one of the platoons. The attack on the right on 'B' Company was supported by tanks which found the going firmer on that side, but 'B' Company managed to drive them off. Not until daylight, and with the assistance of a couple of Shermans which had come up in support, was Major F. D. Jones MC, commanding 'D' Company, able to restore his position and rescue his platoon by a quick counter-attack.

But while 'D' Company was beginning to breathe easier again, the situation on the rest of the battalion front was going from bad to worse. The battalion log presents a graphic picture. '0530 hours, Enemy near battalion headquarters.' An hour later it was clear that the end must be in sight: '0638 hours', ran the log, 'Enemy tanks approach from the north-east'. '0652 hours, Enemy tanks approach from the east. 0704 hours. More enemy tanks.' And there was nothing to deal with them. The PIATs, unreliable and inaccurate anyway, were out of bombs. The anti-tank guns had long since fired all their ammunition and now were silent. The German tanks approached with impunity. By eight o'clock in the morning, the full weight of the German attack had built up and in one tremendous wave 'B' Company was consumed and eliminated.

Now that the right flank of the battalion position had been destroyed, 'D' Company was in a critical state. The rain was pouring down and visibility was minimal, but it was not too poor to see a grey line of Germans advancing from the wood a bare 350 yards to their front. They were wearing long waterproof coats and appeared to be carrying no weapons. The previous party of Germans who had entered their position had surrendered with the greatest alacrity. Was it possible that these too were surrendering? The company commander ordered his men to hold their fire. Steadily the German line came towards them, and then on some hidden signal, every man fell to the ground and started shooting. The next moment the whole company position was enveloped in thick smoke, and, ominously, tanks could be heard approaching down the road from the former 'B' Company area. The company's anti-tank guns fired their last rounds, but they were shooting blind. Slowly and inexorably the tanks came down the road and then at point-blank range set about blasting the farmhouses around which the company had its positions. While the Berkshires were sheltering from the tank fire, the German infantry closed on them from the wood.

At battalion headquarters the brigadier had just arrived. Colonel Baird was engaged in a serious telephone conversation. At length he laid down the receiver and turned to Brigadier Davidson. 'That was Jonah [Major Jones, commanding 'D' Company] on the phone, Sir,' he said 'and he says tanks are coming through again and he does not think he can hold them this time. It looks to me as though my battalion has gone.' Then he took a deep breath, banged his fist on the table and said, 'But I still have my battalion headquarters, and they won't get past us. Don't worry, Sir.'

Now Colonel Baird with his battalion headquarters, the remaining troops from his rifle companies—only a couple of sections from 'C' Company by then—a few mortar men, the drivers of the carriers and anyone else who was around, waited for the inevitable. But the inevitable did not happen for the Germans appeared content with occupying the forward positions and there they stayed for nearly two days. Little did they realise how close they had been to piercing a hole through the defensive front of the division. Their objectives had been the lateral road which ran through the Berkshires' positions and then the Guardapassi bridge over the Fosso della Ficoccia. These they had now secured and having faced the fire of the Royal Berkshires, were reluctant and wary about venturing too far forward.

In the afternoon came orders for the remainder of the battalion—although 'battalion' was a misnomer, almost all they had left was their spirit—to pull back to brigade reserve. At six o'clock they withdrew, unhurriedly and, as the Regimental History proudly recalls, 'in their own good time'. The Germans made no attempt to follow and their place was taken by a battalion of American infantry.

The London Irish had also found themselves the focus of a lot of attention. The men were very tired by now. There had been no sleep since landing at Anzio four days before and ever since then they had been under constant harrying mortar and shell-fire. Because the Factory completely dominated the area north of the Carroceto bridges the Germans intended to take, and hold it. Shortly before midnight on 7 February, 'D' Company, so exposed north of the Factory, made the unpleasant discovery that their forward position was no longer occupied. The platoon occupying it had just disappeared during the night. There had been no sound of firing, and it was assumed that sheer exhaustion had lowered their alertness and a German party had quietly approached and taken them all prisoner. Already the Germans had worked round the totally isolated 'D' Company and during the afternoon the Scots Guards to the west reported that they had seen enemy troops in the Factory itself. They weren't believed, but it was true. Although the enemy were not in sufficient strength to cause much trouble it was a disturbing development. 'B' Company of the Irish were also beginning to feel themselves unpleasantly alone for clearly there were Germans in the hut area where long before No. 3 Company of the Grenadiers had found themselves involved, and all communications with the Royal Berkshires on the right beyond the Fosso della Ficoccia had ceased. Colonel Good of the London Irish could do nothing to stop the infiltration, nor to help his isolated companies. The London

Scottish, or what was left of them, were acting as a long-stop between and to the rear of the Irish and the Berkshires. Otherwise the London Irish were completely on their own, horribly exposed and clearly about to become the focus of a full-scale German attack.

As with the Berkshires to the right, precisely at midnight of a very dark night General Gräser's attack started, with two battalions of 29th Panzer Grenadier Regiment determined to eliminate the Irish north of the Factory. A 'bloody affair', the Germans described it, 'one of the worst of the war'. Although temporarily held up by some mines north of the positon, by the early hours of 9 February they were getting close. Around three o'clock came a message from 'D' Company that they were being heavily attacked. Five minutes of running commentary ensued, but the listeners at battalion headquarters knew that it could not last. 'D' Company wireless suddenly went silent. The adjutant turned to the commanding officer, 'I am afraid they've gone, Sir.'

With the elimination of 'D' Company of the London Irish, the enemy were now able to move into the Factory at their leisure and rapidly work their way through the buildings, although thanks to treatment by both sides, some were hardly more than anonymous piles of rubble by then.

Dawn brought on attacks of even greater intensity than before, supported by very heavy artillery fire and even air support. 'B' Company bore the brunt and they found that not only were they being attacked from the Factory but that by nine o'clock in the morning the Germans had been able to take the Guardapassi Bridge over the Fosso della Ficoccia and were attacking them from the right and right rear as well. Fighting stubbornly, the company were forced back to a road south-east of the Factory itself. 'A' Company tried to struggle forward to help their comrades, but after gaining several hundred yards of ground, they too were pinned down by very heavy fire and could go no further. Every spare man of the Irish had been brought up for what looked like being the last stand of the battalion. Their 3-in. mortars were firing almost vertically at Germans less than one hundred yards away and a small outpost in the last buildings of the Factory found that the much-maligned PIAT, although inadequate against tanks, was a highly effective weapon against buildings. As the Germans occupied those to their front, a blast of the PIAT brought them running out straight into the fire of a waiting bren gun. Thus they were able to survive through the morning and well into the afternoon, but the Germans finally eliminated the nuisance.

Now the plight of 'B' Company was critical. 'I am doing all I can, but it looks as if this is our last fight,' the company commander of 'B' Company was heard to say as German tanks and infantry set about eliminating his final position. But the counter-attack by 'A' Company with tank support produced over thirty prisoners—men only too happy to surrender when the occasion offered and who spoke of crippling casualties in their battalion—and also relieved the pressure on 'B' Company, and the company commander was able to say 'I must apologise for my earlier despondency.'

With the Factory now firmly in their grasp the Germans paused. The London Irish could only wonder at their deliverance. Later they were relieved by American infantry—only one company was needed. The Germans, though, were gradually achieving their objectives. Bit by bit the front of 1st British Division was being eroded from the east. There was now only the 1st Battalion Scots Guards north of the vital Carroceto bridges.

The fall of the Factory meant that the forward companies of the Scots Guards in the area of Carroceto were at the end of what had become a vulnerable and narrow salient, and the right flank of the rest of the battalion was completely exposed.

Carroceto consisted of some dozen stout-walled houses. For the most part they were single-storied, but the largest, with two storeys and a capacious cellar, was the railway station. Here the Scots Guards established their headquarters and enough stores and ammunition to withstand a considerable siege. In and around the station building was No. 4 Company of the Irish Guards which had been sent forward to their support some days before. To the left, towards Vallelata Ridge was 'B' Company while 'C' and Right Flank were nearly half a mile forward up the line of the railway near Milestone 25.

For the most part they had been unaffected by the German attacks on the night of 7/8 February which had virtually wiped out the North Staffords and so thinned the Berkshires beyond the Factory, but their peace was not to last. The first incident was on the afternoon of 8 February when observers in one of the upper windows of the station saw a group of enemy gathering in a ditch some six hundred yards away. As they watched, more and more appeared. Hurriedly a fire plan was evolved for the mortars and guns, while a Vickers machine gun was dragged to the upper window, firmly propped up on a number of meal sacks and made ready. On a signal the ditch was subjected to a savage pounding and in moments was clear save for dead and dying Germans. The rest made off as fast as their legs could carry them to a near-by farmhouse—which was none too safe as they soon found out. Hardly had the Scots Guards congratulated themselves on breaking up that attack so effectively, than to their utter astonishment the Germans repeated precisely the same performance. Again fire was brought down, and again a few survivors managed to struggle back the way they had come. This time some stretcher bearers appeared carrying Red Cross flags and started to collect the casualties. There seemed to be a certain hesitation about the way the Germans were going about their

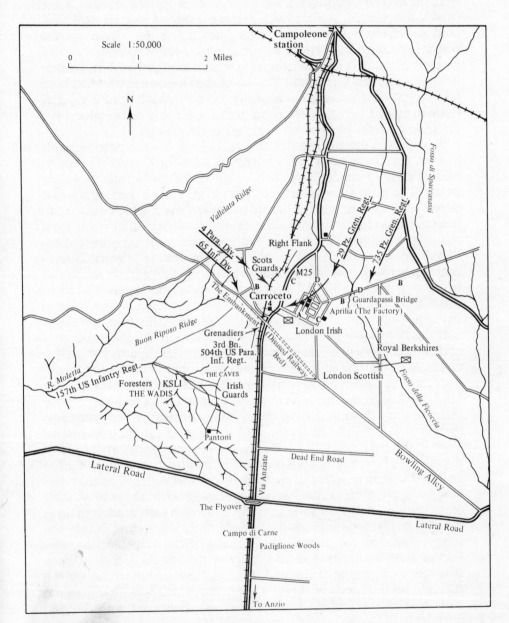

The fall of Carroceto, 9–10 February

business: it was almost as though they wanted to surrender, so a party from the nearest company ran forward to collect those they could. Some twenty-five started to come back, but were shot at by their own side. Only seventeen duly returned to the lines. Later that afternoon, the whole procedure was repeated; but this time the surrender was to a party from the Irish Guards company, who, although they didn't realise it, all but rescued Lieutenant Hussey of the Grenadiers who had been taken with other wounded to a farmhouse below Vallelata Ridge. The German guards were only too eager to surrender to their casualties, but the Irish Guards' party never came quite far enough.

By means of these aggressive tactics, Colonel Wedderburn was able to keep the Germans at arm's length throughout 8 and 9 February. Midnight on 9 February was the hour chosen by the Germans for their attack. The Scots Guards had received warning, for a German warrant officer was captured bearing the orders for the attack which was to have been mounted that morning. This showed that 65th Infantry Division was to attack down the line of the Embankment while a regiment of 4th Parachute Division tried to bite off the forward Scots Guards companies by assaulting from the direction of the Vallelata Ridge and by-passing them to take on Carroceto from the north. Meanwhile, when 29th Panzer Grenadier Regiment had secured the Factory, they were to swing towards Carroceto and assail the Scots Guards from the east.

It was depressing news in a depressing situation and the real gravity of their predicament became apparent shortly after the attack started at midnight. To everyone's horror they discovered that a German tank had 'come to call' and was sitting outside the front door 'shooting the house down over our heads.' This tank, by making use of the little cover there was, and accompanied by about twenty infantry, had worked past the Factory, through the sparse out-buildings on the exposed eastern flank to the station building itself by way of some houses at the end of the drive where the Scots Guards Regimental Aid Post had been captured complete with the medical officer and padre. The tank was now firing point-blank, the heavy shot causing havoc to the thick walls of the station, and its machine guns, fired through each window in turn, causing heavy casualties as the bullets whistled around inside the rooms. Satisfied that it was in command of the situation, the tank backed away and started methodically to destroy the building. Each shot tore a huge hole in the wall. One of the first brought down the staircase on the heads of those in the cellar which was rapidly filling with dead and wounded. There seemed no way of getting rid of the intruder.

The only hope of saving the situation rested on the timely arrival of armour, and Colonel Wedderburn came to the conclusion that only he could ensure getting them by going back to brigade headquarters himself. Accompanied by his Support Company commander, he climbed out of the back window to the station and made his way towards the Carroceto bridges.

For nearly four hours he pleaded, cajoled, entreated that some tanks be released to go to the aid of his stricken battalion. But none were forthcoming. The tanks were loath to try their hand in the dark—although there was a handsome moon at the time—and the higher commanders were reluctant to let them. The Scots Guards' wireless log laconically recorded, '0430 hours, Commanding Officer returns having met with little success.'

Shortly before the tank had made its unwelcome appearance Colonel Wedderburn had received permission to bring back his forward companies before it was too late and to make a tight perimeter around the vital Carroceto bridges. There was no secure way of passing this message to the forward companies so the adjutant went off to tell them. He returned to find the tank outside the headquarters and lay low until it decided to go away. This it eventually did. It was never clear whether by then the German tank commander had decided that he was perilously vulnerable among close buildings at night, or that he just wearied of the sport of trying to bring down the solid station building, or whether he expected that something was being collected to deal with the nuisance—little did he realise that there was nothing.

Through the next hours the Scots Guards consolidated behind the Embankment, where the Grenadiers' and the Scots Guards' headquarters joined forces and Colonel Wedderburn took command of the remains of both battalions. The Grenadiers totalled about sixty men in all, and as the last hours of the night passed it looked as though the Scots Guards, come the dawn, might not number very many more. Only a handful of men of 'B' Company on the left flank came back after a number of hair-raising experiences. Only a platoon of sappers made their escape of the party which had been left to hold out in the station for as long as possible, and which originally consisted of the remains of the Irish Guards Company and three platoons of Royal Engineers who had hurriedly been sent up during the night to fight as infantry. However, the two forward companies of the Scots Guards, although by now with Germans behind them, managed to fight their way back down the railway line. 'C' Company arrived almost intact, but Right Flank, which were caught by Germans firmly entrenched on their return route came back only twenty-five strong after a succession of hand-to-hand fights.

The combined Grenadiers and Scots Guards settled down around the Embankment. It was a depressing place. In a culvert under the bank the Grenadiers' Regimental Aid Post lived an unhappy existence in ankle-deep water. In the middle of the morning the boxes placed to provide a firm floor started to float away and the whole culvert had to be suddenly evacuated as what was described as 'a miniature Severn Bore' swept into the place. Those out of immediate cover had an even more unpleasant time of it. As one highly disgruntled Grenadier officer exclaimed, 'It's very awkward, if we lie on our stomachs we are hit in the arse, if we lie on our backs we are hit in the balls!' The shelling was more or less continuous, and if anyone was unwise enough to show their heads above the Embankment the whole place was treated to a bombardment of mortars and a cascade of small-arms fire. But the remains of the two battalions managed to hold on.

A composite platoon tried to fight through to relieve those marooned in the station building, but it was beaten back by heavy German tank and SP gun-fire for by then the Germans had moved in some force into the rubble of Carroceto. But by this and other small-scale counter-attacks the Germans were prevented from getting any closer. This offensive defence was expensive in casualties, but it bought time, and time was a vital commodity to those in the beachhead. And it achieved its object. The War Diaries of the German Parachute Division testify that they had a very healthy respect indeed for the fighting qualities of those around Carroceto, and also speak of the great number of casualties they had suffered during the previous twenty-four hours.

Most of the prisoners captured by the Scots Guards turned out to be Alsatians who had been press-ganged into joining the German army and were only too delighted to get out of it again. The officers, though, were made of different stuff. One, who asked in poor English, 'Ver is der sea?' replied when it was pointed out, 'Tank you very much, I vanted to know for you vill soon be in it.'

The position on the Embankment was sound enough by day and covered most of the likely approaches, but by night it was obvious that it would not last long, for the Scots Guards were only 120 strong by then. But relief was in the air.

For some time they had been informed that a visitor was on the way. The visitor turned out to be Colonel Webb-Carter of the Dukes. Immaculately dressed as ever and treating the parlous situation with total composure and a kind of disdain which was highly comforting, his presence, always welcome, was doubly so as he came to say that his battalion was to relieve the two Guards' battalions that night. He later wrote:

It was the afternoon of the 10th February. It was raining steadily and it was cold. The Battalion, or what was left of it, was huddled in an American-built slit trench system on the Campo di Carne, trying, quite ineffectually, to keep dry. Occasionally an air-burst from an 88-mm gun arrived over our heads and everyone mechanically ducked rather like worshippers at some strange rite. It was five days since the Battalion had fought its way out of the trap at Campoleone. We had not had time to recover and little chance to refit . . . At about 1500 hours a message came from Brigade that the Battalion was to come under command of the Guards Brigade and that I was to report to that Brigade Headquarters at once for orders. I warned the Battalion to be prepared to move, observed with gloom that a large section of trench had fallen in, entombing my exiguous bedding and set off for the Guards Brigade Headquarters. This was situated in a battered farmhouse about a mile down the road that runs across the Campo di Carne. The Guards Brigade Headquarters always occupied a house in the beachhead. During the peaceful days in North Africa, following the end of the campaign there, when everybody who could crammed into a building, nothing would induce them to live anywhere but in wild and inaccessible wadis (indeed on one memorable occasion the entire headquarters was isolated for twenty-four hours by a raging torrent). Now we all shunned houses, as they inevitably drew shells, they seemed to exert an irresistible attraction, towards the Brigade. As each building slowly crumbled round their heads, so the intrepid band made its way to the next house, where the process was immediately repeated. I do not think they suffered any more casualties than anyone else!

At Guards Brigade Headquarters, the state of the Grenadiers and Scots Guards was painted in sombre colours; everyone agreed that the situation was desperate although no one seemed to know precisely what it was. So Colonel Webb-Carter decided to go and find out for himself.

We drove along the Campo di Carne road in the steady rain, [he wrote] turned right at the Flyover Bridge and set sail down the Rome road. This was in full observation from the Factory and under sniper fire, so we crouched low in the vehicle . . . a sudden right turn told us that we were at the Railway Bed and under cover of view from the Factory. A scene of peculiar desolation met us. The area was littered with broken and burned equipment and vehicles. The rain poured down on shattered ammunition and a derelict tank or two. Lying on his back was a gunner officer shot through the head by a sniper. He had subsequently been run over by a tank. He was not a pretty sight. Up on the Embankment, lurking miserably in their slit trenches were the remnants of two proud Guards battalions. Battalion Headquarters was in a culvert driven into the Embankment and we made our way to it. It was knee-deep in water and crowded to capacity. The Regimental Aid Post was there and a few wounded men were being treated. A heterogenous mass of officers and men were milling about, all talking a trifle hysterically. Looking tired, but utterly unmoved in the babel was Colonel David Wedderburn, the

Commanding Officer of the Scots Guards. He was surrounded by Americans, Sapper and Gunner Officers, all of whom were under his command in the composite force which had been scraped together to hold the position.

That evening the Dukes moved up towards the Embankment. It was dark and raining heavily as the battalion moved into their positions. 'A' and 'C' Companies were well behind the Embankment, but with patrols forward to warn of any enemy movement. Slightly to the rear was 'B' Company and a Beach Group Company which had been rushed up from Anzio port two days before and flung into the line, despite being almost completely untrained as infantry. The Dukes' headquarters was in a house some 300 yards behind the Carroceto bridges.

[Here as Colonel Webb-Carter wrote] seated in a corner and smoking a singularly evil cigar was an American officer. He was the liaison officer from the Tank Destroyers. There was a gunner representative and that seemed to be about all. The medley of Sappers and Anti-Tankers who had been with the Guards had gone. A large tank was firmly stuck in the mud outside the front door and, very successfully, rendered it practically impossible to get in or out. A few signallers huddled on the steps and tripped up anyone who had achieved the manoeuvre round the tank.

The relief complete, the Grenadiers and Scots Guards moved back to the merciful haven of Padiglione Woods. The Grenadiers' Intelligence officer wrote:

The troops turned over the railway line into the dim area of the trees and scrub which comprised 'B' Echelon. Everything that was possible in the way of comforts was prepared. A vast, hot meal was doled out and taken in mess-tins to the little bivouacs dotted round the area. The only thing left was sleep and that with a clear conscience, without the prospect of a midnight alarm. A chapter, which had opened on the 21st of January was closed. Now we were back where we had started.

8

Setting the Net

11–15 February

For days past General Penney had been feeling increasingly isolated and forgotten. It appeared to him that no one truly understood the grave plight of the British 1st Division and he gloomily studied the casualty returns which revealed that his battalions were down on average to half their strength, and in some cases to much less. The division had been continually in action for a fortnight and more, for the most part in bitterly cold and constantly unpleasant weather in a country where their enemy, as well as outnumbering them, could overlook their every movement. There was no 'safe' place in the beachhead; and 'rest' was a misnomer, for there was no respite from din and danger at Anzio. It was hard on the men, it was incomparably harder on the officers, particularly company and battalion commanders, who were always on call. After the unfortunate experience of the Grenadiers when their second-in-command and commanding officer were wounded in qick succession, battalion seconds-in-command were kept well back and as far out of battle as was practicable.

Some commanding officers operated a first and second eleven system, so that key officers could from time to time be taken out of the front line, if and when the occasion offered. But no commander found much sleep, apart from that brought about by sheer physical collapse. Some commanding officers could not, or would not, operate the system. But irrespective of that, 1st British Division was slowing down. The confusion of the war around them, the uncertainty from hour to hour about what was happening, the shelling, the mortaring, the strafing from an increasingly active Luftwaffe, the steady drain of casualties was beginning to tell. The corporate life of a battalion had been likened to a barrel of Napoleon brandy. As long as the cask is still intact, topping up can continue almost indefinitely and the resulting drink will still taste of a high-class spirit. But once the cask has gone, then no amount of replacement will bring back the former flavour. The 'cask' of many battalions in the 1st Division was nearly broken.

But morale was high, there was no sense or feeling of defeatism among the troops on the ground. The experience of a Grenadier officer who went the rounds of his platoon just before they were overrun, was typical of the experiences of many. After telling one of the few old soldiers still left, a lance-corporal, that artillery support was coming and that a counter-attack was expected at any moment, the latter looked quizzically at his platoon commander. 'Well, it's very nice of you to say that, Sir, but there ain't no —— artillery, is there?' 'No, I don't think there is, really,' came the reply. 'And there ain't no —— counter-attack, is there, Sir?' 'Well, probably not actually just yet,' the platoon commander answered. There was a pause, and then the old soldier spoke, 'Oh . . . well, Sir, it's very nice of you to speak to us. Don't worry, we'll go on sitting here,' patting his bren gun as he spoke.

The men suffering in their slit-trenches accepted what happened with stoical good humour. There was a feeling of bewilderment, of some resignation, but no sense of defeatism or despair among the troops on the ground. They knew only what was happening on their own immediate front. Events elsewhere on the beachhead were reported through rumour, usually garbled at that.

They heard, in the way that such information spreads, a little of how things were progressing on their flank. They heard in due time of the annihilation of the Rangers and bitter fighting on the Yanks' front. They heard that so-and-so had copped it, poor buggers overrun by tanks with no defence. But they were in truth like fleas in a blanket seeing no more than the next nearest wrinkle. Nevertheless morale in the 1st Division was high, although sapped by fatigue, wet and the perpetual din of battle. At times their immediate front was amazingly peaceful and the war seemed miles away, at other times it broke with unbelievable ferocity and with no warning that they could see. Around early February, though, there was a feeling that things had gone wrong. They recalled those halcyon hours on the beachhead when Rome appeared ready for the taking and just over the horizon. Now battle areas were no longer clear-cut. The hotch-potch of reinforcements, clearly stuffed into the line as a last resort and in some urgency, was evidence enough that things were none too happy. There were tales of battalion headquarters being attacked, even of brigade headquarters coming under fire and there seemed to be a general state of confusion.

No one seemed to know what was happening. Time after time General Penney sought, entreated, demanded information not only about the enemy, but even about their own plans and objectives—in vain. Much of this lack of information was attributed by those on the ground to their divisional headquarters; some of the criticism was aimed at the divisional commander himself. Those who criticised had no conception of how he fought for their interests, or of the burden placed upon him by a corps headquarters which he was increasingly coming to look upon as inefficient and inadequate. For such a conscientious man as General Penney it was fast becoming an intolerable situation.

The further up the ladder of command, the lower morale, the greater the sense of defeatism. Corps headquarters had gone to ground after an all-too-close German air attack. General Lucas lived a troglodyte existence with his staff in the catacombs under Nettuno surrounded by the macabre and cheerless relicts of early Christians. The atmosphere at headquarters was of almost unrelieved gloom. Officers found it a depressing place. As the tide of battle flowed the Germans' way Lucas became, and worse appeared to become, more and more despondent. His diaries tell of a man worried and almost at the end of his tether. The trouble was that he had been tired before it all began. In a moment of candour on sailing from Naples he had noted that this was his fifty-fourth birthday, and he added 'I feel every year of it'—and he also looked it. He and Penney had been on the friendliest terms before the assault. Both in their diaries speak of a mutual confidence, trust and liking of one another. But as the beachhead battle wore on a growing sense of frustration and dissatisfaction pervaded Penney's relations with his corps commander. It was a mutual process, for Lucas also expressed doubts about Penney and the British way of conducting war, which he had never experienced before and had severe doubts about.

Part of this lack of understanding may have been due to Penney himself, who did not suffer fools gladly, or for long. A highly-strung man, with a great deal of energy and very much a frontline general, he could find no common ground with Lucas. He was apt to be brusque with those who did not see things his way. Montgomery was his beau ideal as a commander, and he may have inherited the latter's distrust of the American way of command. But it is clear that Penney was not alone in his loss of confidence in his corps commander. General Truscott, despite the unswerving loyalty he showed to his superior general, fretted at the lack of decisive command shown by Lucas. Others who came in contact with the corps commander began to feel and express their misgivings, misgivings which were eventually to see on 16 February the appointment of Truscott as Deputy Corps Commander*, and Lucas's eventual removal.

General Lucas may not have understood the British way of war, but nor was he curious enough to find out. The corps commander rarely emerged from his dismal catacomb and, during the course of the beachhead battle, he seldom came to visit 1st Division's Headquarters, which was little more than a brisk walk away from his own. His lack-lustre presence and apparent indecisiveness militated against him,

*At the same time Major-General V. Evelegh was also appointed Deputy Corps Commander with the specific responsibility of smoothing inter-Allied relations. It was the start of an era of total accord.

and people now recalled the unfortunate impression he had made on the officers of the Gordons when he had concluded his address to them with the words 'Well boys, I hope you are looking forward to this operation as much as I am, for I tell you I have never fought a battle before.' This may have been, and probably was, intended as a piece of self-deprecation and self-effacing candour but the effect was not healthy. Nor was Lucas's admission strictly true for, after taking over 6th Corps at Salerno he had commanded it with distinction in the fight up the leg of Italy. But it was true that he had never handled a set-piece battle of the type being fought at Anzio, and this lack of experience was becoming more and more evident.

The clear decisive command was not Lucas's way. His conferences were meetings—likened by some to those of an inefficient company. They began with a general survey and ended with a general discussion. On many occasions Penney, after attending one of these marathon sessions, having gone to seek information or orders or even encouragement from his corps commander, would return increasingly discouraged and disillusioned. Repeatedly he tried to hammer home to his corps commander that only God and superhuman courage and resolution were keeping the Germans from breaking through his thinning line; that his numbers were being whittled away daily and that those still standing were all but asleep on their feet through sheer exhaustion. Already some units of the 45th U.S. Division had taken over the flanks of the divisional position, but tactically it was essential that a counter-attack be mounted on the Germans in the Factory before they took up permanent residence there—and 1st British Division were too weak to undertake it.

But Lucas remained remote, both physically and spiritually, from what was happening on the vital axis of the beachhead—the Via Anziate. It was this remoteness that at last prompted General Penney, when the fall of Carroceto and the Factory were expected hourly and when 1st British Infantry Division had no more resources left, to make a final plea for help before it was too late.

It was successful. On the morning of 10 February a distinguished group, consisting of Generals Lucas and Penney, with Major-General William W. Eagles, commanding the 45th U.S. Infantry Division, which had now arrived complete in the beachhead and had already started to take some of the strain off the 1st Division, gathered at the headquarters of 24th Guards Brigade. After Penney had outlined the parlous situation, Lucas sat silent for a moment or two. Then he turned to General Eagles, 'OK, Bill, you give 'em the works.' Seven words which were to cost the 45th Division grievous casualties in a sacrifice which was to blunt and slow the German attack and do much to save the beachhead.

That evening General Penney decided to write a formal letter to his corps commander. It is a remarkable document, partly for its contents but also for the circumstances surrounding its dispatch. Taken at its face value it makes depressing reading and reveals how crippling had been the casualties sustained by the division since the landing on 22 January. It also reveals a total loss of confidence in the higher headquarters. It is a plea for positive command, a yearning for information on corps intentions, and a heartfelt *cri de coeur* for news about the enemy—for Intelligence had a habit of sticking at corps level and never seeping down. But taken in the context of its author's increasing doubts about the competence of his corps commander, it is a formidable indictment of Lucas as a field commander.

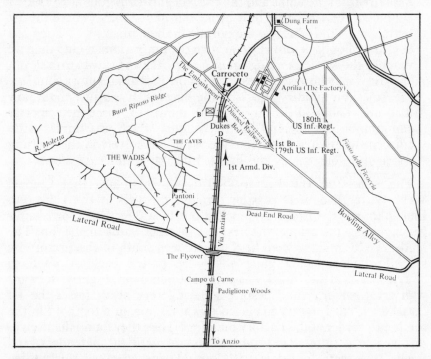

The counter-attacks, 11–2 February

Already, on 9 February, the 180th Infantry Regiment had relieved the British 2nd Brigade and 'C' Squadron of the Reconnaissance Regiment in the area of the Fosso di Spaccasassi. Now, during the night of 10 February, a battalion of the 179th Infantry Regiment replaced the 168th Brigade on what the Germans called the East–West Road which they had intended to capture days before. This was the Line of Departure for the attack next morning.

Setting the Net

At 0630 hours, after a fifteen minute bombardment, the 1st Battalion 179th Infantry duly advanced against the Factory across open fields supported by tanks of the 1st U.S. Armoured Division. At dawn Colonel Webb-Carter near the Carroceto bridges saw

. . . a long column of tanks advancing towards the gap in the Embankment which led to Carroceto and the Factory . . . We could see about seventy tanks in all in file on the road, and before long the leading one reached us. The column paused, and then three tanks rolled through and out of our sight. Hell then broke loose. The enemy brought his guns down on the road and his guns down on the Embankment. On the far side of the Embankment we could hear the Besa fire from the tanks and the crash of anti-tank guns at work . . . Sounds of furious battle now broke out to our right (where the 1st Battalion 179th Infantry were putting in their attack) . . . Then one Sherman shot back into view through the Embankment, and then we watched the whole clanking column turn back and slowly trundle out of sight . . . from a very unsafe OP on the Embankment we could see the American infantry attacking the Factory. It was just about now that an enemy shell hit a small dump of three-inch mortar ammunition, left behind by the Guards, which was unpleasantly adjacent to my headquarters. We sat in the culvert in the swirling water up to our ankles and listened bleakly to the explosions.

The attack on the Factory failed. Of the tanks that Colonel Webb-Carter had seen passing through the gap in the Carroceto Embankment, the first was knocked out by a direct hit shortly after passing under the bridge, the next less than 200 yards further on. The hard-pressed infantry were held up still well south of the Factory by skilfully-sited machine guns and were pulled back at noon to reorganise. A further attack was put in one hour later. Fighting forward with great gallantry and despite suffering very heavy losses the 1st Battalion 179th Infantry managed this time to gain a foothold in the south-east corner of the Factory buildings. Here they found themselves involved in a bitter hand-to-hand contest with the defenders, and finally they were forced to withdraw. They had taken thirty-three prisoners, from 725th Regiment of 715th Infantry Division, and from them they heard that the attack that morning had been no surprise. An intercepted wireless message had tipped off the enemy.

At two o'clock the following morning, 12 February, the gallant battalion tried again. By 0430 hours two companies had gained a tentative hold on some of the houses on the southern side of the cluster of buildings, but dawn brought a strong German counter-attack which drove them out again. The Germans too were nearly spent; they allowed the shattered 1st Battalion, down now to nearly half their effective strength, to establish themselves near the east–west road where they had started twenty-four hours before.

Shortly after the Americans mounted their attack on the Factory on 12 February, the Dukes, behind the Embankment, who had been wondering when it was going to be their turn, were kept wondering no longer. At 0330 hours the shelling on the Dukes' position, which had been intermittent all night, suddenly became a crescendo. Then those at battalion headquarters heard the sound of heavy small-arms fire coming from the forward companies and it was clear that the attack which had been expected for so long was upon them. It soon became evident that during the darkness the Germans had worked their way round the forward companies and were now busily trying to cut them off. On the right, 'A' Company, who were well dug in on the southern side of the Embankment, fought off all attacks, but on the left two platoons of 'C' Company were overrun almost immediately. Only the company headquarters survived, but they were surrounded as was one platoon in a house behind the Embankment.

With the elimination of 'C' Company the way now lay open for the Germans to take 'A' Company from both sides as well as from the Embankment to their front. Dawn revealed the unpleasant fact that the Germans were in command of the Embankment along its whole length west of the Carroceto bridges and had also been able to take the bridges themselves. Only one officer and five men remained of the reserve company—the others had disappeared in the night. The Dukes were now in an impossible position. 'A' Company still existed but under a hail of grenades from the far side of the Embankment itself, which was no more than a long throw away. 'B' Company had managed to stop the Germans from making progress to the south, but were powerless to stop them attacking 'A' Company to their right, and could not move out of their trenches themselves for they were in full view of the enemy in the Factory, while to add further insult German snipers and a tiresome tank on the near slopes of the Buon Riposo Ridge kept their heads well down. If the battalion had stayed where they were for long they would have been eliminated before the day was much advanced. The only answer was to try to retake the Embankment and gain some peace that way.

At the point of the bayonet, and supported by a troop of tanks and some tank-busters which had stayed loyally with them throughout, 'A' Company started to rout out the Germans who had been causing them such trouble all day. The spirited attack seemed to take the Germans by surprise. Sweeping forward, the Dukes regained the Embankment along its length, and a boldly handled tank passed under the Carroceto railway bridge and started to spray the Germans clustering on the northern side with machine gun fire. In a matter of moments they were running away in disorder. A few well-directed shots at the houses in Carroceto flushed out more Germans, and with this success the German artillery fire lifted and comparative quiet settled over the Carroceto area.

The gallant Dukes had suffered heavy casualties including all the company commanders, but no one was more grieved than Major Benson who had been the inspiration behind the successful defence of his company over the last few days. On the evening of 12 February the Dukes were reinforced by a company of the Gordons. They had suffered terrible casualties, but they had held firm for nearly thirty-six hours when totally isolated. Three days later, the Dukes were relieved in this vital position by 'E' Company of the 2nd Battalion 157th Infantry.

The Germans had beaten off all attempts to retake the Factory. They were now poised to eliminate the Allied troops forward of the Flyover as a prelude to the grand attack on the main beachhead defence line.

12 and 13 February were comparatively peaceful on most fronts, but there were reports of the enemy digging in and consolidating on the Buon Riposo Ridge and on 12 February a battalion of the 157th Infantry on the left flank in the area of La Cogna were subjected to heavy probing attacks. All the indications were that the enemy were testing the ground in preparation for something more substantial. During the following night the Foresters and KSLI, still in the area where they had reorganised after their own attack, also found themselves involved in very active patrolling by the Germans. Another German practice which started to increase about then was the bombardment of the forward positions with literature. One which was of special delight was a short news sheet which advised them not to suffer the same fate as the 1st British Division. 'It is not fair to be asked to fight against such superior formations while you are led by such amateurs,' was how it went on. It was a rare moment of light relief from a situation which was becoming awesomely depressing.

To the staff officers at corps and divisional headquarters, the map revealed a picture of ever-deepening gloom. Slowly, inexorably, and seemingly unstoppably, the beachhead was being squeezed tighter and tighter. Only opposite Truscott's 3rd Infantry Division was the line static and reasonably secure. In the centre, Carroceto and the Factory were already in German hands. Soon it would be the turn of the Dead End Road and once that was taken, only the Flyover and the Lateral Road stood between the Germans and complete victory, for the Flyover was only seven miles from Anzio itself, and only four miles from the sea. And there was nothing more to throw into the battle.

East of the Via Anziate the country was flat; good tank going it appeared

from the map or a casual glance. But in reality it was intersected by a
number of deep gullies impassable to tanks and usually with a foot or so
of water in them. Elsewhere the water was never very far from the
surface and when this was churned by shell-fire and the passage of
vehicles, the whole area soon became a bog, impassable for wheels and
nearly so for tracks. Cutting diagonally and dead straight across this
deceptive piece of country ran the disused railway bed—the Americans
called it the Bowling Alley—to the south-east this linked with a road
south of Padiglione, to the north-west lay the bridge at Carroceto and
the Embankment, which had seen so much suffering and sacrifice over
the past days. The line of the Via Anziate itself (see Map 18 page 182) was
the most direct approach to the heart of the beachhead. Here, bounded
on the east by boggy fields and to the west by two wadis, the Fosso di
Caronte and the Fosso di Bottaccia which came within 300 yards of the
main road, the front of necessity must be a narrow one.

To the west, though, from the direction of Buon Riposo Ridge,
where the Germans were in certain occupation, there were two routes
which pointed like arrows towards the Lateral Road and the Flyover.
One passed south from Buon Riposo Ridge, crossed the Fosso di
Carroceto and continued, skirting the deep wadi which became known
to the defenders of Anzio as the North Lobster Claw, for three miles to
join the Lateral Road less than one mile west of the vital Flyover.
Another route, after crossing the Fosso di Carroceto diverged to the
south-east and then cut back to pass through the middle of the cluster of
buildings called Pantoni, and met the previous track north of the
Lobster Claw. It was in this area, bounded to the south by the Lateral
Road, to the east by the Via Anziate, to the north by the Buon Riposo
Ridge and below it the Fosso di Carroceto that was to be fought what
became known as the War of the Wadis. A war which was to see enemy
attacks in strength and which, largely thanks to the dogged courage of
the defenders, faded into a static and peculiarly bloody battle of
attrition when survival was the paramount need, as February ran into
March, and March crept towards the final break-out at the end of May.

Right of Pantoni, in and around a formidably deep wadi, lay the
KSLI who were severely under strength, not only as a result of their
attack on the ridge four days before, but also due to the impressive
amount of mortar fire with which the Germans greeted any movement
at all. Their battalion headquarters had now been driven from the house
they had occupied by unpleasantly accurate German fire and had gone
to ground in a nearby gully where slowly as the rain continued the water
began to rise. They were out of touch with the brigade headquarters, a
not infrequent happening, for wireless sets behaved in a mischievous
manner in that country and it was only too easy to find oneself screened
by some twist in the sinuous course of the wadi.

Setting the Net

To the left of the KSLI, astride the Pantoni track and around a ring contour, which was one of the few easily recognisable features on their front, the Foresters were established. Now reduced to two weak companies, they set about making the crumbling buildings of what had been a once prosperous farm into a miniature fortress. There was only one approach road and this was liable to encroachment from the enemy, so every evening a tank would trundle forward bearing with it rations and ammunition for the following day. Also in support was a platoon of the faithful 2nd/7th Middlesex who set up their machine guns 200 yards behind the Foresters' headquarters and prepared to defend their own position to the last. The happy days when supporting machine gunners could rest assured that their own security was firm in the hands of those they supported were a distant memory. In the wadi country no one was secure, fields of fire were only too often minimal, covered approaches abounded and no one was safe from attack forward of the Lateral Road. Even on the Lateral Road itself, as one Regimental Aid Post discovered some days later as a German patrol came right into it, took some cigarettes and beat a hasty retreat.

In their uncomfortable and exposed positions the Foresters remained for the next four days. The weather appeared to become fouler and fouler, although in their generally exhausted state every twist of fate which made their lives more disagreeable became exaggerated to tired minds and bodies. Someone remembered the optimistic forecasts of the meteorologists before landing that 'February is the turning point of the winter season. Temperatures begin their annual climb from the January low. Precipitation reaches a minimum. Cloudiness and rainfall are lower than at any time since October. . . . In Rome South area there are frequent periods of rainless, partly cloudy skies that justify the term "Sunny Italy".'

It had rained unceasingly since their attack on the ridge, and the cold seeped into wet and tired bodies to numb the mind. To the wet, cold and exhausted men of the Foresters it was difficult to even remember a day when it had not rained.

A number of men from the overrun 'C' Company dribbled back over the next days, with cheering reports of confusion in the enemy ranks. And to add credence a number of miserable Germans who had been captured by one of the forward platoons spoke of not having eaten for three days. But the Foresters knew that the merciful peace could not last and that their enemy was only readjusting himself. On 14 February the long-awaited attack began. It was a haphazard affair, they recalled, and it was evident that the enemy confusion was more profound than they had thought. First to appear were some Germans marching down the track towards the forward positions, evidently confident of a peaceful occupation of Pantoni for they were carrying their packs, great-coats and even some blankets—the latter proved most welcome. Then a heavy mortar concentration struck the forward companies a little before midnight and it became clear that during the previous hours of darkness the enemy had worked their way right inside the battalion position. This could have proved serious had not 'D' Company been confident that the impressive wire barrier they had built over the previous days would be impervious to anything but a barrage of phenomenal proportions. It was the wire which brought the Germans up short, and caught by the machine guns of the Middlesex and the bren guns of the company it was on the wire that most died. In the morning twenty-four dead and wounded members of 4th Parachute Division were counted.

It continued to rain without cease. There was no sleep. Frequent enemy patrolling saw to that by night; shelling and mortaring rendered sleep impossible by day. They were conditions to sap everything, but courage and morale remained amazingly high throughout the ordeal. Fortunately their rations continued to come up, usually more or less on time. In fact throughout the Anzio campaign one of the most significant features was that on very few days, and only in the direst of emergencies, did troops go without a hot meal sometime during the twenty-four hours. The feats of the quartermasters' staffs back at the 'B' Echelons in the Padiglione Woods were remarkable. Often under fire themselves and subject to frequent night attacks from the air, they cooked and prepared meals under almost impossible conditions. Even then their task was not half done for what followed was the often hair-raising drive up the Via Anziate to the nearest point to their battalions which they could reach with some impunity; then the transfer into carrier or jeep, or to carrying parties, and the steady slog up to the line carrying rations, heavy ammunition boxes, even NAAFI goods and the precious bottle of rum. The last portion of the journey was the worst, for in the wadi country no one ever knew if the route was clear or if, encumbered as they were, they might be ambushed on the way.

The 56th (London) Infantry Division was fast assembling in the beachhead. 168th Brigade had been there since 3 February, now it was the turn of 167th Brigade. Like the rest of the Division they had been closely involved with the Mount Damiano battle. For six months they had not been out of the range of German artillery; everyone was very tired. They, too, had looked for some rest, but they were told it was not to be. It was a toss up between Anzio or Cassino where they were destined to go and there was little to choose in unpleasantness between them. On 10 February the 167th Brigade, consisting of the 8th and 9th Battalions the Royal Fusiliers and the 7th Battalion the Oxfordshire and

Buckinghamshire Light Infantry, under command of Brigadier J. Scott-Elliott DSO, assembled near Naples and embarked on LSTs for Anzio. They were little heartened by the sight of small urchins selling the U.S. Army paper, *Stars and Stripes*, which bore banner headlines, 'Anzio worse than Salerno'. Hurriedly the officers were sent to buy up all the copies they could and hide them.

All three battalions were weak in numbers, and more so in experience. Coming out of Damiano none could muster more than three rifle companies, and those reinforcements hurriedly brought in to make up depleted numbers came from a miscellany of different regiments and few of these men had ever heard a shot fired in battle. Of the rest, in the two Fusilier battalions, an 'experienced' man was one who had been with them for three months. As so often happened with reinforcements for those battalions bound for Anzio there was hardly time even to know the names of the new arrivals, before the whole unit was pitchforked into some of the fiercest infantry fighting of the whole war.

Under a waning moon the convoy carrying the 167th Brigade sailed peacefully up the leg of Italy, feeling very exposed and expecting to be sunk at any moment. Just as a sunny dawn was breaking, they arrived off Nettuno. Not a gun could be heard and the many barrage balloons floating over the harbour gave the place, despite the shell-shattered houses, an almost serene appearance. The serenity was rudely interrupted by four FW190s which screamed out of the sun, and weaving between the balloons appeared to come straight at them. As Lt.-Col J. Cleghorn on board one LST related:

> The Captain and his Number One took a flying leap under a table on the bridge. The commanding officer would have followed except that being a rather large man there was no room. Instead, he helplessly watched the harbour wall coming nearer and nearer until there was a crunch and a groan and the prow of the ship mounted it. Whereupon the Captain remarked, 'Well, you've got a dry landing anyway.'

In fact a bomb had landed only fifty yards behind the ship. No LST can have been unloaded in such record time. It was hardly an auspicious beginning to their stay at Anzio. The other battalions of the brigade had a more seemly arrival.

With the arrival of 167th Brigade General Lucas could complete the relief of the 1st British Division for a long overdue rest and readjust his line. Thus the two Fusilier battalions took over from the 157th Infantry who were bolstering the line to the left of the remnants of the Foresters and the KSLI, while these two battalions of 3rd Brigade in the area of Pantoni were in turn relieved by the 7th Ox and Bucks. In the centre of the sector astride the Via Anziate, the 45th U.S. Infantry Division now

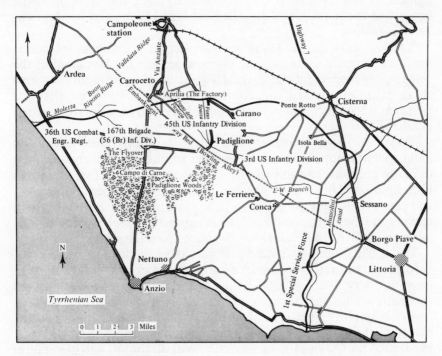

Situation, 15 February

took over the area from the Caves south of Carroceto and west of the main road up to the line of the Bowling Alley and to the village of Carano on the east. Of their three regiments, the 157th Infantry lay astride the road itself, with their 2nd Battalion in the Caves and Company 'E' forward near the Carroceto bridges; the 179th Infantry were south of the Factory, and the 180th Infantry covered a wide front straddling the Fosso di Spaccasassi. Headquarters of 56th Division under Major-General G. W. R. Templer was now operational, and he took over command of the western sector embracing the whole area from west of the Via Anziate, the wadi country and the line of the River Moletta to the sea.

The battalions of 167th Brigade moved up to their new positions in the dark. The commanding officer of the 9th Fusiliers had been greeted by some men of the 36th U.S. Engineer Battalion who had been guarding the extreme eastern side of the beachhead for the last two weeks in their unaccustomed role as infantry. They were referred to as the Moletta Home Guard, and their front was a fairly peaceful one, but that was largely because they ensured that it was so. On the occasions when they were hard-pressed, they had proved themselves fine fighters. Their infectious confidence that there was nothing to be concerned about at all, and that the Krauts had been quiet for days was very reassuring.

A take-over in the dark is never the most comfortable of moments, not least when the country is totally strange. But the battalions of the brigade achieved it without too much difficulty; by midnight they were all in position. Indeed the American engineers' promise that the Germans were very quiet here seemed to be true as hardly a shell passed overhead.

They had been informed that their positions were based on independent company areas. It sounded an interesting formation, not to say an ominous one and wholly different to the sort of war they had been fighting high up on Damiano. The next day was peaceful enough and gave a chance for the positions to be prepared more thoroughly with mines and wire. Night came at last; it seemed set to be a peaceful one, when without warning all three battalions were attacked.

The nightly tank had hardly departed from the Ox and Bucks' headquarters when, preceded by a fighter-bomber attack and a stonk of heavy artillery, the Germans started to form up opposite the forward companies. This was the prelude to a succession of withering attacks by line after line of German troops. Totally isolated by distance and the nature of the country, 'C' Company, the most forward and the most exposed of the Ox and Bucks suddenly went off the air, and gloomily at battalion headquarters they assumed that they had been destroyed. This laid open the way to the flanks of both their other forward companies. At 1100 hours 'A' Company were also reported as being overrun and soon 'D' Company, a bare 200 yards ahead of battalion headquarters itself, reported that one of its forward platoons had been lost and that they were under very heavy attack.

The commanding officer had been wounded and evacuated before even the battalion had come into the line, and early in the afternoon the second-in-command had been killed. The next senior officer still standing was the adjutant, Captain R. Close-Brooks, and he ordered all available men to pull back to the area of his headquarters. Here, in a saucer-shaped depression, a natural defensive position made stronger by dannert wire, mines and any other obstacles they could find or create, the remnants of the 7th Ox and Bucks Infantry withdrew and prepared to resist all boarders. Somewhere off to the right, in tenuous and occasional communication, was the sole surviving rifle company, 'B' Company. But by the middle of the afternoon they went off the air, and could not be raised. Runners sent to find them returned without any news, and it was feared that they too had been wiped out. Determinedly, the little party settled down to a siege of very doubtful outcome. The greatest worry was the ammunition situation and all depended on it being possible to get supplies up during the hours of darkness. And that eventuality began to look increasingly unlikely when the battalion mortar sections, which had been doing sterling work throughout the day from a position 400 yards behind the headquarters in another wadi, were rudely disturbed by a party of Germans who shot their sentries and started to throw down grenades from above. Hurriedly the mortars were abandoned and the mortarmen fought their way out of the trap in which they had found themselves. Only seven men escaped to join Captain Close-Brooks. In less than twelve hours, the battalion had been reduced to a handful of men.

Meanwhile the Fusiliers to the west had been subjected to vicious attacks since dawn. The 'independent company areas', which the formula of space to available men made inevitable, were a godsend to such skilled infiltrators as the Germans. During the night they had managed to slip between the forward companies of both Fusilier battalions. In half-an-hour's vicious fighting, the inner companies of both battalions, shot at from three directions including the rear, had been overrun and a huge hole punched in the middle of the line of the 167th Brigade. By nightfall the 8th Fusiliers had lost both forward companies—only two officers and some thirty men escaping. The 9th Fusiliers were even unluckier, for a tragic mistake when German helmets were taken for those of American paratroops allowed the enemy to penetrate right into the middle of their position before they were discovered for what they were. The best part of both forward companies were overrun, only a single platoon escaping and remaining undetected while the battle swirled and eddied around them. Gloomily, 'B' Company of the 9th Fusiliers, well back in reserve, reported that the only troops on the former positions appeared to be German and that a large column of prisoners had been seen being led away to the right.

Meanwhile, the Germans continued their thrust towards the Lateral Road. Some even managed to reach it, before being dealt with by some tanks of the armoured division which had come hurriedly up in support. But the position of the whole brigade was critical. Within a matter of hours 167th Brigade was in tatters. The Ox and Bucks, consisting of a swollen headquarters and practically nothing else, were holding the key position and barring the way from the west to the Flyover. The 8th Fusiliers to their left comprised some remnants of 'Z' Company with 'R' Company—a reinforcement company which had arrived just before they had sailed and which had been kept together. The 9th Fusiliers, on the left of the line, had only a single company left plus a mixed party of drivers, orderlies and anyone else they could muster. That was all from three proud and battle-worthy battalions which had each arrived at Anzio nearly 600 strong. But weak though

159

they were they were still holding, and it speaks volumes for the defence they had put up that the Germans made no further attempt to oust them from their acutely tenuous position for several days.

Nevertheless, the situation was critical. Hurriedly the survivors of the London Scottish and the London Irish, who had been attempting to recuperate after their own adventures of the last days, were pushed into a reserve position north of the Lateral Road. Even with their help, though, the line was hardly secure, and there was a gap between the two Fusilier battalions down the line of the wadi La Cogna. The only thing that could be done here was to bring down artillery fire on this approach, which threatened the whole of their precarious line. At two minute intervals throughout the night a single gun fired into the wadi, with some effect, as the number of dead Germans which a patrol found there the following morning amply testified.

At corps headquarters they anxiously studied the map of the western sector and could only fervently hope that the staunchness of the British infantry would be enough, for there was no one else to send. By then, too, all attention was directed on the Via Anziate which was clearly about to become the scene of the real test for those in the beachhead.

9

Operation 'Fisch Fang'

('Catching Fish')

16–19 February

The heavy air attacks of the past few days had done little more than hamper the German build-up for the decisive test to come. For the first time German artillery was at parity with Allied firepower, and although their ammunition supply was considerably less than that available to 6th Corps it was nevertheless on a more lavish scale than ever before. For nights past a steady stream of vehicles had brought up ammunition and it had been put in two huge dumps north of Carroceto. It took longer than had been planned as nearly a third of the available vehicles were laid off due to a shortage of tyres.

The great attack was now set for 0600 hours on 16 February. The first phase was the elimination of all Allied troops north of the Flyover, and then the panzer divisions, held back behind the German lines in the area of Cisterna and Velletri to disguise as far as possible the point of the main attack, would be let loose to burst through the beachhead line in one remorseless drive to the coast. Once again 3rd Panzer Grenadier Division was to take the brunt, and General Gräser, who had just been awarded the Oak Leaf to the Knight's Cross which he had won in France in 1940, was to be in command. In support, in separate operations, 65th Infantry Division were to push forward from the Buon Riposo Ridge, while 715th Infantry Division tried to make their way south along the Fosso della Ficoccia and 114th Jaeger Division attempted to do the same down the line of the Fosso di Spaccasassi. Further to the east, in the area of Cisterna and Ponte Rotto the Hermann Goering Panzer Division were to create a diversion.

Under command of 3rd Panzer Grenadier Division was the Infantry Lehr Regiment. An élite demonstration regiment which had just arrived, this crack formation was to be the spearhead for the great break-through. Hitler himself placed great store on the undoubted courage of the Infantry Lehr, but the General Staff, who had authorised the move, had failed to take into account that half of them had never seen service at all, and none of them had ever fought in Italy against Allied artillery and air power; nor was their administrative tail adequate. Thus vehicles, even field cookers, had to be borrowed, and the supply chain broke down at the most crucial moment in their attack.

Operation 'Fisch Fang'

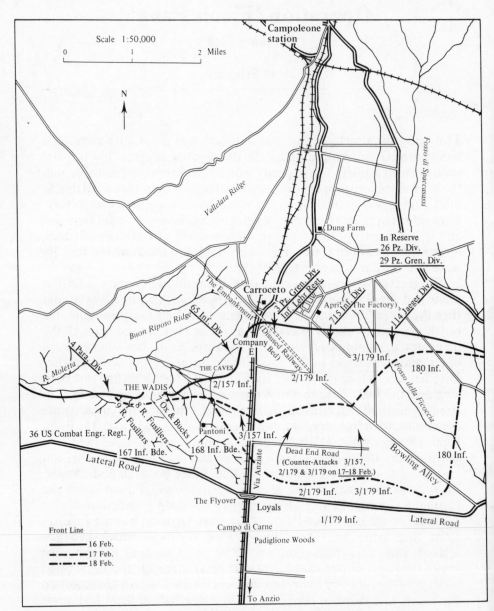

Operation 'Fisch Fang', ('Catching Fish') 16–19 February

Worse, they were unfamiliar with the ground. To attack at night was unthinkable, so a daylight assault became inevitable, and whatever help and surprise darkness might have brought was lost. To those in the divisional headquarters of 3rd Panzer Grenadier Division, sunk deep in the cellar of a farmhouse near old Dung Farm and who had no illusions about the spirit of Allied resistance, it all looked rather hazardous.

Hopes of a resounding success ran high in the German camp. How far this euphoria was justified is open to question, and von Mackensen had expressed grave doubts about the wisdom of attacking on as narrow a front as the ground dictated, with many of his units below strength and full of raw troops who certainly had not tasted the shattering effect of the murderous Allied artillery fire. Nor was he entirely happy about the ammunition supply, which was not plentiful enough to allow a full barrage but had to be limited to specific tasks and counter-battery fire. He requested a postponement to give his new units time to reconnoitre and plan, and for more ammunition to be brought up, but he was overruled. Despite von Mackensen's misgivings, there was supreme confidence that victory would be theirs. The ground ahead appeared inviting enough and a regimental commander in 26th Panzer Division, who were chosen to inflict the final crushing defeat on the Allies, was convinced that his tanks would have no difficulty crossing the flat country south of the Factory—he was killed in a road accident before he could be proved wrong.

As preparations for the German attack advanced, so the Allies stepped up their already impressive air activity. The weather stayed good; by day Kittyhawks, Mitchells, Marauders, Mustangs, Baltimores and Fortresses flew over the battlefield and plastered the German positions, and by night Wellingtons and Bostons took their place. Air attacks on the great railway guns which had been regularly blasting Anzio and the shipping off the port were particularly successful. One in a tunnel in the Alban Hills was damaged, while two on the track north of Campoleone received direct hits, one being derailed, the other destroyed. The German presence in the air was also more noticeable, and they met with success for an LST loaded with fuel was set on fire and a Liberty ship slightly damaged. There was a noticeable increase in their artillery fire, too, a foretaste of what everyone guessed was coming. And if they hadn't suspected it, they knew for certain when, on 15 February, a loud-mouthed prisoner captured near Buon Riposo revealed the German plans for the attack, and the start of 'Big Things'.

It froze hard during the night of 15/16 February, which enabled the German tracked vehicles to come forward, but soon, as a beautiful and sunny day dawned, the ground thawed and once more became a quagmire. Preceded by a massive bombardment of the American forward positions, the German attack broke on the 45th Division. The 2nd and 3rd Battalions of 179th Infantry south and south-east of the Factory bore the brunt, and soon the significance of holding the rubble which now constituted Mussolini's showplace, became apparent, for the Factory completely dominated the position of the two battalions. Throughout the day small groups of enemy tanks and SP guns issued forth to pour point-blank fire on the American positions, which were under continuous observation. When the force of their onslaught was spent, the German troops could reform and regroup and replenish under cover until ready to try again. At the same time, groups of enemy infantry tried to work their way down the Fosso della Ficoccia which transfixed the American positions. Despite almost crippling casualties the battalions of the 179th were able to hold on until the onset of evening brought a blessed relief and the German efforts slackened.

The enemy were having troubles of their own. For the heavier Tiger and Panther tanks to go off the approach roads and tracks was to risk immediate bogging, and every approach to the front was under continuous and savage artillery fire. Thus reinforcements usually arrived having sustained heavy casualties even before being committed to battle, and the state of armoured vehicles in Gräser's division was acute. There were no armoured ambulances left; the wounded stayed where they had fallen or where their comrades or immediate medical attention could tend them. Under Allied artillery fire of an intensity such as no man had experienced before, even the veterans of Stalingrad where 3rd Panzer Grenadier Division had fought before coming to Italy, could do no more. Gräser's attack slowed, then halted. The divisional history records that they captured only eight prisoners during the entire day's fighting, such was the stubbornness and gallantry of the American infantry. And in the middle of the afternoon, after losing most of their officers, Hitler's pride, the Infantry Lehr Regiment, cracked under the strain of such resistance as they had never believed possible and pulled back in disorder to their Start Line.

On the left of General Eagles' line, astride the Via Anziate, the 2nd Battalion 157th Infantry took the full force of the enemy attack. They had only moved that night into their positions among the Caves and north towards the Embankment and had not time to get their bearings before they were attacked with ferocious force at 0730 hours the following morning. The first attack fell squarely on Company 'E' south of the Carroceto bridges and in a matter of moments tanks had overrun their left-hand platoon. Gallant action by one of their tank-busters destroyed two German tanks and frightened off a third, and then ruthlessly the machine guns of the tank-busters shot down the German infantry until the rest turned and fled. This was the start of almost continuous attacks mounted on the 2nd Battalion through that warm sunny day of 16 February. The Germans came from the north and from the east from across the main road; then to their horror, they discovered that more enemy had worked their way through the gully behind their position from the Buon Riposo Ridge, and they were virtually cut off. The nearest troops to the west were the Ox and Bucks nearly one mile away and with innumerable problems of their own. As the 45th Division's history records, 'All morning long the German infantry moved across the open fields, into our interlocking fire. Hundreds died, but the assault waves never ceased.' In fact the casualty returns of 3rd Panzer Grenadier Division showed that over 1,000 men were killed and wounded on 16 February and the following day.

Elsewhere, warned by an intercepted wireless message, diversionary attacks on six different points on the 3rd U.S. Division's front around Ponte Rotto, the Cisterna Creek and the Mussolini Canal, after gaining some ground, were eliminated by the evening, and comparative peace once more returned on that part of the front. Thus by the end of 16 February, the corps line was still intact and in fact had been hardly dented. South of the Factory the Germans had gained about 500 yards, but only after sustaining very heavy casualties, particularly by 29th Panzer Grenadier Regiment of Gräser's own division and 735th Regiment of 715th Infantry Division under his command, both of whom had run up against the stubborn resistance of the 179th Infantry.

Such had been their casualties on the first day of the great offensive that a change of plan became imperative. So the Germans reverted to their highly successful infiltration tactics, and almost immediately achieved what they had been striving for. During the night, they managed to prise open a gap down the line of the Via Anziate and the country immediately to the east between the 157th and 179th Infantry. The highly vulnerable Company 'E' of the 2nd Battalion 157th had been their first target. Groups of twenty to thirty Germans, with close tank support, methodically proceeded to eliminate the company foxhole by foxhole, disregarding their own heavy casualties. At length the only survivors were the company command post and three tanks, which had stayed throughout, a total of eighteen men. At five o'clock in the morning they were told to withdraw, and under cover of smoke the gallant band pulled back to the little safer area with the rest of their battalion in the Caves.

By dawn on 17 February, there was a long, narrow salient plunging into the very centre of the line of the 45th Division, and with daylight the Germans set about widening it. Aided by the close air support of up to thirty-five aircraft—the largest gathering of the Luftwaffe seen for many a day—and with a force of sixty tanks, the German attack struck south from the Factory and down the Via Anziate, intent on enlarging the gap between the two American regiments. Shortly before nine o'clock in the morning the regimental commander of the 179th Infantry gave orders for the remains of his two battalions to pull back 1,000 yards to the further side of a branch of the Fosso di Carroceto. Under cover of a heavy smoke screen they attempted to extricate themselves from close contact with the enemy, but the Germans gave them no respite. Attacked from the front and from the flanks, the 179th Infantry were unable to reform until just north of the Dead End Road. By noon a break-in two-and-a-half miles wide and one-and-a-quarter deep had been established. The Allied line was beginning to crumble.

It was at this crucial moment in the life of the beachhead that General Penney, who had commanded the 1st Division with such distinction from the day of landing, was wounded by a shell when in his caravan in the Padiglione Woods. Command of both British Divisions devolved on Major-General G. W. R. Templer, of the 56th Division, who was no stranger to the men of the 1st Division, having commanded them briefly in North Africa.

Flown out of North Africa into the middle of the Salerno battle when the then commander of the 56th Division had been wounded, Templer immediately set about exerting his own very positive method of command. The divisional sign was the black cat, a rather fat black cat, and in his first address to his officers the new divisional commander pointed to the animal and said that in future the obese beast was going to be somewhat slimmer and then he added, 'When the tail is pointing to the left, then we are going to the left. When the tail is pointing to the right, then we are going to the right. And when the brute has a bright red arse-hole, then we are going straight up the middle.' He was known as the Scalded Cat, a nickname hiding a growing respect and admiration as the Battle of Anzio wore on. Here, there and everywhere in the days that followed, and always accompanied by a copious quantity of evil wine in bottles of every shape, size and parentage, there were very few British troops in the beachhead to whom General Templer did not become a familiar sight. He was to command all the British forces for the six most crucial days of the beachhead.

In this dire emergency, all the resources of Allied air power were called in to support the hard-pressed 45th Division. Wave after wave of fighters, medium and heavy bombers, Fortresses, Liberators, Mitchells, Marauders and anything else that could give close support to the troops were used. Their orders were to fly in below cloud cover. There was nothing more cheering to the soldiers on the ground than to see formation after formation of aircraft coming in, completely oblivious to the holocaust of flak which billowed around them, keeping meticulous, arrow-straight courses and plastering the enemy rear areas. The German fire took a heavy toll. Plane after plane was destroyed or severely damaged. It was a scene which those at Anzio never forgot, and the veterans of those days still speak warmly of the courage of the aircrews who time and again flew into the most intense flak that many had ever experienced. Their admiration for their comrades in the Allied air forces was unbounded.

It seemed that nothing could survive the incredible air attacks flung on the German rear areas and incomplete casualty returns show the Germans suffered 2,569 casualties on 16 and 17 February, but the Germans were not to be denied. Notwithstanding their colossal casualties, fourteen battalions were committed on the Anziate front that day. As soon as a unit was decimated by the air attacks and staggering artillery fire, with that of every available ship, including two cruisers, another took its place, while the survivors withdrew to reform and then return again to the fray.

Some German battalions were told that the Allies were already re-embarking and that their forthcoming effort would be decisive. Others understood that already plans were being made for a parade in Berlin where the British prisoners would be led through the streets as part of a massive victory march. To a dispassionate observer, such an idea might have appeared none too fanciful.

All afternoon the sorely pressed companies of the 179th Infantry fought their individual actions supported by the tanks of the 1st Armoured Division. But they were gradually being forced back. Worse, the 179th were also being forced to the side, to the east. The gap between the two American infantry regiments was widening visibly. Already the 2nd Battalion 157th were all but isolated in their caves with their perimeter contracting hourly as men of the German 715th Infantry Division attacked them from the north, while troops of 65th Infantry Division closed in on them from the west. On the Via Anziate, elements of the Infantry Lehr Regiment, smarting under the disgrace of the previous day and flung once more into battle, had reached the western end of the Dead End Road and established themselves in some houses. From this tenuous toehold they attempted to work their way forward, and two tanks bolder than the others were stopped only just short of the Flyover. Throughout the morning, the Scout Troop of 'A' Squadron of the 1st Reconnaissance Regiment, from a position just south of the Dead End Road, managed to hold up the German advance. They found they could deal adequately with events to their front, but when enemy infantry started to work their way round behind them they were forced to withdraw. Further back, south of the Flyover, General Templer had ordered every available anti-tank gun and anti-aircraft weapon now used in a ground rôle, to be placed in herringbone fashion down the Via Anziate so that the Germans would have to fight for every inch of the main road before they could get through. Rumours of a German parachute landing led to night patrolling of all roads in the rear areas and the beachhead being divided into zones. Fortunately the Germans had no such idea, or capability.

In reserve for night after night, the tanks of the 1st U.S. Armoured Division stood in readiness at half-hour alert, fully loaded with ammunition and fuel, with their engines warmed and their crews sleeping no more than fifty feet from their charges. They came to be known as the Firemen of Anzio. Further back, in four separate stop lines stood every available able-bodied man in the beachhead capable of handling a rifle: drivers, engineers, mechanical fitters, stevedores, signallers, members of the Pay Corps and others, who had, and expressed, strong views on being involved in such warlike activity. But the situation was desperate. Those at higher headquarters knew that practically nothing lay between the Germans and the sea.

Preparation was made to blow huge holes in the Via Anziate: cavities were dug in the surface and were only waiting for the charges to be inserted. The road verges were mined, and the rest of the area forward of the Flyover made into a 'sea of mines'. Lurking behind the Flyover itself were lorries loaded with concrete ready to drive under the bridges and plug them. The codeword for the mining to commence was 'Kitchener—blocks on.' It was issued shortly after nightfall on 17 February.

The German salient had become a wedge and soon a massive hole which thrust right down the Via Anziate. As darkness fell on 17 February there were virtually no Allied troops forward of Dead End Road, except for the gallant 2nd Battalion 157th Infantry Regiment still staunchly holding out in their Caves.

A counter-attack by units of 1st Armoured Division, one up the Via Anziate and the other up the Bowling Alley to relieve pressure from the reeling 179th Infantry did little more than delay the inevitable. Unable to get off the roads due to the boggy nature of the ground, they were forced to advance on what was virtually a one-tank front and caught by enemy tanks and SP guns they could make no headway.

To gain time and a better defensive line, the 2nd and 3rd Battalions 179th Infantry, both down to barely a quarter of their former effective strength, were ordered to counter-attack during the night, while the 3rd Battalion 157th Infantry were to try to regain contact with their sister battalion in the Caves. On the eastern side of the Via Anziate they barely crossed the Dead End Road and had to confess failure. Neither attack succeeded and the effort did little more than leave the attacking battalions in appallingly exposed positions come the morning. The Germans were quick to react. By-passing some of the forward positions they were able to force the 179th infantry back to the final beachhead line, and were also now firmly behind the position in the Caves.

Also during the night von Mackensen decided, despite the relative failure of his battalions to break through, that the time had come to commit his armoured reserve to make the final penetration and crush the beachhead. 26th Panzer Division were chosen for the thrust down and to the east of the Via Anziate in 3rd Panzer Grenadier Division's sector; while 29th Panzer Grenadier Division was selected for the attack on 715th Infantry Division's sector down the Bowling Alley, and an additional regiment was allotted to 65th Infantry Division with a view to improving their thrust west of the main road from the Buon Riposo Ridge, the success of which had taken the German command somewhat by surprise, and was never fully exploited. 0400 hours was the time chosen for the attack, but Allied artillery fire had so hampered the assembly of the panzer divisions and disrupted German communications that the attack was postponed for two hours.

There was no doubt where the blow would fall, the enemy intentions had been clear for days; besides the Via Anziate was the only really practicable approach for tanks. All along the final beachhead line, the Allied troops stood-to, waiting for the attack which was to resolve the Anzio battle. To the east, astride the Bowling Alley and the Spaccasassi creek, 180th Infantry were well-established and had suffered comparatively few casualties over the past days; to their left, the remnants of the 2nd and 3rd Battalions 179th Infantry and their 1st Battalion which was still fresh, covered the ground to within 2,000 yards east of the Flyover. To their left, reaching to the Flyover itself stretched the thin line of the 1st Battalion the Loyal Regiment—it was on these regiments that the full weight of the German attack was to fall, and without the unexampled sacrifice, courage and fortitude of these regiments the beachhead would have fallen.

All through the dark, still, portentous night of 17/18 February the men of the 1st British Infantry Division, the 1st U.S. Armoured Division and the 45th U.S. Infantry Division heard the rumble of wheels and tracks in the rear areas. It was quite clear that the moment of truth was upon them.

On 10 February the Loyals had moved up to positions to the east of the Flyover along the Lateral Road, which they promptly christened Wigan Street. Of all the battalions of the 1st Division, the Loyals were the least battle-scarred. Although they had been continuously in action since arriving at Anzio—indeed, prior to moving to the Flyover, they had been in the line for seventeen days on end—but on fairly quiet parts of the front. Although exposed to constant night work, occasionally subject to artillery and mortar fire of varying intensity, yet they had not been subjected to a major attack. They had suffered casualties, a total of 137 including five officers, but these had been made good by reinforcements and on 15 February the Loyals mustered thirty-one officers and 747 men. Of greater import, though, was the fact that their

original team of officers and non-commissioned officers—a good solid
leavening of tough fighting Lancashire men—was still intact. The 1st
Loyals was a hardened, experienced and supremely self-confident
battalion and although tired like everyone else in the beachhead, they
were the freshest battalion in the 1st Division. It was as well they were.

The area along Wigan Street was completely treeless. To the north
the country sloped gently downwards and crossed flat fields to a slight
dip where there was dead ground and some deep ditches. Beyond was a
slight slope until the Dead End Road was reached 1,100 yards north of
Wigan Street. Further away there were more fields and beyond them
the conspicuous bulk of the Factory with its menacing chimney from
where, they felt, and with some justification, the Germans could see
their every movement. It was the dip in the ground only 300 yards in
front of their position which was the greatest concern, for here the
Germans could form up unnoticed and undetected. The dip merited
half-a-dozen fire tasks from both the gunners and their own mortars.

Along Wigan Street itself were a number of houses on either side of
the road. On the north side lay a substantial farm, Carne Farm it was
called; midway between the Flyover and a scruffy wood, which was
soon given the name of Stonk Wood, was another building rather larger
than the others and to the south of the road. This house was called
Todhunter Lodge. A wind-pump stuck like a gaunt skeleton on the
ground behind Stonk Wood and 300 yards behind the wind-pump a
gully crossed the front at right angles. Here Lt.-Col. E. Fulbrook DSO,
commanding the battalion, established his headquarters.

Their front was 2,000 yards long and with such a distance to cover it
was necessary to have three of their four companies forward along the
line of Wigan Steet. 'A' Company was in the immediate area of the
Flyover; 'B' Company took up residence in and around Carne Farm,
while 'C' Company found a cluster of houses short of Stonk Wood
where they established themselves. To provide some depth to what was
a perilously shallow position, 'D' Company and the carrier platoon were
put in the area between the wind-pump and Todhunter Lodge. But
there was practically no cover anywhere, they felt, and they were under
constant observation. The ground they were on was reclaimed
marshland and below two feet there was standing water.

As soon as they arrived the Loyals set about improving their
unpleasant position. The battle still seemed a long way off. The Factory
had only just been lost, Carroceto was still in Allied hands. Indeed,
there seemed to be so little urgency that one company was taken away to
build a reserve position to the west of the Flyover beyond the Via
Anziate—which was gratefully received by a company of the Gordons
before long—but as the Germans remorselessly started to work their
way southward, it was speedily decided that the Loyals' company had

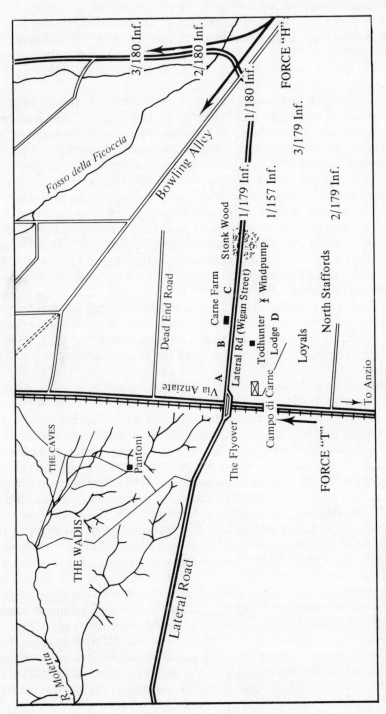

The last stand, 18–19 February

more pressing labour nearer home. No work was possible by day, but as soon as night fell, like moles, the men of the Loyals set to building up their wire, laying mines, reinforcing their slit-trenches and generally making their position as defensible as possible. There was little rest for anyone, but at least they were spared from the nerve-racking job of patrolling.

As the days passed and as the battle grew closer the Loyals began to realise that they might well have to use the position they had been developing, and all too soon. On 16 February they stood to and watched anxiously as the American infantry regiments sought to resist the mounting German pressure. By dawn on 17 February it was clear they could no longer do so. By 0930 hours the first wounded began to pass through the 'A' Company positions near the Flyover. By mid-day they could see enemy armour moving around in the area of the Dead End Road and had started to come under shell-fire themselves. Around four o'clock some American tanks came along Wigan Street from the east and joined noisy battle some few hundred yards up the Via Anziate, and it became painfully obvious that what had started as a second line of defence was now well and truly in the forefront of affairs. And if any had held doubts or hidden hopes that this was not so, they were rudely put to rest when towards dusk a strong German patrol, which had crawled into the dip in front of 'A' Company, suddenly attacked their forward platoon. The battle which was to save the beachhead was about to be joined.

The survivors of the 179th Infantry took up position to the right of the Loyals between Stonk Wood and the Bowling Alley. To the Loyals' left beyond the Via Anziate, the Gordons were dug in. Behind the Loyals, the 2nd North Staffords were acting as long-stop; behind them came the miscellany of corps stop-lines of varying solidity and manned by anyone and everyone. Behind them was the sea. But it was on the Loyals, and on the forward companies of 179th Infantry to their right, that all the fury of the German attack was to break—and was to founder.

All through the night of 17/18 February, the Germans kept up a steady bombardment of the Loyals' positions. At five o'clock in the morning 'B' Company were suddenly assaulted and the company were engaged in a savage battle. At dawn it was discovered that one of the forward platoons had just vanished in the night. Their kit and equipment was still in their trenches, but of the men there was no sign, except some casualties. Then it was discovered that Todhunter Lodge was also in enemy hands. At the same time 'A' Company on the Flyover had also been attacked but had managed to beat off their enemy. With the assistance of some tanks and a spirited attack by 'C' Company Todhunter Lodge was recaptured and a number of prisoners taken. By 0930 hours the position was restored in the centre. Now it was the turn of 'C' Company themselves to face the German onslaught. But the line held, as did that of the 179th Infantry beyond Stonk Wood.

By 1130 hours the German artillery fire slackened, and it seemed as though they were pausing for breath before trying again. The time seemed ripe to try to retake the lost half of 'B' Company's position. So the reserve company with the carrier platoon on foot and preceded by a short, fierce five-minute bombardment swept forward. They routed out some Germans who had gone to ground unpleasantly near the battalion headquarters and rescued those men from 'B' Company who had previously been captured, including the company commander, and drove the Germans from the 'B' Company area at the point of the bayonet. 'D' Company was then ordered to fill a rather large gap between the depleted 'A' and 'B' Companies. This meant that the Loyals now had all four of their companies in a long thin line on either side of Wigan Street. The reserve position formerly occupied by 'D' Company was taken over by a company of the North Staffords.

Promptly at five o'clock that evening, and heralded by a thunderous bombardment, a full battalion of Germans was thrown against 'A' Company. One of the forward platoons was immediately engulfed, but the rest hung on grimly, fighting a hand-to-hand battle with grenades. Some tanks and a company of Gordons from across the Anziate came to help, and together they managed to check the attack. In the middle of the fray the battalion adjutant tried to find out what was happening at 'A' Company, only to be given short shrift by the acting company commander: 'Will you get off this —— thing. I want to shoot Germans.' For over an hour the battle eddied round the isolated platoon positions and the company headquarters of 'A' Company, but at nightfall it was clear they had won. They had only fifty men left by then, but in the gathering darkness the Germans could be seen running back. With the grateful thanks of 'A' Company, the tanks and Gordons returned whence they had come.

In the centre, meanwhile, 'D' Company with the remains of 'B' Company were in firm occupation and had been left in peace on this occasion. To their right 'C' Company could muster sixty men, and that was all of the 1st Battalion the Loyal Regiment.

In this extremity every member of the Loyals was collected from the echelons—cooks, drivers, the quartermaster's staff—until every able-bodied man of the regiment was forward with one of the companies. Further back, the echelon men of the other battalions of the 2nd Brigade were mustered to create another *ad hoc* 'thin red line', should the Loyals not be able to hold. And the likelihood of their succeeding in this receded during the night when it became clear that the scattered and depleted elements of the forward companies were one by one being attacked and destroyed.

Operation 'Fisch Fang'

For once, with the companies in close contact with each other, with the front straight enough and the country flat enough, it was possible to provide a degree of mutual support. A full company of machine guns of the Middlesex Regiment had a magnificent position and were able to fire across the whole front. From the top of a haystack, one of their platoon commanders was able to gain a grandstand view of the engagement. 'Let us have a go by ourselves', he besought and that day 32,000 rounds of machine gun ammunition were fired by that one detachment. The toll taken of Germans as they advanced repeatedly to the attack was staggering. Someone likened their conduct to a Charge of the Light Brigade without the horses. As soon as the enemy emerged from the dip in front of the companies they were deluged by a staggering weight of shell and caught by the machine guns of the Middlesex in enfilade fire. For every man who managed to get into the Loyals' position at least six lay dead or dying. Yet the Germans never let up. It was sheer slaughter, but there wasn't a single man in the Loyals who did not honour the courage and incredible fortitude of their enemy.

The German casualties had been crippling. Some battalions were only 150 strong, yet few flinched from the contest. Still the attacks continued in quick succession, battalion after battalion were thrown into the fray, those who had just come out of the fight were reorganised and committed again. The defenders were allowed no rest. Some of the German units sent up as reinforcements were almost destroyed before they could join the fight. If the shortage of men was assuming dangerous proportions, the shortage of equipment was causing equal worry. Time and again communications were destroyed or disrupted as the concussion of Allied shells shattered the delicate wireless valves. Ammunition was still available, but there were no ammunition lorries to bring it forward. When the tanks or SP guns had expended what they carried, they had to return themselves to collect more, frequently bringing out casualties, for there were no ambulances left, even the armoured ambulances were bogged, destroyed or too valuable to commit forward when their services were equally desperately needed behind the front line.

The supply situation was acute. Few road convoys were getting through by day, as Allied aircraft ranged the approach roads from the north, so the Germans resorted to the use of horse and donkey carts to bring up ammunition and rations. All convoys needed protection from the air, and increasingly from the ground as the partisans in the Alban Hills became more active. For the most part theirs were small-scale forays by groups of four or five men. They collected explosives from the Germans' own dumps through the hands of friendly workers and made attacks on dispatch riders, individual trucks or staff cars. In total their efforts were not much, but in their small and willing way they helped by diverting German troops who would otherwise have been engaged in the beachhead battle.

18 February was crisis day on the German side. 26th Panzer Division were able to push forward some 500 yards, but were then pinned down by heavy fire. To their east, 29th Panzer Grenadier Division, thrusting forward on the road north of Padiglione, were themselves caught in the open by flanking fire. Their advance, too, came to a halt, with two battalions of 15th Grenadier Regiment in an exposed position well forward of the rest of the division and out of contact. On the afternoon of 18 February, armour of 26th Panzer Division tried to attack down the Bowling Alley itself. But a blown bridge prevented any advance in that direction. The end of the day found the Germans masters of a breach five-and-a-half miles wide and two-and-a-half deep, but in only one or two places had they reached their first objective, the Lateral Road, and none of their positions there were really firm. The Allies showed no signs of crumbling, and the German attack was making little progress.

At 1930 hours that evening a lugubrious voice on the wireless, which was never identified, announced that the Flyover had been captured. To this the Scots Guards quickly came back to say in that case their quartermaster—who drove around wearing massive yellow gauntlets and armed to the teeth, and had just passed by—had recaptured it with their ration train.

At a noon conference at corps headquarters on 17 February, Truscott, Harmon and others pressed on Lucas that now was the time to make a counter-attack. The Germans, they stressed, were fully committed. Their reserves of armour had already tried and failed, but there was no let-up in their efforts and for the Allied part, their line was reeling. The Loyals and the men of the three regiments of 45th Division had stood firm and could be relied on to fight to the end, but they were exhausted after nights and days of combat and their numbers were thinning dangerously. Further, to counter-attack now might catch the Germans off balance. They were not expecting anything so aggressive, it could halt them in their tracks.

Shortly after midnight on 16 February Truscott had been woken by his aide and given a signal to the effect that he was to give up command of the 3rd Division to Brigade-General John W. O'Daniel, 'Iron Mike' as he was known to the troops, and proceed immediately to take up appointment as Deputy Corps Commander to Lucas. Truscott's feelings, as he wrote, were mixed. On the one hand he had commanded the 3rd Division for nearly a year. He knew them and they knew him, and he felt that with them he had both 'command authority and responsibility', both of which he would have to give up for a job which had neither. Further, he had strong feelings of loyalty for Lucas, who he liked as a man, although he too had had misgivings about him as a commander. These misgivings were intensified when he duly arrived at corps headquarters the following morning. He had been warned to some extent of what to expect by a staff officer at corps but he was still not prepared for the prevailing sense of dejection and hopelessness in the catacombs in Nettuno. The situation was far worse than he had conceived.

It was compounded by Lucas's reluctance to go to see things on the ground for himself. During his first tour as Deputy Corps Commander, Truscott found both American divisional commanders confident that they could hold on, and radiating reassurance. For their part, the British 1st Division was tired and had few resources left, but in the crucial wadi area which threatened to unpin the whole front if the Germans should penetrate there—what General Templer described as the 'keybrick of the arch'—Templer was equally confident that the Germans were held. In the 45th Division sector, General Eagles, although anxious about the casualties to 179th Infantry, and concerned about the physical fitness of the regimental commander—in fact Colonel Bill Darby of the Rangers, which had not been able to reform after their disaster on Pantano Creek, was shortly afterwards placed in command of 179th Infantry—was also of the opinion that the Germans could be held. Further, there were still some resources left and substantially uncommitted. Before leaving his 3rd Division Truscott had had the foresight to bring the whole of the 30th Infantry Regiment out of the line and they were in reserve a mile or so east of the Fosso di Spaccasassi. In, addition General Harmon had the 6th Armoured Infantry as yet uncommitted, and General Templer's third brigade, the Queen's Brigade, of 2nd/5th, 2nd/6th and 2nd/7th Queens were expected hourly at the port of Anzio. As Truscott put it, 'We still had assets and I advocated a counter-attack.'

Lucas hesitated. Looking objectively at the Anzio campaign, there is occasion after occasion when it appears that action was taken hurriedly and belatedly. There is a woeful lack of a master plan. In many instances it is clear that the Germans were calling the tune and that 6th Corps reacted only after the enemy had shown their hand. Time was lost and ground was lost, and much of this must be laid at the door of the tactical handling of his troops by the corps commander. Now, in the extremity of the beachhead, Lucas still hesitated about committing his reserves. At this crucial moment General Clark joined the conference. After hearing the situation, he authorised the counter-attack and over-ruled the corps commander. Lucas agreed and plans were put into effect.

They were simple. Force 'T' under Templer, with the newly arrived 169th Brigade and support from tanks of the 1st Armoured Division, were to thrust straight up the main axis to the ground north of the Dead End Road, with a view to blunting the German efforts and relieving the beleaguered battalion in the Caves. On the right, Harmon's Force 'H', consisting of the 30th Infantry from 3rd Division and his own 6th Armoured Infantry, would attack up the line of the Bowling Alley from a jumping-off point south of Padiglione. Both attacks were to start at dawn on 19 February.

There was one thing that had been puzzling Truscott since he had taken over his new job. On the front of the 3rd Division the massed fire of his own artillery had been able to break up attack after German attack well before they reached the forward positions of his infantry. Yet on the front of 45th Division, on ground which was if anything more open, time after time the Germans had been able to approach and actually reach the foxholes of the infantry. He asked to see their ammunition expenditure, and to his astonishment discovered that the entire division had fired less ammunition than a single artillery battalion of 3rd Division and at a time when their own front had been comparatively quiet. He initiated an examination into the artillery procedures in 45th Division. When the counter-attacks went in the next day it was to the accompaniment of supporting artillery such as few had ever experienced before.

As darkness fell on 18 February the troops of 30th Infantry and Harmon's 6th Armoured Infantry started to move forward towards the foot of the Bowling Alley. Already the planned counter-attacks had received a severe set-back because the convoy bearing part of 169th Brigade had been delayed by a mine and torpedo attack which had sunk the cruiser HMS *Penelope*, and rendered Anzio port inoperable until the approaches were cleared. So Templer's part in the plan had to be restricted to an attack with tanks only up the Via Anziate—and in the event it did not get far. A further hitch occurred in the early hours of the morning, for when the attack on the Loyals began to assume serious proportions, corps headquarters became anxious about losing their only reserve for the attack up the Bowling Alley, and suggested the whole thing be called off. For hours, through ankle deep mud, Harmon's infantry had been making their way forward; to turn them around now and make them walk all the way back was out of the question. In any case, by the time the manoeuvre was completed it would be too late for them to influence the battle around the Flyover. He was adamant that the counter-attack should go forward and expressed conviction that this was the way in any case to make the Germans ease their pressure on the Flyover area. Then, at 0400 hours, he was also told that an American battalion was somewhere along the line of his advance and full in the path of the artillery Ladder Barrage which was to accompany his attack. His was an agonising decision; to risk the deaths of his countrymen under their own artillery fire, or, if the counter-attack could not go in, risk the capture and death of many more in the beachhead. There was only one answer, the attack was ordered to start as planned. In the event the battalion turned out to be a platoon, and when the artillery fire came down they had in any case moved away.

'Anzio' is one of the proudest battle honours held by the Loyals from the last war. For those who survived, 19 February is the day they will never forget. For their stand that day, and that of the 179th Infantry, their American comrades on the right, was the final and victorious act in the crushing of Operation Fisch Fang.

During the early part of the night the Germans dedicated themselves to eliminating 'A' Company. When that failed they turned their attention to 'C' Company at the other end of the Loyals' thin line. At four o'clock in the morning after a sudden flurry of shelling, German infantry stormed 'C' Company's positions, and those of the 1st Battalion of 179th Infantry to their right. First to go were the forward platoons, still fighting to the very last; then it was the turn of company headquarters. Shortly after a grey and dismal dawn 'C' Company sent their last wireless message.

With 'C' Company's position captured, the Germans then set about dealing with the remains of 'B' Company which had taken up a position in the area of the wind-pump. Soon they were threatening the flank of the next company along Wigan Street, 'D' Company, and had managed to isolate one of the platoons, which gallantly fought on. By six o'clock in the morning, the Germans, despite colossal casualties, not only from the small-arms fire of the Loyals but also from their mortars and those of 2nd/7th Middlesex, plus the entire corps artillery, had punched a huge hole in the position of the Loyals who were now commanded by Major G. A. Rimbault MC, Colonel Fulbrook, who had held every rank in the regiment from drummer to commanding officer being given a well deserved rest.

This was the turning-point in the battle of the Flyover, and in retrospect of the whole Battle of Anzio. Fighting forward with unmatched bravery, although with perceptibly weakening battalions, the Germans were in sight of breaking through the thin line. All that lay between them and the sea was a succession of exhausted and depleted battalions and a motley selection of anyone who could bear arms in the other and *ad hoc* defence lines.

No. 2 Company of the North Staffords occupying the Loyals' reserve company position near the wind-pump were already under small-arms fire from their right where the Germans, having mastered the remnants of the Loyals' 'B' Company, were pushing forward vigorously. But they were the nearest unit able to mount the counter-attack which must go in now if the position was not to be irretrievably lost. At eleven o'clock, under cover of smoke and every gun that could be laid on the area, the North Staffords advanced. Immediately they ran into murderous German machine gun fire. With all their officers and most of their non-commissioned officers casualties, the attack faltered and then stopped within 150 yards of their objectve. Another company of the North Staffords, No. 1 Company, which had been standing by in a long-stop position and fast coming to the conclusion that it was going to be their turn before very long, were ordered to try from a different direction aided by some tanks of the armoured division who shot them in from Wigan Street. At 1500 hours this second company stormed forward with bayonets fixed and with close support from the tanks. Helped by heavy flanking fire from 'D' Company of the Loyals they started to work their way steadily towards the road. As they neared a prominent farmhouse in a heavy thunderstorm they were astonished to see, through the haze and smoke of battle, a party of Germans coming out of the building with their hands up, closely followed by a number of the Loyals who had turned the tables on their former captors. This somehow seemed to be the signal. Suddenly from all around and from the ruins of the farm buildings and houses in the vicinity white cloths started to appear. The Germans had had enough, they were surrendering.

Like a contagion it spread. Even the Germans, tough, battle-hardened and resolute troops—although, like the Allies with a good few fresh, raw reinforcements—could take no more. The continual pounding of mortar, artillery and the might of Allied air power, the cold and the wet, the stubborn resistance put up by the British and Americans and the heavy casualties they had sustained over the past days and weeks had at last proved decisive. The beachhead was saved, but they had been so nearly through.

All along the Loyals' line where the Germans had penetrated, white flags, white cloths, anything betokening surrender was waved. Initial astonishment at the amazing turn of events changed to widespread relief as the Loyals and North Staffords rushed forward to collect their prisoners before they had a chance to change their minds. Patrols from 'D' Company and the North Staffords crossed Wigan Street itself and started to mop up. 200 dazed and bemused prisoners were sent to the rear that day. Their morale was shattered, they were hungry, and exhausted and now that someone had laid down their arms, they did not have the strength or fortitude to pick them up again. They included a battalion commander, his adjutant and three company commanders, but none knew how many men they had, or where they were. They paid tribute to the resistance of those fighting against them and were then hustled to the rear before they discovered that they outnumbered their captors. They were too dazed to comprehend what had happened, for when the break had come, the collapse had been total.

During the day the mortar platoon had fired nearly 5,000 bombs, including what those who witnessed it called a classic smoke screen to mask the first North Staffords' counter-attack. Throughout the battle the intimate support of the gunners had slowed and finally stopped the enemy advance, but none of this would have been enough without the staunchness of the 1st Battalion the Loyal Regiment and their comrades of the 179th Infantry to the east. The Loyals suffered over 200 casualties that day, but had never withdrawn from a single trench. They were justly proud. By 1600 hours the position was completely restored, the only Germans south of Wigan Street were either dead, wounded or captured.

At 0630 hours, and preceded by the Ladder Barrage, Force 'H' had started their attack up the Bowling Alley. Immediately they started to push forward at great speed. Any German resistance had been destroyed by the colossal artillery support. Before them the Germans seemed to be thoroughly disorganised and in retreat. 29th Panzer Grenadier Division, which had been about to mount their own attack southwards down the line of the Spaccasassi creek, ran full into the Ladder Barrage and their efforts were stifled at birth. By three o'clock over 200 prisoners had been taken, the counter-attack had completely thrown the Germans off balance. In any event their activities were ill co-ordinated because the German signal system had been almost wrecked by the Allied artillery fire. For the most part the prisoners were from 715th Infantry and 114th Jaeger Divisions, but somewhere to the west of the Bowling Alley the two isolated battalions of 29th Panzer Grenadier Division ceased to exist. An escaped American prisoner of war described that the German dead in the rear areas were piled up on the side of the roads like cordwood, and that bulldozers were digging mass graves. But the advance by Force 'H' was on a narrow front and in danger of becoming dangerously extended. At 1620 hours General Harmon called a halt. By then the Germans were in disarray. It had been a total success and Clark's insistence on a counter-attack completely vindicated.

For six more days the Loyals remained in the line, until on 25 February they were at last relieved by the 1st Battalion the Buffs, a regiment from the British 18th Infantry Brigade who had come up to taste the pleasures of Anzio and were to relieve the remnants of the 24th Guards Brigade before many days were out. These were comparatively quiet days except for the steady drain of casualties from shelling, air attacks and the infernal Nebelwerfer—massed rockets which made an eerie noise and were called 'The Sobbing Sisters' or the 'Wurlitzer Organ'—an irritation at any time, but to tired troops just another twist to the hell of Anzio.

10

The War of the Wadis

18–24 February

While the Loyals, North Staffords and the 179th Infantry were having their epic struggle around the Flyover and on the Lateral Road, attention had been diverted from the plight of those Allied troops to the west of the Via Anziate. Here, in the area of La Cogna, the 8th and 9th Royal Fusiliers, supported by the London Scottish, were hanging on grimly and beating off all enemy efforts at infiltrating to the south. To their right the Ox and Bucks were still in their position barring the way to Pantoni and the Lateral Road. While forward and to the right of them, Lt.-Col. Laurence C. Brown and his 2nd/157th were holding fast in the Caves despite being desperately short of ammunition, water and rations.

North-west of Pantoni, the Ox and Bucks were periodically completely cut off. Rations and ammunition managed to get through on 18 February, but after that the Germans appeared to be in sole command of the ground behind them, until a tank bearing much needed batteries, water and, of all things, NAAFI supplies, ran the gauntlet three days later, dropped them and departed hastily. There were now Germans on all sides, but their attacks were fortunately indiscriminate. A 'half-hearted' (sic) platoon marched down the road towards them on 19 February but were stopped in their tracks by bren and rifle fire. The next day, when the little water that remained was rationed—it tasted of petrol—spasmodic attacks came in from time to time and from all sides. Later, the Gunner OP post behind them which had stood by since the beginning in a highly exposed and vulnerable position in a ruined house, was overrun by Germans using a flame-thrower. The resident gunner reported that the situation was 'boiling' before silence prevailed. Shelling and mortaring varied from intermittent to heavy, but it was causing casualties, and the Ox and Bucks could not spare a man. Their position was strong; as long as the German attacks were unco-ordinated they could deal with them satisfactorily, provided, that is, their ammunition lasted. They were isolated, but morale was high and they felt themselves still masters of the situation. Nevertheless, it was with huge relief that they heard on the evening of 20 February, that 'Green' (The London Irish) with

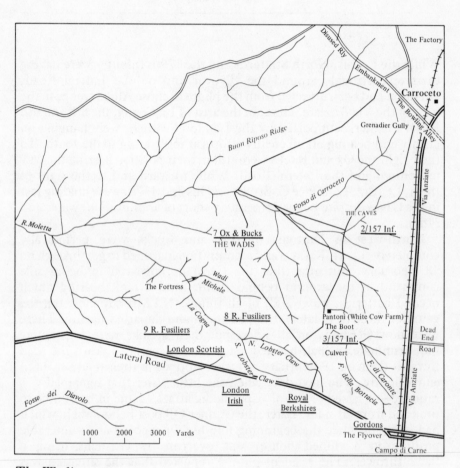

The Wadis

182

'heavy friends' were fighting their way forward to relieve them. But there was no relief that day and the heavy friends found the going quite unsuitable. At nightfall, when it was clear that the Irish were not going to get through that night at any rate, they wirelessed to brigade headquarters, 'St. John II, verses 7 and 8.' ('Jesus saith unto them, fill the waterpots with water. And they filled them up to the brim. And he saith unto them, bear out now, and bear unto the governor of the feast. And they bare it.') But as brigade headquarters had no Bible, it all fell rather flat.

'Green' were having considerable difficulties of their own. After the disastrous night of 16 February, when the two Fusilier battalions appeared to be in imminent danger of being destroyed, General Templer had ordered the remains of 168th Brigade to take up a position behind the Lateral Road to prevent any incursion to the Flyover from the left. The London Scottish filled the gap between 8th and 9th Royal Fusiliers, the London Irish occupied a more or less central position astride the Fosso del Diavolo, what was left of the Royal Berkshires were to the right. Behind them, only the various corps reserve lines stood between the Germans and the sea. All three battalions were desperately tired, and very weak. A few reinforcements had arrived; it had hardly been possible to incorporate them and most were new to battle. Since the end of January the London Irish had suffered an eighty per cent turnover of officers and men. They could muster three rifle companies, but half the men in these had arrived during the last few days.

Hardly had they reached their new position when on the morning of 17 February, they received orders that the Ox and Bucks must be relieved at all costs. But where were the Ox and Bucks? Opinions differed, but it appeared that they were bravely holding out with little more than an enlarged headquarters up the track towards the Buon Riposo Ridge. The more Colonel Good of the London Irish looked at the ground, the less inviting the prospect. Up to the Lateral Road itself there was some scrub and trees. On the road itself were a few houses rapidly being torn into ruins, but beyond lay what appeared to be flat ground, except that by now everyone knew that this was deceptive and the pencil-thin darker marks which were visible hid wadis of unbelievable depth and complexity, although not until anyone had first-hand experience of wadi country did they ever truly appreciate how impossible they were to negotiate.

There were two approaches to the supposed Ox and Bucks' position. Either astride the track itself—and from the clutter of derelict vehicles forward of the Lateral Road it was quite clear that this was in full view of the enemy on the ridge, nor was any close artillery support possible on this route due to the general vagueness about where the Ox and Bucks really were. Or, to try to take what cover the wadis afforded and surreptitiously work forward to the beleaguered battalion. Colonel Good decided that to attack in broad daylight across open ground would be madness; instead his companies must try to use the cover available and winkle their way up.

At noon the three companies of the Irish started across the Lateral Road. All went well. The wadi La Cogna and those known as the Lobster Claws were reached without trouble and only some desultory shelling told that Germans were about. But here they began to experience what moving in the wadis really meant. None of the tangled ditches seemed to run the right way, all were slippery and full of clinging brambles. It was hard work making any progress at all, least of all in the right direction. Cursing, the Irish worked their way across the Lobster Claws and up the far side of the wadi La Cogna and as they breasted the crest were greeted with a storm of shelling, mortaring and small arms fire by Germans who appeared to have the open ground beyond the wadi under observation and complete control. Casualties among officers and non-commissioned officers were very heavy. It was clear that to try to continue the advance in daylight would be suicide. With ill-grace the Irish waited for nightfall.

As darkness fell strong patrols were sent out, partly to find out the strength of the opposition, partly to pinpoint exactly the Ox and Bucks' position. Neither quest was very successful. A patrol penetrated well beyond where it was believed the Ox and Bucks were, but there was no sign of them. The next day, 18 February, the Irish made further efforts to fight their way forward. Once more they were thwarted by heavy and accurate German fire. By now the already under-strength battalion was dangerously weak, and almost beleaguered. By day they felt themselves masters of their particular wadi, but at night with their depleted strength, they were almost pawns of the Germans as patrols roamed on either side. Their position was less than 1,000 yards from the Lateral Road and their brigade headquarters, yet it took two hours' hard and hazardous walking to make the journey. Communications had been by telephone, but a line laid was then discovered to have nearly twenty breaks in it due to shelling and the attempt was given up; communications from then were by wireless.

The next two days saw a similar pattern. Spirited attempts to push forward met bitter resistance by the Germans who were strongly and cleverly sited. The drain of casualties by shelling was continual and the conditions in the wadi were almost unbearable under, ironically for Anzio, a blinding merciless sun. The companies could by now muster barely 100 men between them, so a reinforcement company of a mixture of regiments, hurriedly scraped together from any manpower available in the beachhead, was brought forward at night and immediately thrown into a night attack. At first the new company made some progress, and succeeded in driving the Germans from the end of a neighbouring wadi where they had been a nuisance for a long time, but with the officers nearly all casualties, the attempt was called off until daylight. The next day the Irish were reorganised into one strong rifle company. And this time a succession of platoon attacks with close tank support were successful in capturing the further side of the wadi and a prominent house. The way was now open for the Ox and Bucks to make their way back.

At last, on the evening of 20 February, the Ox and Bucks were given the order to withdraw. A Sherman tank arrived and all the wounded and wireless sets were piled on its back. Then, with a platoon in front, and another behind as protection, they pulled back. The Germans left them alone, perhaps thankful to see them leave, but almost immediately the tank, which was moving backwards, went off the track, depositing the wireless sets in a ditch and severely jolting the wounded. They managed to extricate it, and without further incident reached the Irish behind them. Of the battalion that had been committed to battle, three officers and seventy-eight other ranks returned, and that was all from 600 men of the 7th Battalion the Oxfordshire and Buckinghamshire Light Infantry.

On 21 February it was the turn of the Irish Guards to go to the wadis. Since 8 February, when their two companies had been sent to the help of other battalions, the Irish Guards had moved from position to position as catastrophe dictated. With reinforcements they could now muster two full rifle companies, Nos. 2 and 3. With these it was intended to relieve an American battalion, the 3rd Battalion of the 157th Infantry, in a place which was to become notorious in the annals of Anzio as the 'Boot'. This was a particularly unpleasant wadi which ran parallel with the main road some 600 yards west of the Via Anziate. Halfway up the leg on the left-hand side was a cluster of farm buildings called Pantoni—promptly christened White Cow Farm by the Guardsmen after a large white cow which had been hit by some shrapnel and was lying on its back with its legs in the air, quietly festering in the heat. At the middle of the 'Boot' a transverse wadi—the Wadi Caronte—ran across the front. Beyond the wadi lay open fields and a farm which was christened Carrier Farm; further on was another wadi which comprised the rear of the Caves where the 2nd Battalion of 157th Infantry were still holding out.

The intervening country, and in particular the Wadi Caronte which ran directly to the Via Anziate and the Flyover, was reported as being firmly in enemy hands. On the afternoon of 20 February Colonel Scott went forward to have a look, and as night fell the Irish Guards moved up the Lateral Road.

The War of the Wadis

There was no hope of finding the detailed layout of the American companies they were to relieve, indeed in the labyrinth of wadis it was impossible to know precisely where anything was, as the maps were either inaccurate, incomplete or both. Promptly on time, the Irish Guards met their guides and were led forward in single file in what seemed like a muddy obstacle race, down indistinguishable tracks, round or through shell holes. Coming to what appeared to be a dark and dismal cavern, the guide pointed down and grunted that this was where 'the Colonel' was. Battalion headquarters slithered down a muddy glissade until with a jolt they landed in shallow water at the bottom of what they later heard was called the 'Culvert'. Here indeed was the American command post and a less inviting place it was impossible to imagine. Nor was the situation as the Americans revealed any more reassuring. Their companies were evidently somewhere forward, one near the heel of the Boot, one at the upper end. They had been there for close on a week now and a more 'Goddam place' they never did see. It appeared that a sort of running fight was kept up during the night and that at dawn it was customary to discover that the enemy had established themselves behind them in the dark and had to be winkled out. Sometimes isolated parties would vanish without trace. To bring supplies up at all meant fighting them forward. The shelling was spasmodic, the Guards learned, but unpleasantly accurate, and any feature on the almost featureless banks was a registered target for the German mortars and guns. It was an uninviting situation: quite clearly the Americans were anxious to get out and away.

While Colonel Scott was being regaled with the gloomy details of the Boot, the rest of the Irish Guards struggled on with their faithful guides. No. 2 Company was pointed to a gully somewhere to the right. When they plunged down into it they were greeted by an American company commander who, having made them a present of anything they found in the morning, shouted, 'Come on, Lads,' and vanished in remarkably quick time into the night. The Guardsmen found themselves sole possessors of what appeared to be a muddy ditch some thirty yards wide. With the platoons spread on either side clinging like limpets to the slippery, precipitous sides of the wadi, they waited for dawn.

Meanwhile, No. 3 Company, commanded by Major Kennedy, had trudged on behind their guide. Through the derelict buildings of Pantoni they marched until some 300 yards further on they came to a wadi which crossed their front. Here the American forward companies were situated, plus what appeared to be a mingled mass of other regiments. Major Kennedy had just arranged that the Americans would leave them their three Browning machine guns, a most welcome gift, when two German aircraft flew over their heads, and jettisoned their entire load of anti-personnel bombs (commonly known as butterfly bombs). When the tally was made it was discovered that over seventy men had been killed or wounded. Apart from the Americans and those from other units which had somehow found themselves in that particular wadi, thirty Guardsmen were killed or wounded, a third óf No. 3 Company's strength. It was a bitter overture to an epic story of courage and self-sacrifice.

With the inevitable resulting noise and commotion, the Germans started to fire every gun that could bear on the wadi where the wounded men lay. To distract their attention two Guardsmen ran up the road towards them with a bren gun and kept up a running fight with the enemy while the wounded were taken away.

This was the pattern of activity for the next three days and four nights. As the Irish Guards' Regimental History described:

> It was a savage, brutish, troglodyte existence, in which there could be no sleep for anyone and no rest for any commander. The weather was almost the worst enemy, and the same torrential rain; rain which sent an icy flood swirling around our knees as we lurked in the gullies, would at times sweep away the earth that covered the poor torn bodies of casualties hastily buried in the Boot. Wallowing in a network of gullies, isolated by day and erratically supplied by night, soaked to the skin, stupefied by exhaustion and bombardment, surrounded by new and old corpses and yet persistently cheerful, the Guardsmen dug trenches and manned them till they were blown in and then dug new ones, beat off attacks, changed their positions, launched local attacks, stalked snipers, broke up patrols, evacuated the wounded, buried the dead and carried supplies.

The wadis had to be held. The position at the bottom of the Boot held by No. 3 Company and Battalion Headquarters of the Irish Guards was the last bastion between the Germans and the Flyover. The Scots Guards were a little to the east of the Irish Guards and the Gordons still on the Lateral Road west of the Flyover, but they were in the open with no cover except what they could create for themselves and more than one anxious glance was passed to the left and the Boot. If the Boot fell, the way down the Wadi Caronte and Wadi Bottaccia led straight to the Via Anziate, and it was clear that the Germans, although rebuffed by the strength of the defence of those around the Flyover, had still not given up hope of punching a wedge in the Allied defences and driving to the sea.

At the southern end of the Boot sat No. 2 Company Irish Guards who were subjected to continuous and gnawing enemy shelling as well as infiltration from any and every direction. But the sting was taken out of the German attacks because they could not oust No. 3 Company at the further end of the Boot. As long as they were there fighting the Germans could mount no large-scale attack on the rest of the Boot and the way to the Lateral Road and the Flyover was blocked.

There was still a high proportion of Southern Irishmen in the Irish Guards, volunteers, who caused consternation among the Germans, who could never understand why they were fighting for the Allies. From time to time prisoners, when they discovered who had captured them, would express the opinion that they had no business to be there at all. Commanding No. 3 Company with his own remarkable panache was the effervescent Kennedy. He and his dwindling piratical band conducted the type of private war in which Kennedy and they excelled. He seemed to collect stragglers like a magnet, and his style of leadership was magnetic. He held his men together with a form of private cohesion, and he always seemed to know precisely what was happening. His 'feel' for the battle was unrivalled. To command in this way under such conditions was only possible with superbly trained individualists under equally fine leadership. Kennedy, his men said, had probably personally killed more Germans than any other individual on the beachhead. No. 3 Company's role was to slaughter any small parties of the enemy and to disorganise any large formations; and they were resoundingly successful. They turned the wadis into a murderous maze.

The night of 21 February was one of frequent alarms and incursions by scattered groups of enemy. It was abundantly clear that large numbers of Germans were determined to become masters of the Boot and in as short a time as possible. Dawn at last came and mercifully the German activity died down. But no one was under any illusions that this was truly the lull before the storm; and the storm broke even before they had fully enjoyed their brief respite.

Across the wadis from No. 3 Company German tanks and SP guns started to take an increasing interest in the White Cow Farm area. From the confusion of shouts and detonations it became clear that strong forces were working their way up the Boot to split the company whose platoons were on either bank. Sure enough, from across the road and behind White Cow Farm, 'a solid wedge of German infantry rose from the western gully and, under cover of the 88-mm guns from Carrier Farm, thrust themselves across the track behind No. 3 Company. Kennedy reported cheerfully that he was "more or less surrounded." '

At precisely three o'clock, having been steadily collecting in the western wadi beyond Pantoni, they attacked in massed strength. 'We were lifted out of our slit trenches by a heavy barrage and all the west became alive,' described one survivor. The company fired like maniacs, 'the brens raced wildly; rifle bolts grew stiff and unworkable with the expansion due to the heat'. Despite enormous casualties the Germans pressed on. One platoon position was engulfed completely, and now only company headquarters and a motley collection of other men with Kennedy were left. The remaining platoon abandoned their position on the far side of the wadi and with a fervent prayer that the Germans would not try to come up from that direction in their absence joined their company commander. This had the effect of sealing one flank, but the position was precarious. Then the attack mysteriously slackened, and the odd groups of Germans who had started to try to creep forward using whatever cover they could find, which wasn't much, were dealt with easily.

Half an hour later and with no warning that anyone could remember, a full German company poured across the track towards them. Every weapon was being used at an intensity never visualised by their designers, but nothing seemed to stop them. Kennedy screeched for artillery, 'SOS, Right on top of us.' For hours the gunners had been expecting this fire task would be called for before any other. When Kennedy's desperate appeal at last came over the air, it was only a question of saying the one word 'Fire'. Even in the time it took to shoot the guns the Germans had closed to within 100 yards. The 2-in mortar, which had been firing as never before, only had twelve bombs left. A Guardsman, noticing that the PIAT was sitting idle waiting for tanks which hadn't appeared, picked it up, selected the largest German he could see in the hordes which were running towards them and fired. He afterwards said that he thought he bore a remarkable likeness to the company sergeant-major. But before he could congratulate himself the world to their immediate front erupted in a shattering concusion of stones and mud as the remarkable gunners brought down their shells fifty yards in front of No. 3 Company.

As the last shell exploded, and long before the smoke and dust had settled, the Guardsmen were out of their trenches and running forward to round up any survivors. Fourteen came from as far away as White Cow Farm, three more were picked up on the 'doorstep'. This shattering bombardment had the effect of checking the Germans coming from the west, but almost before Kennedy could realise that they had, if only temporarily, the upper hand, a shouted warning told that another attack was coming in from behind, for the Germans were advancing in extended line down the slope below Carrier Farm. And on that slope most of them died, caught by the concentrated fire of the platoons' massed bren guns and one of the American Brownings which had to be turned 180 degrees to cope with the new menace.

The Germans were not the only ones to suffer. No. 3 company was now reduced to twenty men. To bring the casualties out was the next problem until a Guardsman stepped forward and volunteered to take his jeep to see if he could get them back. With an old bandage tied to his windscreen he carefully drove towards the enemy and from time to time over the next two days he carried out a one-man shuttle service of wounded men, all the way to the Advanced Dressing Station a mile behind the Flyover as no ambulance could get forward. The Germans let him go on his way unmolested.

The last available reinforcements were sent up to the two companies: drivers, storemen, cooks, all the Irish Guardsmen on the beachhead. Those destined for No. 3 company arrived a little before dawn. Steady and very accurate shelling started to whittle away at the remains of the Irish Guards but otherwise the day was without the anxiety of the previous one, although the irrepressible Kennedy gave every appearance of actually enjoying himself. He decided to take a trip to find out how things were at battalion headquarters and on arrival was given orders to prepare for an attack by 2nd/6th Queens that night to clear the road up to Pantoni. Then, gathering what cigarettes he could for his company, he started to return and soon made the discovery that the Boot between his own position at the top and the rest of the battalion probably held more Germans than their own combined strength. This meant that the Germans were within an ace of sweeping through to the Lateral Road and from there into the rear areas of the beachhead.

Shortly afterwards Kennedy also made the unpleasant discovery that there were a lot of Germans in White Cow Farm, together with a small pig which ran screaming backwards and forwards whenever an aircraft passed overhead. It was the best of aircraft warning devices, but the only trouble was that the animal was unable to distinguish between friend and foe. Nevertheless, the pig early-warning system must have saved the Irish Guards a good few casualties. But with the Germans in occupation of the farm, as Kennedy put it, 'We were now surrounded more than we had previously been.' That in itself was all right because it was a state of affairs to which everyone at Anzio became accustomed sooner or later, especially in wadi country. Worse, though, was the fact that they were short of ammunition, particularly of grenades, and they had only three 2-in. mortar bombs left.

They had expected relief in the early part of the night, but the Queens were having considerable difficulty in getting up. Then, at around two o'clock, the Germans started to 'become noisy'. The first attack was on No. 2 Company at the bottom of the Boot; they were seen off without much trouble, but then it became clear that this was merely the *hors d'oeuvres* for the main attack on No. 3 Company who were effectively blocking the Pantoni Road. It was at this vital moment when the forward company of the Queens, who had edged to the west when they heard the attack on No. 2 Company to their front, appeared out of the dark and soon were engaged in hand-to-hand combat with the Germans in White Cow Farm. With the relief now complete and the unwholesome Pantoni area handed over to the Queens, Kennedy and his men pulled back to their battalion headquarters. When dawn came it was to reveal a scene of considerable activity, for a full company of Grenadiers had come up in the night to thicken the defences, and a machine gun platoon of the Middlesex Regiment were ready and looking forward to making things unpleasant for any Germans who showed above ground.

On the same day that the Irish Guards moved into the Boot, the 2nd/7th Battalion the Queen's Regiment were chosen to relieve the gallant 2nd/157th Infantry in the Caves. For eight days now the American battalion, in an epic stand unsurpassed in all the long agony of Anzio, had prevented the Germans from using the main axis to the south. Foxhole by foxhole, platoon by platoon, the battalion had been whittled away. At length the perimeter was confined to a narrow stretch of ground surrounding the Caves, and the Caves themselves. Ammunition was low, water almost expended and the battalion was now pitifully weak. Almost the only resource left was their spirit and under the inspired leadership of Colonel Brown, the 2nd/157th intended to fight on, if necessary, until there was no one left. But it was imperative that they be relieved.

The night of 21 February was pitch dark, and it was raining heavily as the 2nd/7th Queens went forward across the Lateral Road and on over the dead flat ground to the north. For once the German shelling seemed to have subsided and all was going well when the battalion reached the track crossing over the main wadi south of the American position. The intention was for two companies to secure the crossing and for the rest of the battalion to pass through and make for the Caves. Without undue trouble the crossing was duly reached, but at the very moment when the two follow-up companies were passing through a German aircraft dumped its entire load of butterfly bombs on the battalion. One company commander was killed, another wounded, and there were many other casualties. The Queens struggled on, and after meeting a number of Germans, some of whom were killed and some captured, they at length reached the Caves.

The battalion had been heavily cut up by the butterfly bomb attack. It had been hoped to get the anti-tank guns up the road, but this proved impossible. Thus the battalion was in the Caves, but in little better condition than those they were due to relieve. Lt.-Col. D. C. Baynes, commanding the Queens, asked Colonel Brown to leave him his machine guns and mortars, until his own could come up. This was readily agreed.

Around the Caves themselves the Queens were finding life unpleasant and hard, and highly confusing. Thankfully, after their long approach march, the companies fell into their slit-trenches with 'B', 'C' and 'D' Companies on the perimeter of the Cave area, and 'A' Company with battalion headquarters in the Cave complex itself. They were hardly installed when the company commander of 'C' Company found that there were some Germans in a ruined farm in the very middle of his position; all immediate attempts failed to oust them.

22 January dawned to reveal a thick mist covering the area. Somewhere on three sides of the Caves the Queens companies were occupying the former American foxholes, while their previous occupants were gathering in the Caves waiting for the opportunity to slip away. The situation was uncertain and appeared very precarious. There had been no news of 'D' Company, nearest the main road, since five o'clock that morning when they had reported themselves in position. It was assumed that they were merely out of contact, but as the day wore on and no news or runners came to report, it was feared that they had been overrun in the dark or ensuing mist just before dawn—in fact it was probable that the Germans, who were well aware that a relief was taking place, had been lying in wait for them. As darkness fell 'C' Company too reported a lot of enemy movement in the wadi immediately to their south, and it was clear that the Germans were trying to infiltrate from that direction as well.

This was ominous news for the gallant Americans who were ordered to pull out as it got dark. They intended making first to the west, hoping that way to be able to reach the Fosso di Carroceto and find their way back to the beachhead line. Shortly after six o'clock they set off in one long column. Bringing up the rear were the walking wounded, the more serious casualties were left in the Caves. Their route was almost through the middle of the German lines. Heavy fire from some houses along the way split the column; while the leading portion pushed on and most managed by crawling up the many ditches eventually to find sanctuary, the rest broke into small parties and tried to make their way through the Germans who were all around them. Some got back, but most were caught in the open by heavy German fire and were either killed or captured. Of the entire 2nd Battalion 157th Infantry only a quarter managed to make their way back from the Caves, and of those nearly half were immediately packed off to hospital. Theirs had been a gallant, vital stand, but they had paid dearly for their courage and steadfastness. The Presidential Citation which the battalion was subsequently awarded was richly deserved.

At the same time, from the opposite direction, Brigadier L. O. Lyne commanding the 169th Brigade had assembled all the available carriers and jeeps in the brigade in order to make a determined push to reach and resupply the now totally beleaguered 2nd Battalion 7th Queens. Despite heavy fire the column managed to reach Pantoni, but they could go no further as the leading vehicles were stopped by heavy machine gun fire sweeping across the flat ground. In spite of all efforts the attempt had failed, and now the commanding officer of the Queens knew that they were truly on their own.

Shortly after daybreak the Germans turned their attention to 'C' Company. Grimly the company commander reported that he was 'sitting tight, but soberly'. The forward platoons were now almost out of ammunition. They survived until noon, then, with no ammunition left, the remainder were overrun.

With 'C' Company out of the way the Germans then set about 'B' Company to the south of the rapidly diminishing battalion position, but before the company could be completely surrounded Colonel Baynes ordered the remainder to pull back and join him in the Caves. Now with no protecting screen the battalion, or what was left of it, were at the mercy of the Germans. They couldn't get out, but the Germans couldn't get in. All through the long day of 23 February the Germans tried. Troops crept around above the Caves and started to throw grenades inside. These troublesome people were dealt with, but they came back, and eventually it was necessary to pull back away from the Cave entrances. Then the Germans tried the direct approach, attacking down the slope opposite their 'front door', and on those slopes large numbers died. When the survivors went to ground some tanks appeared in their place on the crest and tried to fire shots into the Cave entrance itself. Fortunately, either they were very inaccurate, or they found difficulty in depressing their muzzles sufficiently and no shot penetrated inside. Discouraged by bazooka fire, they also moved off having achieved little.

The din inside the Caves was fearsome. The labyrinths stretched underground for several hundred yards, and in the deepest recesses huddled the wounded, almost deafened by the echo and re-echo as the ground outside was pounded. Here, too, were some Italian peasants, who had sheltered in the depths for days. Badly frightened, they added their wails to the general din. Also resident was a large and ill-tempered pig, who joined the general cacophony.

With the Germans above, around and now threatening to enter the Caves, there was only one thing for Colonel Baynes to do. With his gunner Forward Observation Officer sticking his head through a hole in the top of one of the caves and directing fire, a series of divisional artillery concentrations leading up to the full might of the corps artillery was brought down about their own heads. This was immediately successful. When the dust and smoke cleared the Germans seemed to have disappeared. After a few minutes Red Cross flags started to appear and the enemy came to collect their wounded. The Germans seemed to have learned their lesson, for the rest of the day the men in the Caves were largely left alone.

Ammunition was now dangerously low. There had been no rations and no water for close on thirty-six hours and little likelihood of resupply. Wireless batteries and signal cable were all but expended. In spite of this Colonel Baynes made plans to hold out as long as possible, but in the late afternoon orders came through from brigade to withdraw. During the afternoon some American stretcher bearers came through the German lines to collect the wounded in the Caves. What happened then has never been satisfactorily explained, but on the way back they were seen to be having a parley, and then stretcher bearers and casualties were escorted away under armed guard.

To the survivors of the 2nd/7th Queens, darkness on 23 February seemed to take a very long time coming. Everyone was very tense as the minutes ticked by. Colonel Baynes had reckoned that the only way to get away was to leave in groups of ten or so at intervals through the night and try to make their way back through the Germans, who were clearly in strength on all sides of his position. At six o'clock there were ominous reports that the enemy were trying to force an entry into the rear of the Caves but they were driven off after a short skirmish. Then, promptly at 1840 hours, a heavy artillery concentration came down and as soon as the fire had lifted, the first group crept out and away. At ten-minute intervals the rest followed.

The second group to leave was that comprising the commanding officer and the battalion headquarters party. At first they struck east, along a wadi and over a track, beyond which lay another deeper gully. As quietly as they could they crawled up to the far side and lay waiting. It was very still, there was little shelling and no indication that the first group had yet run into trouble. A German patrol approached their rear. Those in the lead heard a conversation as the battalion's Italian interpreter told the Germans that they were an Italian carrying party. This seemed to satisfy the enemy and after a few moments the Queens' party moved on, straight into a German company position. To go back would be to run into the patrol again and no excuse would pass this time; there was nothing to do but to press on.

To either side were the darker shadows of slit-trenches, occupied by men with ominous-shaped steel helmets, but no one questioned the small party. The occasional muttered 'Offizier' seemed to satisfy the curious. They were almost through the enemy lines when suddenly shots rang out behind them as the last members of the party were challenged. The leading members broke into a run. In front of them was another wadi into which they fell, landing in a heap at the bottom, all except the commanding officer who landed in the centre of an enormous clump of briars. As he struggled to get out there were signs of German activity above, so he told his Intelligence officer, Lieutenant J. W. Sewell, to take the others and try to get away. Meanwhile, the last three men in the group, who had included the medical officer, by pretending not to understand and generally giving the impression of willing stupidity, distracted the Germans' attention and gave time for the others to get away. So Lieutenant Sewell, with his small party, now reduced to eight men in all, continued to work towards the south.

Moving slowly and carefully and avoiding two German patrols on the way they at last hit the Lateral Road and so found their way to safety. They were back by 1030 hours that night. The signals officer returned at three the next morning. The commanding officer, after lying low and then extricating himself from his bramble bush, returned early the following morning, and the battalion's accompanying battery commander, and one gunner the following night. A total of four officers and seventeen men, and that was all of the entire 2nd Battalion of the 7th Queens.

Throughout the daylight hours of 24 February the enemy intermittently shelled the area of the Boot. Around mid-day the Irish Guards learnt that in the evening the Dukes were coming up to relieve them. Before nightfall the Grenadier Company slipped away, back to their battalion. And then at last blessed night fell, and so did the rain to add a final twist to the Anzio story for the Irish Guards. The Regimental History records: 'At dusk a slow file of men plodded up the track. They were introduced as the Dukes, but the first six men denied it and gave the names of six different regiments, till a sergeant said, "You're Dukes now", and then, apologetically, "They're new, Sir, we only got them this morning." '

Colonel Webb-Carter of the Dukes continued the story:

In the evening the battalion set out. With a rather defiant gaiety, the troops climbed into the troop-carrying lorries . . . Going past Brigade H.Q. I saw the Brigadier, standing by the road. He wished me luck. I felt that we needed it. Dusk was drawing in as we drove up the familiar Rome road. Soon in the gathering gloom, we turned up a track into the woods and bumped along in the mud and pot holes which were the twin components of the improvised road forming the channel of communications.

It was pitch dark and the Germans then began to shell heavily the Campo di Carne road. We had to cross this to get to the wadis and the ever-haunting fear, on relief nights, loomed large. Would the troops be caught in the open? It was difficult to judge amongst the trees the exact position of the shelling, and I sent a message through to the leading companies to halt.

Pushing up the track to the fringe of the wood it was possible to see that the fire was coming down further to our left, just on the line of the road. It was a terrifying sight and it made a lot of noise. The Boche knew that a relief was being carried out somewhere in our sector that night and his artillery was diabolically active. At any moment it might shift to our area. There was no option but to press on.

We turned off the main road and plugged up the track. It was dotted with shell-holes. At regular intervals along its first 200 yards were the derelict carriers of the Irish Guards, all knocked out while trying to bring up rations the night before. It seemed an age, but at last we reached a small bridge over a little gully, which formed a culvert. This was our R.V.

The leading companies were already filing off to the right across country to take over positions there. I climbed down the bank into the little gully, and edged past a wrecked jeep trailer, into the culvert. Here was the R.A.P. and also Andrew's [Scott] H.Q. That imperturbable officer, wrapped in a duffle-coat, presented his usual robust and faintly Regency appearance. The little culvert was crammed. The M.O. was dealing with a couple of recently wounded Guardsmen, and the R.A.P. occupied half the space; the rest contained the elements of the headquarters of both battalions, Dukes signallers taking over from the Guards and my own officers trying to contact their opposite numbers. Andrew and I sat on a stretcher propped up on empty ration boxes and discussed the situation. The position was fluid in the extreme and the whole area was cut up by long deep wadis, heavily overgrown, which changed hands nightly. A sort of grotesque hide-and-seek had been played for days in these wadis. The Irishmen would debouch from one particular wadi and assault an enemy held one, and on their return would sometimes find the Boche in occupation of their own positions. The Guardsmen were on top all right, but deadly tired.

Meanwhile at the Boot the first two companies of the Dukes were taking over. As they were out in the open, hurriedly changing over, a concentration of shells and mortar bombs crashed into the Boot. The Dukes suffered worst, they had more men, but the Irish Guards suffered too. The handover was hurried on, and, leaving the distracted Dukes to push their men into position in the blackness and their own stretcher bearers to help where they could, the Irish Guards moved out. Colonel Webb-Carter continued: 'As the tall Guardsmen filed out, leaving us the heritage of death and desolation they had borne so long, a peculiar sense of isolation struck us. In all the long-drawn-out crucifixion of the beachhead, no positions saw such sublime self-sacrifice and such hideous slaughter as was perpetrated in the overgrown foliage that sprouted in the deep gullies.'

For another ten days 24th Guards Brigade remained in the beachhead. But by now all Guards reinforcements in the Mediterranean theatre had been expended and it was decided to withdraw the brigade; the 5th Grenadiers to be absorbed into the other battalions of the regiment in Italy; the 1st Battalion Irish Guards, never to fight again as a battalion but to be gradually absorbed into their 2nd (Armoured) and 3rd Battalions, which were to distinguish themselves in North-West Europe before very long; and the 1st Scots Guards to be joined by men from their 2nd Battalion, and as a reformed 1st Battalion Scots Guards to fight with great gallantry throughout the rest of the long Italian campaign. In all the three battalions of 24th Guards Brigade had suffered the incredible total of eighty-nine officer, and over 1,900 Other Rank casualties in their seven weeks at Anzio.

It was to be on the Scots Guards that the evil genie of Anzio played his last trick. For on 27 February, while the battalion was resting in the shelter of the Padiglione Woods, a shell burst in some trees above the officers' tents. The second-in-command of the battalion, a company commander and two other officers were killed instantly; the commanding officer died later that day of the wounds he received.

Colonel David Wedderburn had taken command of the Scots Guards only a few days before they sailed for Anzio; thus he was forced to impress his personality on his battalion while in actual contact with the enemy—no small achievement. But it was as a tactical commanding officer that he had been outstanding. His manipulation of the guns in support of his battalion was a virtuoso performance, and saved very many casualties. He seemed to know by some uncanny instinct just where and when the Germans would try next, and many an attack was killed at birth. The aggressive defence which he conducted from Carroceto Station undoubtedly kept the Germans at arm's length for many vital hours. His loss saddened even the blessed moment of at last leaving the horrors of Anzio; it was felt by many people outside the confines of his regiment. It was bitter that the architect of so much of the Scots Guards' success over the previous weeks should be killed in this way and at this time. On 7 March, the first elements of 24th Guards Brigade sailed from Anzio. It was a beautiful morning.

11

The Final Attack

28 February–3 March

The Allied Intelligence Summary for 27 February warned,

> The enemy has now had eight days since the attack down the Albano-Anzio axis in which to regroup and reorganise his badly disorganised forces . . . It is believed that he is now capable of continuing the attacks on the beachhead; and that, when the weather affords him artillery observation and is suitable for the employment of armor, he will resume his offensive action.

He did, on 29 February, but before von Mackensen's forces made their final attempt to eliminate the forces in the beachhead a number of other attacks were mounted against the long-suffering troops in the wadi country. Although staff officers sitting comfortably in their caves in Nettuno, or in warm and sometimes dry ruins nearer the front, could confidently refer to them as diversionary, they were far from diversionary to those who met them, and made yet another gruesome chapter in the War of the Wadis, and the 'Bloody Boot' in particular.

One attack was aimed at the Wadi La Cogna and the Lobster Claws where the remains of the Fusilier battalions and the Ox and Bucks had manfully hung on with steadily depleting numbers. They were sustained there by the remnants of the partially reformed battalions of the London Scottish, the London Irish and the Royal Berkshires, and it was to the last two battalions that disaster fell. The pattern was painfully familiar: the takeover at night of ground no one had ever seen before, the steady shelling and mortaring combined with aggressive German action down the maze of communicating wadis, the gradual isolation of far-flung platoon and company positions, with bad or non-existent communications; the steady gnawing away of already depleted strengths in conditions when the wadis became torrents and slit-trenches so filled with water that they had to be abandoned; the valiant efforts of everyone to keep those up front supplied with food, ammunition, water and what few comforts possible; the heroic fight against heavy odds; the final moment, when relief was impossible and the wireless operator sent his last message; the awful silence as it was clear that no one, save perhaps a few dazed survivors, would ever return.

They hung on, but it was a question of bare survival. Every morning at six o'clock just as the brigade commander of the 167th Brigade was settling down to some overdue sleep after checking the reports of the previous night, from his widely dispersed possessions, General Templer would ring up. 'Hello Jimmy [Brigadier Scott-Elliott], is that you?' The Brigadier would sleepily reply that it was. 'Oh, you're still there then?' the commander of the 56th Division would continue. By that time, the brigade headquarters of 167th and 168th Brigade were sharing the same headquarters. Their battalions were down to at best two weak companies each, and many of these men were quite new. 'Off the boat and into battle,' was the cry. The division was by then at no higher than twenty-five per cent combat efficiency and were literally wasting away day by day. But their morale remained unaffected, the cockney humour of the Fusilier battalions quite unimpaired from the ordeal. Visiting his men in hospital at Anzio one day, the commanding officer of the 9th Fusiliers saw a man from his own headquarters. 'Hello Roberts,' he said, 'how are you?' 'Oh, all right, Sir' came the reply. 'Achieved me life's ambition. Got blue blood in me at last. The bullet went through the adjutant first!' The 56th Infantry Division were known by the Germans as 'Hell's Kittens', they had earned the title through dogged determination and gallantry.

The horror, and the bravery, and a further episode in the saga of Pantoni and the Boot, was encapsulated in the experiences of the 2nd Battalion the Sherwood Foresters.

After taking over Pantoni from No. 3 Company of the Irish Guards, the 2nd Battalion 6th Queens settled down to wadi life. To their rear, in the area of the Culvert, the Dukes were firmly in residence and making existence extremely unpleasant for any Germans around, particularly those in the Wadi Caronte to the north. To the Queens' right, particularly in the extension of the Boot, and often behind them as well, there were a great many Germans. Although stronger than the Irish Guards company, nevertheless the Queens had an exciting and perilous time.

Now reduced to three rifle companies the 2nd/6th Queens had one company in Pantoni itself, by then little more than a ruined shell of some houses and a few out-buildings; another in the wadi to the immediate east where Major Kennedy had made his last stand, and the third further down the Boot, but within reach of the most forward company of the Dukes. For once the neighbouring battalions were close enough to create a coherent line, and even the Germans found it difficult to infiltrate towards the rear.

The story with the forward companies was different. Theirs was a world of continuous alarms, of little sleep and a lot of worry, and it was a very weary 2nd/6th Queens who heard with delight that the 2nd Foresters were to relieve them during the night of 27/28 February.

There had been some dispute among the Foresters, none of whom had been able to go forward to see their new positions, as to where precisely the Queens actually were—a not infrequent occurrence in wadi reliefs. And when the time came for the change-over it was a pitch black night and the rain, which had poured down unceasingly for four days and nights, showed no sign of abating. Floundering in the heavy mud, the Foresters, still under strength despite receiving considerable reinforcements, made their way forward with their guides from the Queens towards Pantoni and the Boot. They had heard unpleasant tales of ration parties failing to get through, of fixed-line machine gun fire crossing the track they had to travel, of Pantoni itself being the most popular registered German target in the district, but at first things seemed to be going all right.

Battalion headquarters of the Foresters took over from that of the Queens on the edge of some trees south of the Lateral Road, and there they waited for what seemed hours. At last, at six o'clock in the morning, the Foresters' anti-tank platoon commander returned with a harrowing tale.

All had gone well on the move up, apart from the normal problems of keeping to the track and fairly heavy shell-fire on the last stages of the journey. The take-over had gone smoothly enough. The two companies in the Boot had moved in; it had been almost like clockwork, and the Queens, after bidding them good-night and good luck had moved silently off in the dark. In Pantoni itself, which was the key to the whole area, 'C' Company of the Foresters too had arrived safely. The Queens had shown them where their own platoons were, the anti-tank and machine gun sections were settling down when suddenly everything seemed to happen at once.

No sooner had the last Queens' man vanished into the night, than from the west a mass of Germans using a flame-thrower mounted on a half-track vehicle attacked Pantoni. The anti-tank platoon commander, Captain T. G. Gould, who had gone forward to see his guns sited, heard German voices coming from where one of the Foresters' platoons should have been. From then matters became confused. Using the flame-thrower to rout out any Foresters in the houses or in their slit-trenches, the Germans set about methodically eliminating 'C' Company. Those who were not killed or wounded were captured; the company commander was last seen standing on the parapet of his trench with a tommy gun, defending his headquarters. Half-a-dozen rather bemused survivors, including the company sergeant major found their way back to their battalion headquarters, and that was all from the entire company.

The loss of Pantoni was a very grave matter indeed, and threatened the safety of the whole Boot position, so next day the reserve company was ordered to re-take it. They were to attack from the Boot itself and in the late afternoon set off in torrential rain. The way was deep, and the German shelling across the open country which they had to cross distressingly accurate, but they reached the Boot and started to make their way forward. In view of their difficulties it was decided to postpone the attack until early the following morning. Shortly before 0200 hours they moved out of the Boot again and to their Start Line on the forward edge of the wadi. Whether the Germans had suspected this all along never became clear, but on the Start Line they were soundly and comprehensively shelled, and forced to scatter.

There were very few men left by now, far too few to take on Pantoni which had been steadily reinforced by the Germans during the previous day, so the attack was called off and the remnants pulled back into the Boot itself, to join the rest of the battalion who had consolidated as their casualties had mounted. When dawn broke on 28 February Captain P. A. Hewitt, the sole surviving company commander, discovered that he had exactly 100 men left from the rifle companies of the 2nd Foresters.

It was a grim situation made worse by the rain which came down without cease. Soon there was a raging torrent running down the Boot. Miraculously, the nightly ration train arrived, running the gauntlet of shells and ambush parties, bringing with them ammunition, food, weapons, dry socks and rum.

After seven days and nights in the Boot, Captain Hewitt and his party were at last relieved. They were almost past noticing what went on around them, a number had to be bodily lifted from their slit-trenches and it took days for some to walk normally, so used were they to crouching in their slits. Those in the towns of Anzio and Nettuno referred to the hunched shoulders and wary look which they found themselves adopting in the 'Rear' areas, as the 'Anzio shuffle'. They would have called it something different if they had ventured to see the shuffle of the very gallant men who had been sitting in flooded wadis for days and interminable nights keeping the Germans at bay.

It took the survivors four hours to make the walk back to the Lateral Road, the weaker being carried by their comrades. Of Captain Hewitt's 100, forty returned.

By then 18th Infantry Brigade, consisting of the 1st Buffs, the 14th Sherwood Foresters and the 9th Battalion the King's Own Yorkshire Light Infantry (The Yorkshire Dragoons), had relieved 24th Guards Brigade in 1st British Infantry Division. Also the 9th Commando and 40th Royal Marine Commando, with a total strength of 600 men, had been brought up to Anzio with the specific task of carrying out

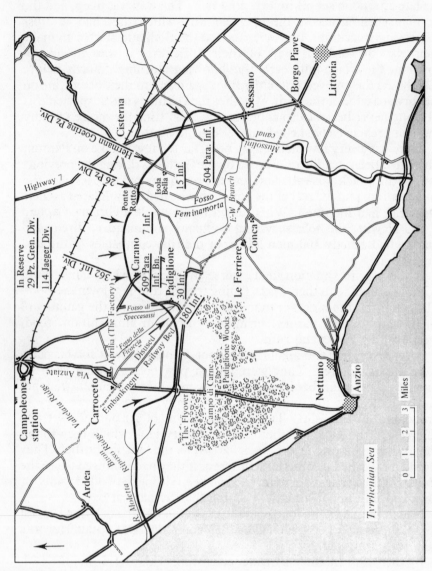

The final German attack

small-scale incursions into the German lines in the wadi country. They had demonstrated that the enemy were not the only experts at infiltration.

But before this the Germans had made their last major effort to eliminate the Abscess; it was designed to fall this time on a four-mile front between Isola Bella on the east and the Fosso di Carano on the west.

The plan was for the *Hermann Goering* Panzer Division, supported by a battalion of Tiger tanks, to strike south from Isola Bella towards Le Ferriere. In the centre 26th Panzer Division, with a battalion of Panther tanks, had the task of securing and strengthening the bridge south-west of Ponte Rotto over the Fosso di Feminamorta so that it could carry the 50-ton monsters. On the German right, 362nd Infantry Division were to undertake the main attack. Lurking behind and ready to exploit any gain were 29th Panzer Grenadier and 144th Jaeger Divisions.

A complex deception plan was devised to show that 1st Parachute Corps in the wadi country were preparing to make a major offensive. Dummy tanks were to be sited around Ardea. There was to be increased patrol activity during 27 and 28 February along the whole corps front, and roving guns were to spread havoc and dismay south of the Buon Riposo Ridge. Behind the ridge convoys of vehicles from 3rd Panzer Grenadier Division were to simulate the movement of reinforcements by blinking their lights when driving, but 'not in a clumsy way', the German orders specify, while a more solid attack was to be made to take two small hills west of the junction of the Dead End Road and the Via Anziate. On the extreme east of the beachhead, strong forays were to be made all along the Mussolini Canal and a lot of artillery movement simulated to give the impression that a strong attack was mounting in that quarter as well.

In the event, the deception plan was a failure. The 3rd Infantry Division was well forewarned. Wireless intercepts had told 6th Corps precisely where the next German blow would fall. For days past enemy gun positions had been plotted, their tank concentrations located, supply dumps and approach routes identified. The division were in a strong position to sustain anything the Germans threw at them. They had three defence lines, and as events were quiet elsewhere on the front, 6th Corps had ample reserves to deal with any emergency. Further, there was now a feeling of quiet confidence in the Allied camp. The great attack on the Via Anziate had been the main German blow; and it had been defeated. The co-ordination of artillery fire across the whole Beachhead Defence Line was now at a peak of efficiency, and a number of reinforcements had arrived, fresh troops who had not experienced the grinding privation of life on the beachhead. And it was a confidence which spread from the top for, on 23 February, Truscott had relieved

The Final Attack

Lucas. The move, which had been smouldering for some time, was eventually made by Mark Clark, who was a long-standing personal friend of the corps commander. In Clark's words, 'Johnny Lucas was ill—tired physically and mentally from the long responsibility of command in battle, but I was determined to do nothing to hurt him.' Lucas was made deputy army commander to Clark, and then given command of an army in the United States. He died in 1949.

People felt that now the worst was over, that their affairs were in firm hands and that the Germans had little offensive life left in them. The many prisoners recently captured had told of appalling casualties in their ranks. An increasing number of German reinforcements were of a lower quality; many were little more than youths. They were being flung into this, the grimmest of battles, with no previous experience of war. It appeared that the mighty German war machine was grinding to a halt. Thus it was with determination and confidence that the 3rd U.S. Infantry Division waited for the coming battle.

The attack had been planned for 25 February, but the preoccupation of some units of 26th Panzer Division in the Battle of the Caves, and the impossibility of bringing all the attacking troops into their assault positions in time, meant that the attack must be postponed. Exploratory efforts from the line of the Fioccia and Spaccasassi creeks and towards Carano, supported by the heaviest weight of artillery fire the Germans had yet mustered, had failed to dislodge the men of the 180th Infantry Regiment. It was clear that the Allies would take a good deal of shifting before any appreciable hole could be made in their defence line.

The new time chosen for the grand attack was 0400 hours on 28 February, but once again the fates intervened, this time in the shape of heavy rain which forced another postponement. Later on 28 February the skies began to clear and the wind rose. But would this be enough to dry the ground for tanks to operate? Kesselring was doubtful, but having visited the forward units he found them so full of confidence that he ordered the attack for the following morning.

All day 28 February the German rear areas had been shrouded in smoke, as their build-up progressed. Low cloud cover prevented any appreciable Allied air effort, so the precise details of what was occurring were concealed. In a pre-emptive strike designed to disrupt the German preparations, at one hour before dawn on 29 February, the entire might of the corps artillery brought down a shattering bombardment of the German forward and rear areas. In all on that day the Allied artillery fired over 66,000 rounds—to the German 1,500 tons—more than had been used on the fateful days of 18 and 19 February. The Allied shelling, though, was not enough to halt the German attacks. All across the 3rd Division front reports started coming in of enemy attacks being pressed forward vigorously.

The approach of 362nd Infantry Division opposite Carano had been badly delayed by heavy mud which slowed and almost prevented their accompanying tanks from getting into position. To add to their problems the divisional communications were out of action for some hours due to the Allied shell-fire. Thus the raw, fresh troops of the division were thrown piecemeal into battle. The congestion in the rear areas was indescribable as weather and Allied gun-fire made movement off the roads wholly impossible. Traffic jams, particularly in the area of Ponte Rotto, reached mammoth proportions.

Despite these handicaps the Germans pushed forward with great gallantry against a skilful and stout American opposition. All along the four-mile front they made slight inroads, but the only breakthrough of consequence, and which penetrated the first defence line, was on that sector occupied by the 509th Parachute Infantry Battalion in the area of Carano where a full regiment of three battalions and other supporting units were thrown into battle. Suffering staggering casualties; the Germans swarmed into one company position, singing and shouting. A fierce hand-to-hand battle ensued and then they swept on towards the company in reserve. And here they foundered. Pounded by artillery and mortar fire and torn to tatters by the unrelenting small-arms fire of the Parachute Infantry, the surviving Germans were forced to find shelter in what ditches they could find. Later that afternoon a counter-attack was mounted to regain the lost ground. During the afternoon of 29 February the weather cleared enough to allow some of the massed might of Allied air power to come to the aid of the defenders.

Near Ponte Rotto 26th Panzer Division failed in their task as their bridging vehicles were unable to get through the press of traffic which stretched almost to Cisterna. Elsewhere across the front the pattern was of isolated infantry attacks unsupported by armour, which could not come up in time to help, being blunted by spirited American resistance. The mine-fields, which were spread in cheerful profusion on all and every likely approach, proved an added bugbear as some of the mines had sunk so deep in the mud that they could not be located by the mine detectors, but were not so deep that they did not explode when tanks passed over them. Although the weather was unpleasant for the Allies, it virtually brought the German attack to a halt. 150 prisoners were captured and fourteen tanks destroyed on that first day.

During the night there was more heavy rain. 362nd Division reported more than fifty men actually drowned in the flooded gullies and ditches on their front. Mechanical transport was useless under such conditions, even horse-drawn carts became bogged axle-deep in the mud. The pattern of attacks on 1 March was repeated. In places the Germans managed to dent, but nowhere penetrate the first defence line, and it was clear that their efforts were weaker now. And the prisoners were coming in. Over 300 were counted that day, and some sizable formations had surrendered *en bloc* as soon as their officers were killed. It was heartening information. The enemy was slowing down and breaking up.

It dawned bright and clear on 2 March. Now the full array of bombers and fighter-bombers could be brought in to help the 3rd Division: 241 Liberators, 100 Flying Fortresses and several hundred other aircraft—even more than had helped to break the great attack on the Via Anziate—pounded the German forward positions and the rear areas around Cisterna, Velletri and Campoleone with fragmentation bombs. Other aircraft strafed and attacked the German tanks and gun positions nearer the front line. It all helped discourage the Germans from further efforts; in fact their attack was fading fast. The attacks on 2 March were only limited attempts, desultory and unco-ordinated affairs beaten off with some ease, and principally in the Ponte Rotto area where German armour continued trying to fight forward and were destroyed in satisfactory numbers. In all, between 29 February and 4 March, the German forces had suffered over 3,500 battle casualties. The 3rd Division had lost heavily too, the almost continuous fighting over the past six weeks had taken a heavy toll of men and machines.

On 1 March von Mackensen had reported that he was unable to break the Allies with the troops he then had. At 1840 hours that day, Kesselring accepted the truth of his army commander's report and ordered all large-scale offensive action to cease. The Allies had won, the beachhead was safe. The Abscess must stay, until it was joined with the festering sore which the Germans were soon to see creeping up the leg of Italy.

A few weeks later, in an almost unprecedented step, Hitler ordered that a dozen front line officers, who ranged from the commander of 29th Panzer Grenadier Division down to company commander level, should report to him personally. How convinced he was from their arguments and explanations must remain a matter for conjecture, but the truth was that four-and-a-half years of war had bled the German army white. They no longer had the moral fibre, nor the material resources for offensive action.

12

'Call de Roll, Kesselring'

Now ensued for the troops at Anzio what was euphemistically referred to later as the 'Stalemate'. Each side paused for breath. The Germans acknowledged that the Allies were too strong to be driven into the sea; for their part 6th Corps were not strong enough to capture the Alban Hills. It was now conceded that the drive to Rome had become stuck in the mud of Anzio. Not until the 5th and 8th Armies down the leg of Italy could prise the Germans out of the Gustav Line would the men in the beachhead be asked to renew their attempt to cut the German communications. Then, or when the mud dried.

Meanwhile began for the British and American forward troops at Anzio the sort of war which their fathers had fought in France and Flanders nearly thirty years before: trench warfare at its most unpleasant, when success was an enemy dugout taken or some hapless patrol destroyed, when survival was the paramount need, and it required a supreme effort of will to keep going. Along the thirty-two mile front took place a war 6f patrol and counter-patrol, of mine laying and mine lifting. Dominating no-man's-land it was called. In the wadi country no-man's-land was so narrow that sometimes it was possible to hear what their enemies said and it was suicide to raise a head by day. This was a personal war which private, sergeant and junior officer fought without specific orders, for none were possible, where their world was the range of a grenade, the field of fire for bren gun, tommy gun or rifle the width of a couple of rooms, and their horizon the top of the next scrub-covered ditch.

'Normal patrolling' was how the wireless described the nightly hazards of Anzio. But if there was one thing that was not normal on the beachhead it was patrolling in the wadi country. In places the wadis were fifty, sometimes 100 yards across the top, but narrowed down to little more than the width of a thin trickling stream at the bottom, which overnight could become a torrent, driving the unhappy troops of both sides up the wadi banks. On these slippery, thorn, bramble and scrub-covered slopes dugouts were constructed—their crumbling sides reinforced by soggy blankets—which afforded minimal fields of fire. These were the troops' homes for days on end until blessed relief took place and other unfortunates found it was their turn. The little platoon positions looked impressive on the map, and by dominating the many wadi junctions the occupants might assume that by doing so they dominated the country; it was a misleading impression which could prove fatal.

For the Germans were adept at going across country. In small parties at first, perhaps laying telephone line as they went and taking with them a couple of Spandaus, they would establish themselves behind the strong-points and would call up the rest of their number. The first inkling to the defenders that anything was amiss would be when messengers 'going down the drain' failed to get through and vanished without trace. A reconnaissance party would discover the Germans in residence and then it would take a full-scale attack by tired troops to dislodge the nuisance.

Thus, on the western sector of the beachhead the next months were a tale of bitter fighting in the tangled wadis; of small unknown and unseen acts of heroism—by both sides—and occasionally of chivalry; of parties going forward being split by action, and then lost altogether; of men straying and disappearing for ever into the night. With the familiarity of a strong dislike the wadis sprouted names—the 'South Lobster Claw', the 'Redoubt', the 'Fortress', the 'Starfish', the 'Boot' and many others. Their titles were often chosen for the resemblance to these shapes on the map and each, in its own inimitable way, was a small portion of Hell on earth.

The wadis were approached from the Lateral Road which was under observation and almost continuous fire by the Germans, and no safe movement on it was possible by day. A number of tunnels had been burrowed under the roadway to lessen the danger of crossing it, but there was still a stretch of open country beyond which must be negotiated. Those who were rash enough to try to do so by day spoke of the awful feeling as they were chased across this bit of country by shells and the wonderful sense of relief as at last they were able to plunge into the muffled sanctuary of the wadis. By day it was an eerie experience to walk up the well-trodden routes, past a rifle, its butt sunk in the ground, a steel helmet which had once belonged to a German paratrooper and now hung in a bush, a particularly gaping shell-hole, a tree snapped off at head height as though by a freak storm. The unhappy occupants of the wadis came to know these markers well. As the weeks followed each other in painful succession the mindless, endless trudge along the sinuous wadi bottoms became as ingrained on the memory as the glutinous, boot-hugging mud. But there was a feeling of security in the bottom of the wadis. And there they endured days of peace and nights of the utmost ferocity.

For the nights were worst. The form up in the dark amid a blur of dimly seen shapes. The search for the shadowy figure of the guide in the gloom and the grunted recognition. Crossing the open ground and the fear of being silhouetted by an enemy flare. The plunge down into the slippery, foetid blackness of the wadi where all sounds were deadened. The long single-file walk up the gully bottom, pacing out the distance in case the guide should lose his way or be killed, the one as likely as the other. The arrival at the further end greeted by the resident platoon commander anxious only about how soon he could hand over and slip away. The interchange on enemy positions, such as they were known, DF tanks and fields of fire. The entry of the platoon sergeant to report that all was ready. The mutual wishes of good luck, and then the departure of the old guard leaving the new platoon commander in charge of his own little empire, blessing his stars that this relief had gone without disturbance. They were not always so; sometimes a relief might take two nights to complete, so close were the Germans. On one occasion as the second night was nearing its end, a voice in the purest English spoke up from the German trenches not a cricket-pitch away, 'For God's sake hurry up with your relief, you've kept me awake for two nights!' They hurried, but not to please the German.

The long nights at Anzio are vividly remembered by the veterans. The eerie feeling of men moving about in the dark, the uneasy sensation that their enemy were around not very far away and could see them, even if they were invisible themselves. The horrible knowledge that all depended on which side was most alert. The long hours with nerves at concert pitch. It became too much for some. The night noises became painfully familiar: the distant rumble of shelling towards the Alban Hills, the pop-pop of the mortars or the hissing rush of air as shrapnel passed close by. Almost as agonising in their effect were the dud shells which landed with a plop. There was an awful sense of thankful anti-climax when they did not go off—and vast numbers of dud shells were fired by the Germans (it was believed they had been sabotaged at the factories by the forced labour in Germany).

The British battalions were now forced to rely on reinforcements of raw, untrained soldiers, in many cases straight from England. It was a rarity to find any who had been in action before. Some came up in the night, were killed within hours or never seen again. Officers were particularly scarce. Some cavalry officers attached to infantry battalions found themselves now flung into a purely infantryman's war. A number of magnificent volunteer South African officers were attached as occasion offered and were in great demand. Commanding officers even now speak highly of their calibre. The essence of leadership then was to absorb the motley collection of men, not only of all regiments, but of all arms as well—on one memorable occasion a draft of thirty men included representatives of no less than twenty-eight different regiments. On the whole the reinforcement units, when they could, sent Scots to Scottish regiments, north countrymen to northern regiments, but in the crisis days of the beachhead any man who could handle a rifle was sent where the need appeared most pressing. In the early days it had been possible to distribute the new arrivals between the rifle companies, so that at least a leaven of experienced men existed, now there was no one to distribute them to. They were formed as platoons and called companies.

Behind the Lateral Road and down what was called Artillery Lane—a track which became more perilous as the pot-holes became deeper, despite the efforts of the sappers to keep them filled—in the trees and scrub of the Padiglione Woods and the Selva di Nettuno were the echelons, and the gun lines of the 'remarkable' (it was an expression of respect, admiration and thanks used on countless occasions) Artillery. Every brigade commander swore that his own gunners were unique.

'I can assure you', [wrote one later when the beachhead was no more,] 'that no brigade has ever been so magnificently "looked after" (and I use that term in its full sense of intimate help and co-operation) as this brigade has been by your grand Field Regiment. Throughout the Brigade, the feeling of confidence and trust in your Regiment is quite phenomenal and, of course, entirely due to the results your Regiment has produced. I should be most grateful it you would convey these remarks to all ranks of your Regiment.'

It was a tribute echoed by every infantryman who fought at Anzio. The close fire support of the guns broke up enemy attack after attack, but it was the knowledge that this intimate support was always there, that the guns were ready and more than willing to bring down anything, from a few smoke shells to help a single man get back, to a colossal concentration of every gun that could bear to break up a weighty attack, which was the most sustaining feature of their support. The unfortunate soldier in his slit-trench, wondering when and from which direction the next German attack would come had little enough encouragement in the tough early days of the beachhead, but he knew, and they never let him down, that the guns were behind him and able to respond at a moment's notice. It was very reassuring. Indeed the Germans reckoned that seventy-five per cent of their casualties were caused by artillery fire; a further fifteen per cent were due to air activity.

Gunnery was a field where at first British and American practices differed widely. Rarely did the American artillery conform to infantry movements or infantry rates of advance. The careful orchestration of war, the close co-ordination of time and distance which was the essence of British artillery practices were quite foreign to the Americans. There were other differences between each nation's gun procedures. Most significant, perhaps, was that American forward observation officers (FOOs) or Observation Post officers were more often than not very junior officers; the more senior ones remained on the gun lines or in command posts directing fire. The British used their more senior and more experienced officers forward. These men, tested in war and with the experience of several campaigns behind them, were of invaluable assistance to the companies or battalions they supported, and not only in their own roles. On many occasions they commanded infantry companies, even at times battalions, with skill and distinction.

Behind the Lateral Road dwelt a fine battery of American 155-mm guns, manned by coloured troops. Not for them the prosaic British fire procedure, the steady 'Shot Over,' 'Shot Out'. Instead, when all was ready, the cry would go up 'Call de Roll, Kesselring! Here we come,' and with a mighty roar the guns would fire.

Observation points over the flat Campo di Carne were at a premium. Insecure ladders were propped against the highest trees—and had to be removed at phenomenal speed when spotted, which inevitably, sooner or later they were—the few houses still standing with an upper floor intact held eagle-eyed gunners scouring the plain to their front for targets. The Flyover, with its raised embankment, was the most dominating feature on the southern side of the plain. Here tunnels had been dug right through to the other side and a slit left to give observation towards the Factory and Carroceto. Try as they might the Germans were never able to shoot through the slit openings, and the OPs remained undisturbed.

The 'eyes' of the beachhead were the Air OP planes, the Cubs of the Americans—'dehydrated flying fortresses' they were sometimes called; the Austers of 'A' and later 'C' Flight of 655th Air Observation Post Squadron, RAF. Theirs was a particularly hazardous task. Flying slow and very vulnerable aircraft they flew high over the Allied lines spotting the fall of shot or enemy movement in the rear areas. They had little protection except a steel sheet under the pilot's cabin—passengers felt strongly inclined to sit on their steel helmets! Their armament was the pilot's pistol, and if attacked they had to rely on their remarkable manoeuvrability. To the Germans they were a constant menace. They were always there, apparently seeing right into their positions and they felt, even if it was not always the case, that their every movement could be seen. The observation planes and the naval gun-fire with its flat trajectory and terrifying noise were to many Germans the most lurid and unpleasant memories of the Anzio campaign. So dominating were they over the battlefield that after a while no German field gun would fire for fear of being spotted.

No matter the weather, no matter the conditions, the pilots of the Air

OP planes courageously carried out their role. Without their help the value of the Allied artillery fire would have been drastically reduced. Pilots were killed during the Anzio operation. Flying at the height of the mean trajectory they were at greater risk from their own guns than from enemy action. One plane lost its propeller, shot off by a shell, but managed to get down safely; another was hit by a ranging round and was unfortunately destroyed, the pilot killed.

The wadis were a particular problem to the gunners as the sides of the gullies were too steep for the relatively shallow trajectories of field guns. Mortars were the ideal weapon under such circumstances, but other novelties were tried. Experiments of setting guns at their highest angle or digging in the trails were attempted with varying success, but the use of air burst high-explosive shells was far more effective. For dealing with troops advancing up the wadis the Bofors anti-aircraft gun with quick-firing shells proved highly successful.

A perennial problem was the hiding of the muzzle flash. With the Germans occupying all the best ground for observation, there was hardly anywhere where gun flash could be totally hidden from view. Thus, as the weeks passed the gun positions, and particularly living quarters, receded deeper and deeper into the earth, until some reckoned that they were immune from even a direct hit. Nevertheless, so close were the gun lines to the enemy that the gunners had an unusually high casualty rate; never were they out of range of immediate retaliation by counter-bombardment.

Special events were celebrated in special ways. To mark Hitler's birthday, an area where a German cookhouse was purported to be was left strictly alone for some weeks, then at the appropriate time, when it was reckoned the local residents were about to enjoy their breakfast, 51 shells from some American 150-mm guns were loosed off towards the target, followed by a hail of leaflets wishing the Führer happy returns. Other shoots were timed, as they cheerfully put it, 'to shoot the breakfast plate out of his hand—the luncheon fork out of his mouth—the evening rations while still in his vehicle.'

Other incidents enlivened the 'stalemate' period. On one occasion the troops had to stand-to as fifty German paratroops had been spotted landing—an ever-present anxiety. It later transpired that the fifty paratroops had been two baled-out airman reported by twenty-five different sources. In April Italian midget submarines made a sudden attempt on the assembled shipping around Anzio port, and anti-tank guns were swiftly brought down to engage them, as they were for an 'invasion' scare when a number of barges were spotted on the radar heading south. These were later identified as coal barges on the Tiber.

Movement along the Coastal Road was severely restricted. Ominous notices declared that 'Dust Brings Shells', and lurid cartoons emphasised the point. Elsewhere on the beachhead, particularly on the Lateral Road itself, it was sometimes possible to gauge the stereotype German response. A wait at the end of the road, while the last unfortunate ran the gauntlet, the timed pause and then the dash to the far end where cover could be obtained. It was a nerve-racking process, which some became quite adept at. Others were not so good and for them it proved fatal.

From the air, the beachhead resembled an area where a vast army of moles had gone mad; at night the moles of Anzio came to life. In the daylight hours the wise kept out of sight and movement was reduced to the minimum, except at the port where the business of unloading continued without pause. At nightfall the whole beachhead came alive. The starlit nights were disturbed by the clatter and scream of cranes working at the port. Tracer hung over the forward lines like luminous cobwebs; further back, the sky was lit by arcs of leaping flame; brighter jets and balls of light climbed lazily into the sky towards some attacking aeroplane. From a distance, Anzio at night resembled a particularly magnificent show of the Northern Lights or a crazy, noisy firework display. The anti-aircraft guns in the beachhead had achieved a signal success over the Luftwaffe. By 1 May 186 enemy aircraft had been shot down by anti-aircraft fire, and now German high-level raids were almost a thing of the past. So sophisticated and slick was the anti-aircraft technique in the beachhead that the Germans were losing nearly one-third of their attacking force on each occasion. The last major attack by German aircraft involved fifty planes; of these thirty turned back, from the remainder nine were shot down.

Life was nearly as tense in the 'rear' areas as it was at the front—and many reckoned a great deal less safe. In an area smaller, as was pointed out, than some American ranches, a vast conglomeration of military paraphernalia had gathered. The small rudimentary airstrip on the outskirts of Nettuno was shelled sporadically, and heavily whenever any aircraft landed, so that it was by now only used for courier planes and as an emergency field. Below Anzio and Nettuno, staffs lived a troglodyte existence in the capacious wine cellars and catacombs beneath the towns.

In this, the most difficult of battles, there was a further sustaining factor of substantial importance—particularly for the British troops. This was the appearance of General Alexander in the beachhead. Even after the span of thirty-four years veterans recall the visits of Alex, as he was always known. His presence was not the flamboyant one of a Montgomery or a Patton. His approach was one of discreet showmanship, which succeeded. Those who recall these visits recall too the indefinable impression that if Alex was there things were 'all right'. The confidence and trust they placed in their commander-in-chief was complete, his presence very comforting. On one occasion he came to call on the 5th Grenadiers who were resting and sorting themselves out after the Carroceto battles in the woods behind the front. After chatting with one or two officers and men, Alex saw a lance-corporal whom he recognised from many years back. Together the two old soldiers sat down, shared the same lunch and discussed the campaign. When he left what he had done and said was round the battalion in no time at all.

Alex's presence also sustained the commanders of the beachhead. At the height of the crisis when 6th Corps seemed on the verge of having to swim for safety, General Penney had been wounded, and General Templer was in charge of the British forces, General Alexander flew up to see him, sitting behind the pilot in a fighter. He was greeted by General Templer and taken back to the headquarters. It was around nine o'clock in the morning. For over an hour the two men discussed one thing or another; friends they had known together in Ireland or in Yorkshire, hunting or shooting or any other subject away from the immediate crisis. From time to time General Templer tried to switch the conversation back to matters of more immediate moment, but each time he was adroitly steered back to conversational nothingness. At length, in desperation Templer offered Alexander a drink. To his surprise, for Alex never drank at that ungodly hour, and some dismay, as he had little left, Alex asked for some gin. The commander-in-chief drank it with some avidity and then stood up. 'Gerald, I must be off,' he said, 'I have done all I could to help you, haven't I?' Templer replied, 'Yes, indeed you have, Sir,' and as he later wrote, he meant it. The two men had not discussed one thing about the battle, or any of the other manifold problems which were besetting the 1st and 56th Divisions, but he had instilled 'life and courage and determination into me at the moment when I wanted it badly'.

For the fit the 'rear' areas were bad enough, but for the sick and for casualties they were little less than Hell on Earth, and the medical compounds richly earned the title 'Hell's Half Acre'. For the first time battle exhaustion cases began to appear in appreciable numbers. There was little pattern about the process, sometimes no indication that a man would break. This war was beyond the compass of everyone and some could not take it. Even the most experienced might succumb, having reached the limit of his human resistance. On one occasion a senior soldier and a dozen of his companions 'reported sick'. There was nothing wrong with them but fright; their leader was a man who had fought in the Spanish Civil War, at Dunkirk, in North Africa and on the beaches of Salerno, yet even he had his breaking point, and the constant shelling had brought him to it. In this instance a little exercise at the hands of the regimental sergeant major was enough to bring them back to their senses. Once the remains of a platoon which had been caught by the cataclysmic blast of one of the German railway guns, which had killed a number of their comrades and shorn them of their clothing, were found digging like rabbits under any cover they could find and were quite incoherent. The same medicine worked like magic. But these were short-term experiences which responded to short-term remedies.

Other instances were more serious. At first, for even to the medical staffs this was a relatively new condition, the victims were looked on as malingerers or as men who had temporarily lost their nerve; for them discipline, swift and vigorous, was the remedy. But others were clearly very different cases. The trembling, shambling, incoherent man, perhaps a non-commissioned officer, who was unaware of his whereabouts, gazed about him with a look of uncomprehending shocked surprise and seemed to hear nothing spoken to him, required above all rest, sedation, sleep and food, and later, encouragement. At Anzio, Exhaustion Centres were set up where such treatment could be administered and after a few days' respite the men returned to the line—the figures show that very few came back for further treatment. It was as though the crisis had passed and somehow, even in the hell of Anzio, they had found a form of inner peace. Those few who did not recover after this treatment had to be evacuated to Naples for full psychiatric care.

It was fortunate, in a way, that it was only possible to send out of the beachhead those who were beyond simple treatment and who needed this specialist care. There was little inducement for the malingerer to try his hand if the best that could happen to him would be a few days' rest under even worse shelling than he might have been receiving at the front. The Germans tried vigorously to encourage the breed. Their most effective propaganda device was a book of 'V' matches with the telling label 'Come Back Alive' while on the rear it bore the somewhat Irish exhortation 'Better a few weeks ill than all your life dead.' When opened, it proved a goldmine to any potential malingerer as it gave advice on how to feign sickness of all sorts. 'Bomb Happiness' took on many forms. On one occasion a north countryman resolutely refused to leave his forward slit-trench, and it was too exposed to physically force him out of it. He stayed there for three days, until on the Friday he suddenly turned up at his battalion headquarters; he had come for his pay!

Others would deliberately maim themselves. The sudden single shot in the night was the sound a platoon or company commander most dreaded. All too often it was the signal that some unfortunate had reached the end of his tether and had shot himself in the foot, or shot off his trigger finger. It was the dire warning that his men had been stretched to, and in one case beyond, breaking point. The victim had to be hustled to the rear before the disease could become contagious.

The clinical symptoms of battle fatigue—nervousness, irritability, insomnia, excessive drinking and smoking—were no guide at all at Anzio that a man's nerve was breaking. There were very few who were not nervous; many even now vividly recall that they walked scared most of the time. There was always the oppressive feeling, if one allowed oneself to feel it, that they were in constant danger and that nowhere was safe at Anzio. As exhaustion and privation took their inevitable toll, senior officers were sent back for a few days' 'rest'. Those who knew of it kept the matter a close family secret, protected from outsiders and gained strength from the knowledge that if their own war was bloody enough, how very much worse it was for the older men with the extra strain of responsibility. It was this responsibility, though, which kept many an officer and non-commissioned officer going, that and the fear of being found wanting.

For the more senior commanders, the perpetual worry, combined with a cumulative exhaustion and the overwhelming feeling of impotence over affairs which were being resolved at platoon and company level and which they could barely influence, became oppressive. There was little a brigade commander or a commanding officer could do but encourage the men under his command to stay where they were.

Observers speak of a state bordering on hysteria. It required conscious effort of will to keep going. It helped to busy oneself with some trivial matter, but as time went on battalions deteriorated almost visibly. Sheer cumulative exhaustion had eroded the moderating factor which raises man above the animal, to the point when a mishap appears a disaster, and a minor success becomes a major victory. Now much of the spark had gone. Battalions contained a mixture of wily old birds who had seen it all, and new men who had seen nothing. Sometimes the mixture worked, sometimes it did not.

Not everyone in the Anzio beachhead was a hero. For the most part companies and platoons fought as they should have done, as long as their officers and non-commissioned officers were standing. It was when they had all been killed or could take no further part in the battle and the private soldier was left on his own, that occasionally inexplicable things started to happen. Occupants of isolated forward positions would disappear with no trace and no noise. Patrols sent off into the dark would never be heard of again. Individuals would slip away unnoticed and unremarked until picked up by some roving German patrol. The profusion of German leaflets were rarely the cause of this defection. They usually had a contrary effect and provided rare moments of light relief, but if any had a mind to desert, the opportunities were legion. A good few deserters roamed the rear areas

216

pillaging food dumps when they felt hungry: when challenged there were any of a dozen thoroughly plausible excuses to use.

The German attempts at propaganda were almost wholly ineffective. The rarer and more lascivious pamphlets were collected eagerly, the better ones were kept and the others found an appropriate use. Among of the greatest boosts to morale were the broadcasts sent out by Rome radio. Its seductive-voiced announcer was promptly christened Axis Sally and her companion, George. 'Hello suckers,' she would begin. 'Who has who surrounded?' Then might follow a list of recent prisoners. Although they were intended to show German success, the lists were rather a source of consolation that some officer or man was not killed, as had been feared, but captured. Then would follow relays of the latest popular tunes from America, and the seductive nostalgic never-to-be-forgotten strains of 'Lily Marlene', the adopted tune of both sides. The Germans can have had no idea of the morale effect of Axis Sally's broadcast; rarely can a propaganda effort have so comprehensively misfired.

Throughout the rear areas were stacks of ammunition and supplies of all sorts. It was a near certainty that sometime during each night the Germans would obtain a direct hit on some dump or other; they could hardly miss. At first they were massed too closely, but later separated as widely as space allowed and surrounded by earth banks. Nevertheless, from time to time, spectacular firework displays were effected as an ammunition dump exploded. Hits on other dumps although less spectacular could be of greater inconvenience. A single shell on a bakery reduced the bread output on the beachhead by 28,000 loaves a week, until it could be replaced.

Among the confusion of guns, dumps and storage depots, the Germans could not fail to hit something, and often that something was the hospital complex. No more than 200 yards from a reinforcement camp, less than half a mile away from piles of ammunition and fuel, under frequent air attack and under the constant threat of artillery fire, Hell's Half Acre was aptly named. Patients found it a terrifying experience to be in hospital. In the early days they lay on beds well above the ground. Only canvas was overhead, often showing daylight through holes ripped by shrapnel, indicating that this was no place of rest and tranquillity. When warning came of an attack, as one man they reached for their steel helmets and placed them over their private parts. Little the wonder that lightly wounded men would hasten back to the safer areas of the front line, and others would disguise their wounds as long as possible.

The red crosses which covered the hospitals did not avert hostile actions. In one week two of the faithful nurses who had earlier been brought up to share the agony of Anzio and whose calming presence must have saved the sanity and the life of many a man, were killed. Altogether six lost their lives along with eighty-six other medical personnel and over four times that number wounded in the Anzio battle, although many of these were not in the rear areas.

In his *Memoirs of an Army Surgeon** J. A. Ross has painted a searingly vivid picture of what life was like in Hell's Half Acre. Here in the Casualty Clearing Stations in the early days,

> The buckets placed below caught some of it [the rain], but not all. Gutters dug to catch the excess filled, overflowed, and were crushed in by heavy trampling feet, till the floor became a sea of mud. On either side of the ward were placed the stretchers of the men awaiting operative treatment for their wounds . . .
>
> There the wounded lay, in two rows, mostly British, but some Americans as well, in their sodden, filthy, muddy clothes—greatcoats, pullovers, battledress, all of the thickest, soaked, caked, buried in mud and blood—ghastly pale faces, shuddering, shivering with the cold of the February nights, and their great wounds.
>
> Most had their first field-dressings or shell-dressing on. I grew to hate that combination of yellow pad and bloody, dirty brown bandage and mud-darkened skin. Many men reached us who would not normally have survived long enough to reach a C.C.S. (Casualty Clearing Station) at all. Some unconscious, these chiefly head wounds, whose loud snoring breathing distinguished them. Some (too many—far too many) were carried in dying, with gross combinations of shattered limbs, protusions of intestines and brain from great holes in their poor frames torn by 88-mm. shells, mortars, and anti-personnel bombs. Some lying quiet, and still, with legs drawn up—the penetrating wounds of the abdomen. Some carried in sitting up on the stretchers, gasping and coughing, shot through the lungs. Others, less badly wounded perhaps, looking around with curious eyes, falling back on to their stretchers at the sights that met them there. Some, the least badly wounded, clutching mounds of equipment and 'agitating' about pieces of their kit which had gone astray. All were exhausted through being under continuous fire and lying in the mud for days or many hours before and after being wounded.

The dedication of the nurses was a tonic to all as they went unemotionally about their business, as was the devotion of other medical personnel. One officer's most treasured memento of the beachhead is a note from a medical orderly, a corporal, who after close

---

*Published by William Blackwood & Sons in 1947.

on a fortnight of almost continual action can apologise that he has been unable to check his stores as often as he would have liked. This was what the Anzio veterans spoke of as the Anzio spirit. In the dark days of February, when everyone knew they were fighting for their lives, it sustained them. As the spring months passed, it prospered. Nor was it restricted to the fighting troops. It pervaded every department, from the stevedores who stoically unloaded the ships day or night, aware that at any moment the shells plummeting into the bay might land in the hold of an ammunition ship moored at the quay, to the military policemen on point duty, or the signaller checking his cables. And it was unique to Anzio. Many officers said that they had never seen anything like it during the war; it was what Londoners experienced and felt in the Blitz, in fact the comparison is very close, and it engendered a camaraderie between British and American servicemen which was never exceeded in the Second World War. General Harmon summed it all up as a 'confidence in unity, an unselfish willingness among troops to help one another, that I never saw again. I have sometimes thought that this was, in the end, the electric force which made victory possible.' And it mattered not at all what uniform was worn or the nationality of the wearer.

13

Stalemate

March–May

With the abandonment of large-scale offensive action by both sides, during March and April, it had been possible for the Germans to make considerable adjustments in their order of battle. On the east of the beachhead the Hermann Goering Panzer Division were withdrawn for some long overdue rest and reorganisation and pulled back to a coast watching role on the west coast of north Italy near Leghorn. At the same time, 114th Jaeger Division were taken from the Carano sector and dispatched to the quieter Adriatic front. The two armoured divisions, 26 Panzer and 29th Panzer Grenadier, were taken back into general reserve south of Rome, where they could be sent either to Anzio, or the southern front as occasion offered. In their place a number of extra units were sent forward, including two Italian battalions, but these were of dubious worth. Thus the number of divisions opposing the Anzio 'Abscess' was substantially reduced, although the total number of troops, 135,000, had never been greater even at the height of the German attacks in February. But though the numbers were high, the calibre was variable. Of the divisions facing the Allies in March and April, only the old stalwarts, 3rd Panzer Grenadier Division, holding the front immediately east of the Via Anziate, were considered first grade. The Americans captured one evening a prisoner who was carrying a piece of doggerel which, when roughly translated, read:

'Greiner Division (362)   'The game is up
Steadily diminishing   The bolt is shot
Soon sole survivor   First goes Hitler
General Greiner   Then the lot.'

It was very encouraging.

Despite this scarcity of top-class troops, a lack of ammunition and fuel, and with a crucial shortage of vehicle spares on his hands, Kesselring contemplated a number of offensive plans. One destined for 29 March, on either the Via Anziate or the Cisterna front, was only fully abandoned in mid-April. Once again the perpetual dilemma facing the Germans had become acute, for, while conditions on the southern front were still uncertain Kesselring was reluctant to commit his valuable armoured reserve; for his part, von Mackensen did not consider that any worthwhile attack on the Anzio front could be mounted without them.

On the Allied side, the 504th Parachute Infantry Regiment and the 509th Parachute Infantry Battalion had left the beachhead in late March and early April respectively, bound for England to swell the forces waiting to mount Operation Overlord. On 21 March the 34th U.S. Infantry Division came in to relieve the long-suffering 3rd Division who had by then endured sixty-seven consecutive days in the line—the latter were withdrawn to the area north of Nettuno to prepare for the break-out, and set about absorbing their share of the reinforcements which were streaming into the beachhead—no less than 14,000 in March alone. This influx of new men brought the Allies up to strength and gave them substantial superiority over the enemy for the first time since the early days of the landing.

Also, beginning on 7 March, the battalions and brigades of the 56th British Infantry Division began to be relieved by the 5th British Infantry Division. By then the 56th Division was drastically under strength, their combat efficiency put as no higher than twenty-five per cent in some cases. Low in numbers to start with, the succession of gallant if expensive actions in the wadi country had reduced the division to only a shadow of its former self. On 11 March, the leading elements sailed from Anzio bound first for Naples, and then to Egypt to reform, retrain and incorporate a large number of disbanded light anti-aircraft units and turn them into infantry.

The 5th Division who relieved them were far from full strength themselves, and like their predecessors had been heavily involved in the Garigliano battles. Their three brigades were the 15th Infantry Brigade, of the 1st Battalions of the Green Howards, the Yorks and Lancaster Regiment and the King's Own Yorkshire Light Infantry (KOYLI); the 17th Infantry Brigade, of the 6th Battalion the Seaforth Highlanders, the 2nd Battalion the Northamptonshire Regiment and the 2nd Battalion the Royal Scots Fusiliers; and the 13th Infantry Brigade with the 2nd Battalion the Cameronians (Scottish Rifles), the 2nd Battalion the Wiltshire Regiment and the 2nd Battalion the Royal Inniskilling Fusiliers. In support were the 7th Battalion the Cheshire Regiment with machine guns and mortars, and the 5th Reconnaissance Regiment.

The leading brigade, the 15th, embarked at Naples on 4 and 5 March into heavy seas and the KOYLI arrived off Anzio the following morning a somewhat chastened and very sea-sick battalion. But they were more than a little cheered when they heard of the adventures of their comrades in the Yorks and Lancs who had found themselves making an unscheduled, fortunately unopposed, landing on German-occupied soil some thirty miles south of Anzio due to the captain of their craft losing his way. After hurriedly re-embarking they arrived safely and in one piece, if somewhat late, during the course of the next day. By 7 March the brigade was fully formed in the beachhead and that night they moved into the line, straight into the wadi country. It was, mercifully, an undisturbed take-over.

With the arrival of the 5th Division it was now possible to completely reorganise the western sector of the beachhead. Thus the 1st Division was given the sector from a point a little over one mile east of the Flyover on the Lateral Road, where the 45th U.S. Division were holding sway, to a line southwards from Pantoni in wadi country and which embraced the Boot and the eastern end of the two Lobster Claws. On this sector, 2,000 yards east of the Flyover, operated the battalions of the 2nd Infantry Brigade, with frequent reinforcement from the squadrons of the 1st Reconnaissance Regiment. While doing duty alternately in the tricky wadi world west of the Via Anziate were the 3rd and 18th Infantry Brigades. To the west of that, in the wadi La Cogna and stretching to the Moletta itself, where the 36th U.S. Combat Engineers still reigned, was the sphere of influence of the 5th Infantry Division. Theirs was the dubious pleasure of defending the closest of the wadi country, with able support from Nos. 9 and 40 Commandos, until they were released later in March. In particular they were responsible for the notorious area known as the 'Fortress', where any movement invited fire and men lived a claustrophobic existence in slit-trenches at almost hand-shaking distance from the Germans.

There was danger, under such conditions of cheek by jowl warfare, of developing a 'dugout complex'. Commanders at all levels—and on both sides—were at pains to inject an offensive spirit, even though conditions were more reminiscent of trench warfare in the Great War. For the most part attacks were for limited objectives; the straightening of a piece of line here; the elimination of an over-obtrusive position there; perhaps the opportunity of wiping out a trouble-spot or capturing an isolated post by a carefully planned, well-executed raid. It was a policy which led to casualties, but the alternative was a life of stagnation which preyed on both the spirit and the body and invited fierce and savage attacks from the Germans if they felt that the troops opposite them had dropped their guard.

War in the wadi country remained unchanged. As Lt.-Col. M. Redmayne of the 14th Foresters described later, 'Nothing seemed to have any tactical sense. There was little or no actual support between platoons, certainly not between companies, and indeed in most cases sections were fighting a private war of their own. It was a company commander's battle, and they struggled desperately to find some way of evening things up with an enemy who appeared to hold all the cards.'

The Germans, too, found conditions unpleasant. A divisional report declared 'These places are so bitterly contested because there is so little no-man's-land between us and the enemy. They are covered with low briars and undergrowth, swampy in parts. The enemy had strongly fortified his positions here since the beginning of March, digging trenches and mining and wiring his positions.' From time to time more substantial attacks were mounted than the fighting patrol or platoon-strength raids which were sent out to keep the Germans on their toes and allow them little sleep.

The Allies were not the only ones to show an offensive spirit. In what became known as the Battle of the Woods, the KOYLI found themselves the target for some German aggression. On 24 March they relieved the 36th U.S. Combat Engineers who were pulled back to prepare for the break-out. The 36th were thankful at last to be free of their infantry duties which they had performed so ably on the Moletta River. This was a different form of terrain to the wadi country. Here thick woods abounded, the undergrowth was heavy and both sides had sown mines liberally. The battalion position was on the forward edge of a prominent wood and each company position an individual stronghold, mined and wired and independent of all others. In a neck of the wood, well forward of the rest of the battalion, 'A' Company occupied the most isolated of the company localities with Germans uncomfortably close in some woods to the front. On the night of 31 March, two platoons of the German 11th Parachute Battalion, supported on this occasion by a platoon from a Battle School and with some flame-throwers, moved quietly into position opposite 'A' Company. They had been specially trained and rested for this occasion and were out to teach the Yorkshiremen a lesson.

A pleasant sunny afternoon was passing drowsily when at 1530 hours on April Fool's Day the whole battalion was suddenly and comprehensively shelled, while a shower of mortar bombs fell on the 'A' Company position. Then, under a heavy smoke screen, the German platoons hurled themselves at 'A' Company. For three hours the battle raged. This was close quarter fighting at its worst, using the bayonet and grenade and trying to drive off a persistent attacker in heavy scrub, but the Yorkshiremen held firm. At eight o'clock the Germans had had enough. Next morning twenty of their dead were counted in the area, and many wounded had been seen borne away. 'A' Company had lost one officer killed and eleven men wounded.

Further to the east, the 2nd and 3rd Brigades soon made themselves masters of the ground astride the Via Anziate and up to the line of the Dead End Road. Here the war took on the complexion of trench warfare of a former day, with communications trenches and almost a Flanders' routine. Ahead, the pock-marked landscape came increasingly to resemble pictures of a World War I battlefield, with gaunt wire entanglements, blackened twisted stumps of trees and the occasional pile of rubble of what had once been a house or farm. Mud clogged everything, and even red poppies started to come up to complete the similarity.

To their right was the American sector, in places as peaceful as their own, in places a good deal more noisy. One of the latter was a protrusion at the tip of a wood west of Padiglione which, because it changed hands so often, was christened by the Germans 'Dirne Anna' (Prostitute Anna). It gained a form of unpleasant notoriety with 3rd Panzer Grenadier Division and prompted a German war correspondent to write:

> This is an advanced position which dominates enemy territory and is one of the most bitterly contested places in the Nettuno bridgehead. The opposing sides are very close together. It is the normal daily routine for hand grenades to be thrown across the tiny strip of No Man's Land and to fall in the other side's positions. Heavy concentrations of enemy artillery constantly churn up the ground. The garrison of this strongpoint live under continual strain with hardly a break in the fighting and without sleep. As darkness falls, the enemy sends out his recce and fighting patrols into No Man's Land, constantly trying to find a gap in the iron ring of our defence. In bloody man-to-man combat every foot of the ground is fought over. With machine-pistols and hand grenades the Brandenburghers beat off the constant American assaults.

The 3rd Panzer Grenadier Division were the most outstanding division on the German side engaged at Anzio. They had fought in Poland, France and on the Russian front and were a highly geared battle-worthy formation. Recruited from the Berlin area, theirs was a family formation, and the family and regional tries were maintained throughout the war. When a man from the 3rd Panzer Grenadiers returned to the front after a spell in hospital, there was no question of his being cast into the reinforcement channels. Instead he returned to the 3rd Panzer Grenadiers, to the same regiment he had left, to the same battalion within that regiment, and, more often than not, the same company he had been a member of. When one officer was promoted to command a company it was accepted as normal and inevitable that he would of course command the same company commanded by his great-grandfather during the Franco-Prussian War seventy years before. The 3rd Panzer Grenadiers were an élite formation who fought in the highest traditions of the German army, but these traditions did have their drawbacks. One of these was that if you were to die you should do it wearing your best uniform. At the height of the German offensive, when the battalions and regiments of von Mackensen's army were disappearing before their very eyes and one troop commander found his troop consisted of no more than single figures, he was considerably put out to find that his orderly, unbidden, had laid out his best uniform for the forthcoming attack!

On the east of the beachhead the ground became more open, until the formidable waterway of the Mussolini Canal barred the way. This was the home of a very remarkable body of men, the 1st Special Service Force, who had been brought into the beachhead at the beginning of February and made themselves complete masters of the vulnerable eastern flank. Conceived in 1942, they were a joint American-Canadian unit. At first, as the Canadians had more combat-experienced officers and senior non-commissioned officers they provided a high proportion of these ranks, but soon the unit was totally integrated at all levels. The two nations wore the same uniform, the same baggy parachutist trousers and combat jackets, except that the Canadians sported a small maple leaf. They were volunteers drawn from such professions as forest ranger, trapper, or stockman; they were tough individualists who, under strict discipline, became a redoubtable fighting force. It had originally been intended that the 'Force', as they referred to themselves, would be sent on a death or glory mission to Norway to blow up the German heavy-water plants, and for this purpose they were specially trained in parachuting and skiing, by Norwegian instructors. The culmination of their training was a thirty-mile walk on skis carrying fifty-pound packs and concluding with an assault on a strong-point. As many of the Force had been drawn from the Southern States and included a sizable contingent from the Texas cavalry who had never seen snow in their lives, it was an arduous test. From their inception, their leader was Brigadier-General Robert Tryon Frederick, a small, slim man, more like a small town bank manager to look at than a fighting soldier. Until he spoke, that is. Then the full force of the character of this very gallant soldier—he was awarded the Distinguished Service Cross no less than four times—became apparent. Under Frederick's leadership the 1st Special Service Force became a body of fighting men to rank with any on either side in the last war.

They had arrived in the beachhead on 3 February and were immediately sent to the east flank, where they found the Germans unpleasantly near—far too close, they reckoned, for comfort and well-being. So they set about pushing the enemy back, and within the space of four weeks, by active and vigorous patrolling, the German line had been pushed back for over a mile.

The reclaimed Pontine marches which they overlooked was so flat it was known as the 'Billiard Table'. Barely a tree broke the general monotony of level fields stretching away into the distance. The occasional house stood up like an island, and these would often change hands nightly. The area was too flat to allow patrolling by daylight; instead, night was turned into day and in the dark the Force struck. There was nothing consistent about their raids, except their inconsistency. Place and time varied, as did the weight and direction of the attack. Theirs was a constant offensive spirit and it had a devastating effect on the enemy. Once an order was captured which declared to the German soldier, 'You are fighting the élite Canadian–American force. They are treacherous, unmerciful and clever, you cannot afford to relax. The first soldier capturing one of these men will be given seven day's furlough.' In a diary found on an officer he had written a few days before, 'The Black Devils are all around us every time we come into the line, we never hear them come.' Thus the Force earned the soubriquet of The Black Devils of Anzio.

The Germans had no idea how large the Force was. From the front they covered they computed that there was a full division's worth opposing them, whereas at no time did the Force exceed 3,200 men, and for most of the time they were very much fewer. But by constant patrolling and offensive action they made themselves the undisputed rulers of the eastern side of the beachhead, one quarter of the centre beachhead line.

The Americans took a leaf from the German book and brought their tanks well forward, putting them in the ruins of the houses which had their backs knocked out, and parking them in what had been the front room with their gun barrels sticking through the gaping casements. There the tanks stayed, although the crews were changed. Elsewhere, sheep grazed right up to the rear headquarters and gun emplacements, and cattle and mules wandered among the minefields. The cattle were protected by an army order, but they turned out to be an aggressive breed; many a soldier declared that he had to shoot in self-defence!

Most of the local population had been evacuated by the Germans even before the landing, as they were particularly sensitive about this stretch of coastline. A number stayed on, dispensing evil wine in black market cellars, or tilling their fields and tending their flocks. A good few survived in the Caves, taking stoically the frequent change of ownership from British to American to British and finally to German.

The danger of having civilians wandering about the battlefield was considerable, not least from the security angle, so most were 'frozen', and forbidden to move. Despite the German evacuation there still seemed a remarkable number of Italians about, and for the most part they took shelter in the few surviving farmhouses in the beachhead, and stayed there despite the shelling. As the fighting on the Via Anziate became fiercer, so an increasingly large number fled to the rear, and soon evacuation became essential. Between 18 February and 10 March 11,000 civilians were evacuated back to Naples on empty ships. This left an estimated 8,000 in the beachhead area who declined to move and preferred to stick it out. A number of commanders were becoming concerned about the shortage of local labour so the evacuation was largely suspended, and civilian workers were brought up from Naples.

Feeding the population, which at all costs must have their movement restricted to the minimum, became something of a problem until a mill was restarted using tractor power and fresh flour started to come up from Naples. But by imaginative use of available resources what could have proved a difficult problem in the restricted beachhead was kept well in hand. Carabinieri were brought up to help keep order. A number of civilian doctors and nurses remained on duty in Anzio and Nettuno and to all intents and purposes the local population remained self-contained in the beachhead. Normal diseases and injuries would be handled by the civilian doctors, while shrapnel and shell wounds were sent to the military hospitals. Sometimes the medical officers of units were called on to help, and one delivered a baby using the light of a torch and sixteen candles.

Life in the rear areas assumed a steady monotony. Pervading all was the smoky atmosphere produced by the artificial fog canisters which puffed out their filthy fumes all day, shrouding the Anzio area in a lung-blocking cloud. Recreation was provided by football or baseball matches, while the more hardy bathed in the sea. Concert performers came up from Naples and performed before entertainment-starved troops. The divisional bands were dispatched to the beachhead, a mobile cinema was established and a leave roster worked out so that many people were able to have a change of scene. The Anzio Turf Club held their one and only 'Spring Meeting', using horses made of wood—the betting was fast and furious. Donkey races became popular, and beetle racing became a craze.

A champion beetle could fetch as much as £8, no mean price for an insect. Housed in jam jars for the parade—and there was no shortage of starters—when all bets had been laid, the runners, each with its owner's colours marked with paint, or with small flags mounted on the back of the insect with chewing gum, would be put in the starter's jam jar in the centre of a six-foot circle. The jar would be raised and the first beetle to reach the perimeter declared the winner. Skulduggery was not unknown. One champion beetle met an untimely death under the boot of a clumsy soldier, others mysteriously vanished in the night—and ownership was hard to prove.

The churches were popular. In the Padiglione Woods was an all-denominational cave where 100 men could worship in comparative peace. A mass baptism was arranged in the sea; the huge waves running that day did nothing to deter the converted. For those nearer the front line worship was less easy. The remarkable Father Essig, Roman

227

Catholic Padre to the 1st Special Service Force, who held his services in the open, would precede each with the advice that in the event of enemy disturbance he would be available for personal consultation in the foxhole behind the altar.

By now fresh meat, brought up by ship from Naples, was appearing regularly on the menu, and it became possible to vary what had become a stodgily monotonous diet. The novelty of the variation provided by the different rations given to the British and Americans had begun to wear off; each army was heartily sick of compo and K-rations. Ingenuity knew no bounds. The Force were adept at patrolling, but they were also adept at bringing back food, particularly eggs, and it was not an unusual sight to see a patrol returning laden with food. As the stalemate continued it was possible to keep chickens, and one of the trickiest problems on the beachhead, which at times nearly led to blows, was whether the egg concession in the area belonged to the incoming or the outgoing unit. An organisation calling itself the Beach Research Foundation came to the interesting conclusion, after days of intensive field study, that chickens laid best under shell-fire. Their opinion was divided as to why. Some said that it was because the birds were allowed no rest and thus had their minds fully concentrated on the matter of egg laying. Others felt that sheer terror caused the birds to scratch away at the earth, and that the deeper they went the worms became larger and more succulent. Elsewhere in the rear areas some units turned their hands to a little gentle farming.

There were more positive activities, though, and training began to intensify. Small raids were conducted in different places and at differing times across the whole front. In the rear areas, troops practised assaulting pillboxes and strong-points. And many fertile minds turned to devising ingenious new weapons to defeat their enemy.

The pride of the 5th Division, perfected under the personal midwifery of the divisional commander, Major-General P. G. S. Gregson-Ellis, was a form of catapult designed to cast mortar bombs silently into neighbouring wadis. The range of the device proved sadly below even the most pessimistic hopes of its inventors. Battle sleds, which were narrow steel tubes with high sides to protect a man lying full-length within them proved more successful. These were intended to be towed into battle behind tanks over minefields and through wire. This was splendid, provided the ground was flat, and the tanks were not knocked out before the infantry had passed through the obstacle. Grapnel hooks powered by mortars were designed for throwing over wire entanglements so that they could be pulled down. But the Snake was the most successful of these contrivances. This was a steel trough filled with tubular explosive-filled Bangalore Torpedoes which could be pushed under enemy obstacles ahead of a tank. A number of these linked together could penetrate several hundred yards of enemy defences and could then be set off by the propelling tank. They could also be set off by the defenders to the eternal detriment of those propelling it.

At times artillery ammunition was in short supply and had to be saved, but there always seemed to be unlimited tank ammunition. Tanks were propped up on logs of wood to increase their range. And with considerable success, for the range of their main armament of 11,000 yards was increased to over 14,000 and enabled the tankmen to join the obscure world of the gunner.

And the Italian weather had at last broken. Warm, sunny, drowsy days succeeded one another without cessation. Larks were to be heard and seen over the battlefield and lizards basked on rocks in the sun while the nightingales sang their heads off. As the ground dried, wild lupins sprang up over the minefields and the mud sprouted green shoots. Now when they saw Italians they bade them 'Buona Pasqua' ('Happy Easter') and they meant it.

With the warmth came the tingle of anticipation, a sense of purpose pervaded their activities. They knew that there would be hard fighting ahead. They had an admiration and a respect and some pity for their adversaries, but now they knew for certain that they were 'in the win', and that the 'win' would be very soon. And if they had any doubts, the sight of pile after pile, dump after dump of ammunition, fuel and stores of all sorts filling up the back areas was enough to convince even the most sceptical. 'If you don't move out soon,' one staff officer, beholding the military cornucopia spread around the rear areas of Anzio remarked, 'this weight of stores will push you out.'

14

Springing the Trap

22–25 May

HEADQUARTERS VI CORPS
Office of the Commanding General
APO-306

22 May 1944

TO: The Officers and Men of the Allied Beachhead Force

For more than four months you have occupied the most dangerous
and important post of any Allied force. You have stopped and
defeated more than ten divisions which Hitler had ordered to drive us
into the sea. You have contained on your front divisions which the
enemy sorely needed elsewhere. You have neglected no opportunity
to harass and injure the enemy. Arduous conditions you have
accepted willingly and cheerfully, and you have not failed to improve
in discipline and training and in condition. You have set a standard
that has won the admiration and respect of our United Nations. For
your services during these trying days, I congratulate you.

Now, after four months, we attack. Our comrades of the 5th and
8th Armies—Britons, Poles, French, Americans, Italians—have
achieved a great victory on the south front. They are driving the
enemy to the north. They have set the trap—it is for us to spring that
trap and complete the destruction of the right wing of the German
10th Army . . .

Our comrades in the south are fighting their way toward us. The
eyes of the world will be upon us. Be alert—be vicious—destroy the
hated enemy. Victory will be ours.

L. K. TRUSCOTT, Jr.,
Major General, U.S. Army
Commanding

So Truscott in his Order of the Day heralded the break-out from the
beachhead at Anzio.

The final push on the main Italian front, so appropriately called

230

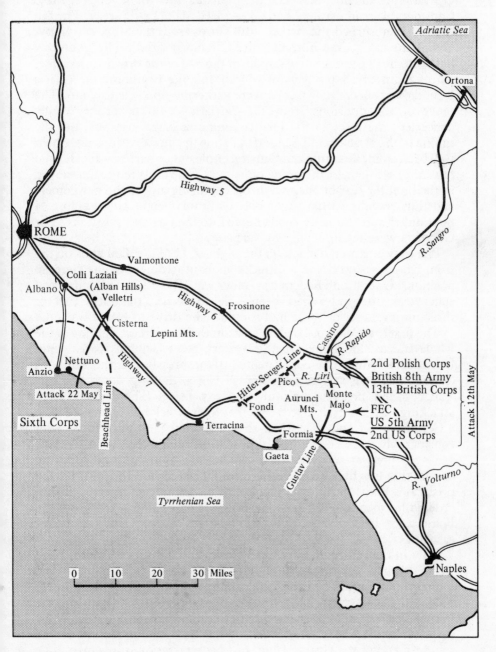

Operation Diadem

Springing the Trap

Operation Diadem, had commenced on the night of 11 May. Considerable readjustment had taken place to the battle array. The 8th Army had absorbed the British 10th Corps from the 5th U.S. Army, and at the same time inherited the Cassino position. The boundary between the two armies now ran down the line of the broad Liri Valley. Throughout the latter days of March and the beginning of April a formidable collection of troops were gathering opposite Cassino. The move of the divisions from the Adriatic could never be wholly concealed, the place of the forthcoming attack was obvious, but the timing of the attack could be hidden. Thus the new divisions were held well back from the front line. Only reconnaissance parties were allowed foward to see their forthcoming objectives. The units in the line stayed in the line, for fear of enemy patrols capturing any of the newcomers and thus revealing what was afoot. Only forty-eight hours before H hour did the attacking divisions move into their assault positions. The Germans were taken wholly by surprise.

Precisely at eleven o'clock on the night of 11 May 2,000 guns on the front from Cassino began a thunderous bombardment of the German positions: Operation Diadem was under way. By brilliant planning and staff work Alexander had been able to secure the local two or three-to-one superiority he had sought. The drive to Rome was on.

The first three days of Diadem saw some of the fiercest fighting of the whole Italian campaign. On the western coast General Keyes's 2nd U.S. Corps found they could make little impression on the stubborn German resistance. The 13th British Corps fighting down the Liri Valley found progress painful, and expensive. The Polish Corps attacking Cassino itself discovered that their attack had coincided with a German relief and that when they assaulted they were faced with considerably more enemy than they had bargained for. A few features were captured after heavy fighting, but the Germans still held the dominating heights and with the daylight proceeded to eliminate the precarious Polish positions. The Polish commander, General Anders, ordered his men to pull back. Twenty-four hours after starting out the Poles were back where they had started, having suffered heavy casualties.

Only in the centre on the Upper Garigliano did success loom. Here General Juin's magnificent French Expeditionary Corps, in one of the most brilliant attacks of the whole campaign, had made remarkable progress. The Germans had felt themselves secure in this sector and the French onslaught took the resident German division completely by surprise. On 13 May Monte Majo, the dominating feature at the southern end of the Gustav Line, had been taken by Juin's men. The door had been forced.

Making swift use of their success, the French swept on. By 15 May the French Expeditionary Corps had shattered the German positions in the Ausente Valley and taken Ausonia. This threatened the flank of the division opposing the 2nd U.S. Corps and forced it to retreat. Then Juin played his master-stroke. The Germans on the southern sector were divided by the all-but-impassable Aurunci Mountains, so he ordered his 12,000 Goumiers, magnificent fighting men from the mountains of Morocco, to penetrate the mountains and drive for the Lateral Road behind the newly constructed Hitler Line between Pico and Formia. Even before the Germans could man this new defence line it became untenable.

Elsewhere the Germans were beginning to yield. In the Liri Valley steady progress was being made as the British 6th Armoured Division was working round behind the Cassino massif. It was slow, methodical work, costly in time and men, as each limited objective was dealt with in turn. But it was succeeding. With the armoured division now poised to cut off Cassino, the Poles attacked again.

On 17 May the second Polish attack on Cassino was mounted. Inch-by-inch, position by position, the gallant Poles fought their way forward against fanatical resistance. As dusk fell on 17 May they captured a dominating height above the Monastery. Next morning, that and the town of Cassino were found to be clear of Germans. At 1020 hours the Polish flag was raised above the ruins of Monte Cassino. It was a symbolic gesture of the greatest significance.

With the Poles now outflanking the Hitler Line from the north, and the French from the south, the condition of the Germans looked precarious in the extreme, but, fighting with great fortitude, they still resisted stubbornly. But matters of greater moment were happening to the south, for, on 19 May, the 2nd U.S. Corps and the French broke through the Pico-Formia Lateral Road, and now the last feasible defensive position opposing them, that between the towns of Fondi and Terracina, lay at their mercy.

The original Diadem onslaught had caught the Germans wholly by surprise. Von Vietinghoff commanding the 10th German Army was on leave in Germany, as was his chief of staff and General von Senger und Etterlin of the Panzer Corps, while General Westphal, Kesselring's own chief of staff, was ill. For close on a week Kesselring considered the attack on the southern front as being nothing more than a deliberate feint designed to lure his reserves from either a break-out from Anzio or another landing somewhere up the coast. For weeks now his intercept operators had been listening to Canadian voices on what appeared to be a corps wireless net in the Naples area. Then, on 17 May, this same corps was located in the centre of the line. Worse was to come when he discovered how far the French had penetrated into the lines of the 10th German Army. Kesselring was still not convinced. Not until aerial reconnaissance had shown that no invasion force was on the seas and that another landing was not imminent was 26th Panzer Division ordered south to support the tottering line. Then, as Keyes's and Juin's advance threatened to unhinge the whole Hitler Line, Kesselring reluctantly ordered 29th Panzer Grenadier Division, his last reserve in the Rome area able to influence the battle at Anzio, to take up a position between Fondi and Terracina. Von Mackensen disagreed and an argument ensued between the two staffs. When Kesselring returned to his headquarters after a visit to the front it was to find that his orders had not been obeyed. Thus when the German division at last reached Terracina it was to find that the Americans were in firm and unyielding occupation of the higher ground. The new German position was untenable. Coming into action straight off the line of march they were too late to influence affairs, and could do little more than slow the American advance up the western coast. The time had come for 6th Corps to break out of Anzio.

General Alexander had reserved the right to dictate the timing of the break-out from the Anzio beachhead. All hinged on progress on the southern front, and how soon the German reserves were lured into the fight for the Gustav and Hitler Lines. Truscott had told Alexander when he visited Anzio of the four contingency plans for the break-out which his staff were working on. Alexander had then said that Operation Buffalo, which encompassed a drive through the Cisterna front and from there towards Valmontone to sever the escape routes of the 10th German Army, was the only one that mattered. Truscott passed on details of his discussion to Clark, who was deeply incensed at what he considered Alexander's interference and his by-passing of the American chain of command. It was a seed of discontent which was to have wide-reaching implications before Rome was captured.

For several weeks past, 6th Corps had been preparing for what one enthusiastic man called the 'Biggest Jail Break in History'. Since the beginning of May there was a heightening tension in the beachhead. On 9 May they heard of the air attacks on the dams at Pescara. Could this be the start? There were now six divisions at Anzio, two British and four American, and the 36th U.S. Infantry Division was about to embark at Naples for the beachhead, while Combat Command 'B' had been brought from the main front in early May, so General Harmon's 1st U.S. Armoured Division was complete again after a break of four months. Surreptitiously, during the previous weeks, there had been a good deal of Air OP activity. What the Germans did not know was that the aircraft carried the company and platoon commanders who were to lead the forthcoming attack. At divisional headquarters of the 1st Armoured Division a huge sand model fifty feet square had been constructed. Daily, officers and men would study this minutely. From early May

American tanks started to go forward at night to fire off boldly at what might or might not be enemy positions and then pull back again. From mid-May more of the tanks went forward than returned: the others were carefully hidden, their crews subsisting on cold food so that no smoke would reveal their new positions.

So limited were the roads approaching the Anzio front that it was reckoned that two full nights would be needed to bring forward the assaulting troops. Traffic control was vital, and worked out meticulously to the finest detail. For some weeks the artillery had fired sudden random concentrations on different parts of the front. The Germans would stand to, and then, nothing further happening, would return to their disturbed sleep cursing the reckless way the Americans squandered ammunition. After this had happened a few times, they hardly bothered to even report the practice.

On 20 May came the first warning to move up; it turned out to be a false alarm and everyone relaxed. The next night the great exodus began. The day had been hot and the land was quite dry; dust, not mud was the inconvenience now. The 3rd Infantry Division moved out of its bivouac area towards the front. At the side of the road was the divisional band, and to the strains of the 'Dog-Face Soldier' they moved up towards the front. The area ahead was quiet. Far away to the south gun flashes lit up the night as the great battle on the southern front neared its climax. For almost the first time those at Anzio could feel that they were no longer alone, that they were part of greater events, that their isolated existence was about to end.

Intelligence had calculated that the Germans were expecting the break-out when it came to be astride the Via Anziate. To strengthen this illusion, a series of diversionary local attacks were to be mounted some hours before the main thrust on the Padiglione and Cisterna fronts. These were to be carried out by the 1st and 5th British Infantry Divisions which had been detached from command of Truscott's 6th Corps and were now under direct command of the 5th Army.

On the 5th Division's front Operation Wolf, as it was termed, was to comprise a battalion strength raid by the 1st Green Howards on the coastal sector towards the little town of L'Americano across the Moletta River. This part of the front was covered with dunes and scrub and had hardly been disturbed since the initial days of the landing. The German 4th Parachute Division had prepared their positions with great care on the further banks of the Moletta. Mines and wire had been distributed with a cheerful liberality, and the Green Howards were under no illusions as to what lay ahead.

On May 22 the Green Howards moved forward to their assault positions behind the leading companies of the Northamptons south of the Moletta River, and at 1130 that night a thunderous bombardment

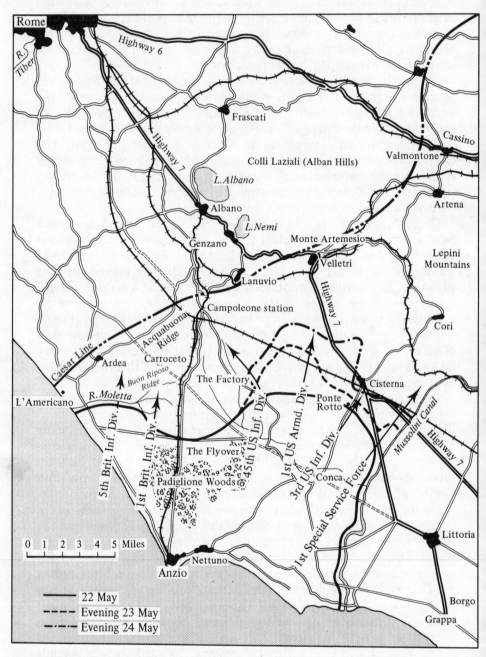

The break-out and the road to Rome

was directed on the German positions across the Moletta by the divisional artillery, some ships anchored off shore and any corps guns which could bear. For hours the massive bombardment continued, then, at 0315 hours, the sappers who were to tape routes across the river, place scaling ladders against the further steep banks and gap the enemy wire, started to move forward, and almost immediately into a newly laid minefield. The engineer officer was killed and the programme badly disrupted. The supporting platoon had also received heavy casualties and with great gallantry the senior surviving non-commissioned officer rallied his men and stormed across the stream in the face of heavy machine gun fire which by then was raking the water and the near bank. They placed the scaling ladders against the bank, and the way was now set for the first assault company to make their attack.

'D' Company of the Green Howards pressed forward with great gallantry. They suffered casualties in the new minefield, and more when they crossed the Moletta which was some two feet deep at that point. Shortly before dawn they reported that they had taken their objective, but were woefully weak having lost nearly three-quarters of their strength, and were nearly out of ammunition.

The way was now clear for the second assault company to take up the running. They crossed the river and started to make their way towards L'Americano, and immediately ran into heavy opposition. By 0730 hours, and despite almost crippling casualties, 'C' Company considered they were close enough to assault the hamlet. This they proceeded to do across flat bullet-swept ground. A few men reached the first houses of the place, but by then the company was down to single figures. They were told to withdraw short of the village.

Piecemeal, the remaining company, 'B' Company of the Green Howards, had been fed into the battle, but a few tanks had also been able to cross the Moletta and enabled the Green Howards to hang on, but only just. But their survival was by now just a question of time. At nine o'clock in the morning the Germans mounted a heavy attack on the isolated 'C' Company near L'Americano. Shouting and singing they advanced on the pitifully weak Green Howards and by sheer weight of numbers overwhelmed them, very few survivors managing to get back. Then they turned their attention to 'D' Company. Soon the surviving men of the Green Howards were struggling fiercely with their backs to the river, sustained by a ferocious weight of fire from the machine guns of the Cheshire regiment on the southern shore and the support of every gun and mortar in the area. The German attack was beaten off and then the following morning the remaining Green Howards were ordered to pull back across the river. This they accomplished under heavy machine-gun fire and a storm of grenades from some German parachutists who had been able to creep up and all but cut them off during the night. Operation Wolf had cost the Green Howards over 150 casualties, including twenty-seven dead, but it had not been a vain sacrifice. By their aggressive action they had prevented any reinforcements being sent from the Parachute Division to the crucial main Anzio front; as did the attacks by the 1st Division, now commanded by Major-General J. H. I. Hawkesworth during the temporary absence of General Penney. These took the shape of a strong raid by the Dukes with support from a platoon of the Foresters, and other smaller efforts by the Buffs and 2nd Brigade.

The Dukes' attack comprised a two-company assault on Pantoni and a heap of rubble to the north-east which rejoiced in the name of the 'King's Arms', while the Foresters' platoon took care of a prominent feature to the east called Green Bush Hill on the junction of the wadis Botaccia and Caronte. During the early hours of the night of 22 May gaps had been cut in the enemy wire and lanes made through their minefields. This enabled the assaulting companies to make good progress at first when their attack commenced at ten o'clock that night. But soon stubborn German resistance brought the attack to a halt. Green Bush Hill proved a harder nut to crack than had been expected and it became apparent that with daylight the forward positions which the rest of the Dukes had been able to occupy would be untenable. However, the line had been pushed considerably nearer Pantoni as a result of their efforts, and shortly afterwards the Germans came to the conclusion that Pantoni itself was untenable and duly pulled back. But the attack had cost nearly 100 casualties.

The other diversions of 1st Division were on a smaller scale. Platoon strength attacks on separate points of the front, and a lot of tank movement along the Lateral Road and other tracks. The Germans had been expecting that the main attack would be mounted along the Via Anziate, and they continued to do so as a result of the British division's actions. By the time they realised they were in error, it was too late for them to influence the main battle which had erupted further east.

Promptly at 0545 hours on the morning of 23 May, while the Green Howards were storming their way across the Moletta, and the Dukes were beginning to realise that Green Bush Hill was an insuperable obstacle, the massed artillery of 6th Corps thundered into action. The 3rd U. S. Division were under no illusions about the stubbornness of the German resistance. Over the last three-and-a-half months the enemy had been digging and preparing their positions. For weeks past patrols had probed these defences, until every pillbox was known, every approach route mapped and plotted, and then left strictly alone. They had discovered that every building, or their remains, had been converted into miniature strongholds, and they came to curse the day when the Italians made their hive-like outdoor ovens so well built. The enemy defences were deep, in places over 7,000 yards, and in this area there were innumerable strong-points, each as prickly as a hedgehog and supported by SP guns.

But the ground had dried and there would be no danger now of tanks bogging. The grass and some crops had grown up; in places it was waist deep, and made excellent cover.

Thus commenced for the 3rd U.S. Infantry Division three days of fighting which went down in their annals as the toughest of the war, and brought this very fine division no less than five Congressional Medals of Honour. On the first day they suffered 995 battle casualties, the highest number in any one day in the war, but it had bought some success. On the left, the 30th Infantry Regiment, despite meeting stout German resistance, had pushed past Ponte Rotto and by mid-afternoon were half way to the railway line; in the centre, the 7th Infantry Regiment attacking Cisterna from the front were inching their way forward against resistance which was at times described as fanatical; on the right, the 15th Infantry Regiment were driving forward with some success to outflank Cisterna from the south-east. And the Germans were suffering. 362nd Infantry Division had lost fifty per cent of its strength, and two regiments of 715th Infantry Division had been badly cut about. Against this thrust, the Germans hurriedly recalled the Hermann Goering Panzer Division from Leghorn, but the battle looked like being over before they could arrive. More local reinforcements were heavily involved opposite the British divisions and could not be released.

Although progress in the centre of the 6th Corps' attack on the first day had been marginal, that on the two flanks was more promising. On the east, the Special Service Force had driven forward against stiffening opposition and had managed to sever Highway Seven south-east of Cisterna. But on the western sector, elements of General Harmon's Armoured Division were all but through the German defences. By noon Combat Command 'A', who had made great use of the Snake to get through the enemy minefields, had closed on the railway line. By dusk they were 500 yards further on. Combat Command 'B', on the other hand, whose commander had declined to use the Snake, was still well south of the railway line at dusk, having suffered heavy tank losses. At first the day had been overcast, but as it cleared so the Allied air forces were able to blast the areas around Albano, Cisterna, Velletri, Genzano and the foothills of the Colli Laziali. And Mark Clark, who had brought his command post forward to Anzio for the great break-out, was well pleased, as indeed he might have been.

On 24 May the attack was resumed. By the end of the day Cisterna had been cut off, 850 prisoners taken and the town of Cori in the foothills of the Lepini Mountains was being fast evacuated.

Meanwhile, on the southern front, the 2nd U.S. Corps were pushing on. On the night of 23/24 May the Germans abandoned Terracina and started to make their way across the mountains towards Highway Six and safety. The way was at last clear. Then, on 25 May, Cisterna itself was captured. It was a moment of rejoicing and euphoria. GIs of the 3rd Division found bicycles and rode around the ruined streets of the town; they picked flowers and stuck them in their helmets, while their prisoners looked on in amazement. It reminded the GIs of Sicily. All around were broken, destroyed or abandoned vehicles and equipment, the derelict debris of war. The only inhabitants of Cisterna now were the prisoners, bewildered flotsam whose world had come crashing down, and a few half-starved cats. By 25 May, 6th Corps had suffered 4,000 casualties and the loss of eighty-six tanks or tank destroyers, but they had taken over 4,800 prisoners and it was reckoned over 2,700 vehicles of all sorts had been destroyed.

But on the extreme right of the beachhead had taken place a matter of greater moment. Here the 36th Combat Engineers and 'B' Squadron of the 1st Reconnaissance Regiment, who had been brought over to this side of the beachhead for the great break-out, had pushed south-eastwards at daybreak. There was little opposition and what there was was easily swept aside. At 0730 hours on the morning of 25 May they met some engineers of General Keyes's 2nd Corps near a place called Borgo Grappa. One hour later, Major R. A. Fortnum of 655 AOP Squadron, on a reconnaissance over the eastern side of the beachhead, saw a long column of vehicles driving north-west. They did not look like Germans. When he landed he discovered that they were indeed men of the 91st Reconnaissance Regiment of the 2nd Corps.

After 124 days and some of the most savage and costly fighting of the Second World War, Anzio had ceased to be a beachhead.

Epilogue

Throughout 25 May 6th Corps pressed relentlessly forward. By the end of the day Cori had been taken and the leading elements of the 3rd Division were approaching Artena, less than four miles from Valmontone and the vital German escape route, Highway Six. All around was the proof of the success of Allied air interdiction; the sides of the roads north from Cisterna were littered with burned and abandoned vehicles.

Now, with the German Army apparently at the mercy of Alexander's troops; with Highway Six about to be cut and the annihilation of the German forces to the south little more than a matter of time, took place one of the most controversial decisions of the entire Italian campaign. On 26 May Clark ordered Truscott to switch his attack from Valmontone towards Rome. Alexander later described Clark's action as inexplicable. In his own memoirs and in later conversations, Clark states that he was anxious about the left flank of his 6th Corps, as it became increasingly exposed to German counter-attacks from the Alban Hills the further north it went; but that pre-supposed that the Germans were by then capable of offensive action, and there was every indication that they were not. The accusation has been levelled against Clark that he felt that 5th Army had earned the glory of the capture of the Eternal City, and that no one was going to rob him of this crowning achievement. This he has flatly denied, but it would appear that the ccapture of Rome before the great invasion in Normandy—which was originally scheduled for 5 June—had long been in his thoughts and had some influence on his actions.

Truscott was informed of the switch of direction by a staff officer from Clark's headquarters. Afterwards, in his memoirs, he uncompromisingly asserted that this alteration of the direction of the 6th Corps attack had 'prevented the destruction of the German 10th army.' At the time he protested strongly and pointed out that the Germans were all but in his grasp. But Clark had left his headquarters and was visiting the front; he could not be reached by telephone. Thus Truscott, as indeed Alexander, was faced with a *fait accompli*; the one had to comply with, the other to stomach, a drastic change of plan which threatened to take pressure off the Germans at the most crucial time. Truscott was also faced with a highly complicated logistical problem of switching his axis ninety degrees in the face of increasing enemy resistance. While the 3rd Division and the 1st Special Service Force continued north towards Valmontone, the remaining formations of 6th Corps were ordered to attack to the north-west, around the western slopes of the Alban Hills and directly towards the seductive goal of Rome itself.

On the left of the 6th Corps the British 1st and 5th divisions had been carrying out extensive patrolling; gradually it became clear that the enemy to their front were thinning out appreciably. On the same day as the link-up with 2nd Corps and when Cisterna at last fell, 18th Infantry Brigade took over from one of the regiments of 45th Division which were now needed for the drive to cut the German escape routes. Then began a slow, steady advance against lessening opposition and a profusion of mines and small deftly handled German rearguards.

On 28 May, patrols of the Gordons retook the Factory. It had taken nearly four months to return, but now there was little left of Mussolini's pride but anonymous heaps of rubble and the burned-out remains of Allied and German tanks and vehicles. At the same time the North Staffords regained the northern end of the Buon Riposo Ridge. It was all now rather eerie. Enemy shelling had all but ceased except in isolated pockets; a stillness had settled on the countryside, interspersed with the occasional distant, and seemingly impersonal, chatter of a machine gun or the flurry of rifle fire. The enemy positions were empty, just lice-ridden dugouts, with the stale crusts of black bread, abandoned equipment and clothing and the foetid smell of decay. It was like walking in another world, as though the living were trespassing on the regions of the dead. And behind the advancing Allied armies the grisly task of reclaiming and burying the dead went on. Some dated from the first attacks in far-off January: The poor, rotting corpses indistinguishable as Allied soldiers save for the pattern of the decaying boots, or the steel helmet lying alongside. By dusk on May 28, the 1st Division had retaken Carroceto and were now up to the line of the Embankment.

Now the 1st Division, with the 45th U.S. Division on their right and the 5th British Division on their left, pushed hard to the north-west and to the last German positions south of Rome on what was known as the Ardea Line which stretched away to the north-east skirting the Alban Hills, embracing Valmontone and merging into the Caesar Line.

But the fighting was by no means over. As the 5th and 1st British and 45th American divisions closed on the Ardea Line, all along the 6th Corps' front the Germans were stabilising their positions. On 30 May the 3rd Division and the 1st Special Service Force, still striving to take

Valmontone, were placed under command of the 2nd U.S. Corps, leaving Truscott's 6th Corps to continue their efforts to push past and over the Alban Hills. To their north, the 10th German Army was being rapidly withdrawn to the Caesar Line, and now it was discovered that the Apennines, which looked such a solid and impenetrable obstacle on the map, were traversed by small roads and tracks down which a retreating army could slip away and which could be blocked for days by small, skilfully-handled rearguards, a type of fighting at which the Germans excelled. There were no grandiose sweeps by armoured formations to round up a tottering and demoralised army, as some had envisaged, instead it was steady grind, wearisomely clearing mines from the paths of advancing troops, winkling out each German stronghold in turn, while all the time the bulk of the German forces were slipping away to fight another day.

By 29 May it began to look as though once again Kesselring had managed to stabilise his line across Italy. The divisions of the 6th Corps were tired, those of the 2nd Corps had suffered heavy casualties as well, but Clark felt that one more effort might be conclusive. By now the 36th U.S. Infantry Division was in the line, sandwiched between the 34th Division on their left and the 3rd Division, now of 2nd Corps, on their right. A National Guard division, the 36th had never fully recovered from the disaster on the Rapido River. Physically it had been made up in numbers, but its morale had been badly shaken and it smarted from the disgrace of the Rapido fiasco, and reluctantly stood the taunts of its Regular counterparts in the American Army. No one felt the odium more keenly than the division's commanding general, Major-General Fred L. Walker. The fates were now to relent, for the 36th Division were to make more than amends for their previous failure. The final triumph was to be theirs.

At the centre of their front lay the town of Velletri, in firm, and very possessive occupation by the Germans. Behind lay the formidable massif of Monte Artemisio, a high point of the Colli Laziali which dominated the country north and south. Vigorous patrolling had been ordered for the night of 30 May, and one of these patrols, to their intense surprise, discovered an unguarded route up the side of Monte Artemisio and that the mountain itself was unoccupied by the enemy. Reacting with great speed, by dawn General Walker had managed to infiltrate a complete regiment on to Monte Artemisio and another was hard on its heels, while his third was endeavouring to outflank the Germans in Velletri itself. The Germans counter-attacked this catastrophic penetration which threatened to unhinge the whole Caesar Line, but the Americans were too strongly established by then to be unseated.

This was the chance Clark had been waiting for. 6th and 2nd Corps, although exhausted, pushed forward driven remorselessly by their army commander. The fighting was fierce but gradually the Americans began to get the upper hand. On 2 June Valmontone was at last captured, and then all along the line the Germans started to pull back to the north.

On 3 June the three divisions on the left flank of 6th Corps began to drive forward in concert, but before they could get far the German positions on the Ardea Line had to be eliminated. Patrols reported that the enemy was withdrawing, but the battalions were under no illusions that there was still a great deal of fight left in them. Reinforced by raw reinforcements; 5th Division had already received a number of unfortunate set-backs to inexperienced companies which had pushed forward too boldly. The sapping experience of life in the wadis had taken heavy toll of men's fitness; theirs was a steady slog forward, never knowing when they might come across another enemy stronghold manned by the ever-resilient 4th German Parachute Division. The 5th division ached for refitting and resting, but there could be no respite until Rome was reached. At last, though, the country appeared to be in their favour. Instead of always being overlooked, now at least they could see something of what lay ahead. Rome was now less than thirty miles away.

The final attacks on the Ardea Line took place on 3 June. On the right, the Foresters and KSLI of the 3rd Brigade, after some stubborn fighting on the Acquabuona Ridge, drove the defenders off it, although not until a number of spirited counter-attacks had fallen on them. With this prominent feature now captured, 18th Infantry Brigade were passed through to take up the running. By dusk they were masters of the ridge, and during the night patrols roaming forward reported 'No Contact.'

On their left the Yorks and Lancs mounted an attack against the southern extremity of the Ardea Line and after resisting desperate counter-attacks held on to their gains. Also attacking were the 2nd Wilts, whose objective was the high ground north-west of Ardea. This turned out to be the last German stronghold south of Rome, but to the attacking Wiltshires it proved a costly objective. Their two assaulting companies were held up well short of the enemy positions having suffered very heavy casualties from German machine gun fire. So depleted was the battalion by then, that the only reserve left to the commanding officer was the carrier platoon. In a gallant attack which was to earn the 5th Division their only Victoria Cross of the war, the carrier platoon advanced through withering machine gun fire and a heavy concentration of German mortar fire to the enemy wire. By this time the platoon was attracting the fire of seven machine guns whose bullets swept the ground in front of the German wire from no further away than fifty or 100 yards. The platoon was pinned down and looked like being annihilated where it lay. It was at this moment that Sergeant Rogers, the platoon sergeant, advanced alone firing his tommy-gun from the hip. As the citation read,

> He got through the enemy's wire, ran across the minefield and destroyed two of the enemy's machine gun posts with his Thompson sub-machine gun and hand grenades. By now Sergeant Rogers was 100 yards ahead of his Platoon and had penetrated thirty yards inside the enemy's defences. He had drawn on to himself the fire of nearly all the enemy's machine guns and had thrown their defences into confusion. Inspired by the example of Sergeant Rogers, the platoon breached the enemy's wire and began the assault. Still alone and penetrating deeper and deeper into the enemy position, Sergeant Rogers, while attempting to silence a third machine gun post was blown off his feet by a grenade which burst beside him and wounded him in the leg. Nothing daunted, he stood up and still firing his Thompson sub-machine gun, ran on towards the enemy post. He was shot and killed at point blank range.

By his action he had destroyed the German position and on 4 June the armoured cars of the 5th Reconnaissance Regiment stormed on, wiping out what little enemy resistance there was. By nightfall they had reached the banks of the River Tiber. Meanwhile to the north, the Germans had been hurriedly withdrawing before the troops of the 6th and 2nd Corps. At 0800 hours on the morning of 4 June, the leading elements reached the outskirts of Rome. Early in the afternoon, men of the 1st Armoured and 36th Infantry Divisions with those of General Frederick's Special Service Force entered simultaneously. Two days later took place the mighty invasion of Normandy—and the Fall of Rome was forgotten in matters of greater moment.

As the Allied armies streamed into Rome, an officer saw a priest silently regarding the military might. He turned to him. 'It is impressive, is it not, Father?' The priest made no reply and looked steadily ahead, then slowly he turned his head and a smile came to his lips. In perfect English he replied in a low voice, 'It is, my son, another Changing of the Guard.'

*   *   *

Was Anzio the greatest lost opportunity of the war? For years the controversy has raged, and it will doubtless rage on for many years to come when two or more soldiers are gathered together. Should General Lucas have pushed on immediately after landing? Was he right to consolidate? Was his mission to sever the German communications with the southern front practicable with the forces he had available?

There seems little doubt that on that first day, units of 6th Corps could have physically reached Rome, could have scaled the Colli Laziali, could have cut Highway Seven, even perhaps Highway Six. But could they have stayed there, could they have been sustained?

The answer to this seems to hinge on two questions. Would the Germans have panicked with a formidable force sitting behind them and withdrawn from the Southern front; was 6th Corps ever strong enough or organised correctly to take on the task given them?

When Kesselring came to view the beachhead that first sunny afternoon he declared that the Allies had missed a uniquely favourable opportunity to take Rome. Whether or not he still adhered to that view when he was in possession of all the facts and had the advantages of hindsight is not known, but he later referred to the landing being a 'half-way measure' and that the landing force was initially too weak. At the time his staff were urging him to pull back from the Southern front, but he was confident that he could hold the beachhead. Further, under the contingencies of Case Richard he felt that he would have enough troops in the immediate future to seal off the beachhead without calling for substantial reinforcements from the main Southern front. (Had simultaneous and continuous pressure been mounted by the 8th Army when the landing took place, as Clark had originally urged, the story might have been somewhat different, for a number of German units were sent from the Adriatic front opposite the 8th Army to help at Anzio.)

As far as the strength of 6th Corps is concerned, Lucas only had a superiority over his enemy on the first three days of the life of the beachhead (until getting on into April and May). Further, this balance and inevitable future imbalance had been forecast before the operation was mounted. If any break-out was intended in the early days of the beachhead and advantage gained of any surprise achieved, it had to take place within the first three days or not at all. Thereafter the greater pace of the German build-up by land would place Lucas at a perpetual and growing disadvantage. The initial landing craft lift was for two divisions, plus the better part of two-thirds of another. No further substantial reinforcement could be expected for three days at the least, and even that was dependent upon favourable weather. The main armoured force was not even scheduled to land until 27 January (D + 5) Inevitably, therefore, 6th Corps were only strong enough to consolidate at first and then, when their build-up was complete, to break out—but by then the Germans were in sufficient strength to oppose them.

For 6th Corps to have tried to break out in the early days before it was possible to reinforce heavily would have been suicidal, bearing in mind the long delay due to the sea passage and the imponderable of the weather—storms could have effectively sealed off the landing for days on end. It would have been suicidal, too, to have pushed rashly into the hills or on to Rome with the forces Lucas had available. Every senior commander on the Allied side who has committed his thoughts to paper, or is still alive, is adamant on that point. None doubted that the mission could have been temporarily successful, but unless the Germans had panicked—and there was no indication or likelihood of that—the force would have been eliminated, and could never have been maintained or sustained. The Alban Hills, twenty miles from the port of Anzio, were a formidable massif in which several divisions could easily have been swallowed. To maintain that long, thin supply thread from attacks from both flanks, and from an enemy who possessed interior lines of communication, would have been impossible. The invading force would soon enough have been severed from its source of supply and those who had reached the hills or Rome would have been destroyed piecemeal. Some consider that the overwhelming might of Allied air power could have been conclusive, but in practice on too many occasions that might was grounded due to bad weather. Although the German resupply and reinforcement was hampered by Allied air action, it was never completely interrupted, and certainly the 'guaranteed' isolation of the battlefield which had once been promised was never achieved.

Much odium and contumely has been heaped on the head of the unfortunate General Lucas. But the balance of opinion is now that he was right not to attempt to push on until he was strong enough. Not until D + 7 had that consolidation been achieved, when the 1st U.S. Armoured Division, or more correctly, its greater half, Combat Command 'A', had assembled in the beachhead. That is not to say that he should not have made every effort, and it would not have taken much, to capture the nodal points of Campoleone and Cisterna at the outset—but even this is arguable. Although it would have given him considerable communication advantages, and allowed his armour room to manoeuvre, which they never had, it would also have lengthened the beachhead line from thirty miles to over forty miles, and even with the smaller perimeter during the crucial days of 16-19 February 6th Corps only just managed to hold on. For the brutal truth about the beachhead battle was that the Germans could attack where they willed, and wherever they chose to mount their principal onslaught; so extended were the Anglo-American forces that, with varying degrees of rapidity, they would be overwhelmed. It was, as one soldier put it, a game of cards in which the Germans held all the aces and jokers. Not until the nature of the ground channelled the German attack into a comparatively narrow, and inevitable, front were their efforts defeated.

A further criticism is that strong mobile patrols should have been sent to range the German rear area and the Alban foothills—a fighting column along these lines was mooted during the planning stages of the operation, but it died along the way. Even if they had not survived long this would have caused considerable disruption and even panic in some quarters, and might have given an impression of strength behind the German lines. But all opinion and criticism aside it cannot be denied that for Lucas to lose contact with the German forces for two and a half days was wholly wrong. One must come to the conclusion that Lucas's tactical handling of his corps was faulty in this respect and certainly his method of command was lack-lustre. It is easy enough to criticise thirty-four years after the event, but the most conspicuous evidence of this was the way in which 6th Corps became galvanised when Truscott took over. It was as though new life had been pumped into the expiring body of 6th Corps, even when Truscott was officially only Lucas's deputy.

In his defence, it can be said that Lucas was clearly the victim of fundamentally misleading topographical Intelligence. The ground to the west of the Via Anziate appeared from the air to be excellent tank-going, in fact he was informed that it was. Thus, in the early days of the beachhead he had expected strong German counter attacks led by armour from that quarter—which goes some way to justify his caution. Also his own plans hinged on making use of this same ground for his eventual armoured break-out with Harmon's Armoured Division. In the event the ground precluded both fear and hope, for the Wadi country was impassable to tanks. But no one at the headquarters of 6th Corps truly appreciated this until, shortly after taking over, Truscott came to view the offending wadis himself. That evening his chief of staff telephoned: 'The General says that now he knows what you mean. You need never mention those Goddam wadis again.' To a lesser extent a similar situation existed on the Cisterna flank. Here air photographs had revealed a country of cultivated fields surrounded by neat hedges, but they did not show that the water-table was within two feet of the surface and that the ground became impassable after a shower of rain. Furthermore the 'neat hedges' turned out to be twenty-foot irrigation ditches full of brambles and scrub. The implications of these revelations, as the troops on the ground discovered to their cost in due time, had incalculable effect on the tactics and planning after the Anzio landing, and Lucas was the principal sufferer.

None the less, it is clear that the unfortunate General Lucas found himself embarked on an adventure for which he was unsuited by temperament, inclination or experience. And it was an adventure which could never succeed, given the prevailing circumstances, the forces and the landing craft available for the landing. The tragic fact is that Operation Shingle was ill-conceived—within the narrow context of the operation itself.

But looked at in the light of the Italian campaign as a whole a different picture begins to emerge. German casualties at Anzio amounted to over 35,000 men killed, wounded or captured—Allied battle casualties were rather less. Some of the German divisions mauled at Anzio were never reformed or reactivated, and German morale suffered a severe set-back, more especially as Hitler had associated himself so closely with the battle. Had the Anzio operation never taken place, a fair proportion of those divisions would have found their way to the main Southern front where defensive positions abounded, and to eliminate them in that ground unfavourable to the attacker would have cost vastly more Allied lives than those lost at Anzio. Anzio was looked on by Hitler as an 'Abscess' but it would be more apposite to call it a vortex, sucking divisions into Italy which might otherwise have fought in Normandy or elsewhere in Europe. On 21 January the German front line in Italy was 85 miles long, on 30 January (D + 8) it had grown to 120 miles. The 'primary task' of Alexander's army was that of 'containing as many enemy formations in Italy as possible'. Looked at in that context Operation Shingle begins to assume a different hue.

But I dare say that when the Anglo-American forces landed at Anzio that crisp morning in January 1944, no one among the invading troops saw himself as being part of an army which would become involved in a battle of attrition and survival as sustained and bitter as any in World War II.

Anzio

Allied Order of Battle

SIXTH U.S. CORPS

British Forces

1st Infantry Division
   24th Guards Brigade
      5th Battalion Grenadier Guards
      1st Battalion Scots Guards
      1st Battalion Irish Guards
   2nd Infantry Brigade
      1st Battalion The Loyal Regiment
      2nd Battalion The North Staffordshire Regiment
      6th Battalion The Gordon Highlanders
   3rd Infantry Brigade
      1st Battalion The Duke of Wellington's Regiment
      2nd Battalion The Sherwood Foresters
      1st Battalion The King's Shropshire Light Infantry

   2nd, 19th, 24th, 67th Field Regiments, RA
   80th Medium Regiment, RA (The Scottish Horse)
   81st Anti-Tank Regiment, RA
   90th Light Anti-Aircraft Regiment, RA
   46th Royal Tank Regiment
   1st Reconnaissance Regiment
   2nd/7th Battalion The Middlesex Regiment (MG)

2nd Special Service Brigade
   9th Commando
   43rd Royal Marine Commando

U.S. Forces

1st U.S. Armoured Division (Combat Command 'A' only)
   1st Armoured Regiment

6th Armoured Infantry Regiment

3rd U.S. Infantry Division
7th, 15th, 30th Infantry Regiments
504th Parachute Infantry Regiment
509th Parachute Infantry Battalion
751st Tank Battalion

1st, 3rd and 4th Ranger Battalions

Principal Reinforcements to April

U.S. *45th U.S. Infantry Division*
157th, 179th, 180th Infantry Regiments
158th, 160th, 171st, 189th Field Artillery Battalions
645th Tank Destroyer Battalion

1st Special Service Force (Canadian/American)

British *56th (London) Infantry Division*
167th Infantry Brigade
8th and 9th Battalions The Royal Fusiliers
7th Battalion The Oxfordshire and Buckinghamshire Light Infantry
168th Infantry Brigade
10th Battalion The Royal Berkshire Regiment
1st Battalion The London Scottish Regiment
1st Battalion The London Irish Rifles
169th Infantry Brigade
2nd/5th, 2nd/6th and 2nd/7th Battalions The Queen's Royal Regiment

18th Infantry Brigade
1st Battalion The Buffs
14th Battalion The Sherwood Foresters
9th Battalion the King's Own Yorkshire Light Infantry (The Yorkshire Dragoons)

5th Infantry Division
13th Infantry Brigade
2nd Battalion The Cameronians
2nd Battalion The Royal Inniskilling Fusiliers
2nd Battalion The Wiltshire Regiment

Allied Order of Battle

15th Infantry Brigade
1st Battalion The Green Howards
1st Battalion The King's Own Yorkshire Light Infantry
1st Battalion The York and Lancaster Regiment
17th Infantry Brigade
2nd Battalion The Royal Scots Fusiliers
2nd Battalion The Northamptonshire Regiment
6th Battalion The Seaforth Highlanders
5th Reconnaissance Regiment
7th Battalion The Cheshire Regiment (MG)

40th Royal Marine Commando

Reinforcements May

U.S.
1st Armoured Division—Combat Command 'B'
34th Infantry Division
36th Infantry Division

Select Bibliography

BLUMENSON, MARTIN, *Anzio: The Gamble that Failed*, Weidenfeld & Nicolson, 1963

BOWDITCH, JOHN, III, *The Anzio Bridgehead*, vol. XIV in 'American Forces in Action' series, Historical Division, Department of the Army, Washington, 1947.

CLARK, MARK W., *Calculated Risk*, Harrap, 1951

The History of the Second World War; The War in the Mediterranean, vol. V, HMSO, 1973

JACKSON, W. G. F., *The Battle for Italy*, Batsford, 1967. *The Battle for Rome*, Batsford, 1969

KESSELRING, ALBERT, *The Memoirs of Field-Marshal Kesselring*, Wm. Kimber, 1953

MORISON, SAMUEL ELIOT, *History of United States Naval Operations in World War II*, vol. IX, Oxford University Press, 1947

NICOLSON, NIGEL, *Alex*, Weidenfeld & Nicolson, 1973

Report by the Supreme Allied Commander Mediterranean to the Combined Chiefs of Staff, HMSO, 1944

SHEEHAN, FRED, *Anzio: Epic of Bravery*, University of Oklahoma Press, 1964

TRUSCOTT, LUCIAN K., *Command Mission*, Dutton, New York, 1954

VAUGHAN-THOMAS, WYNFORD, *Anzio*, Longman, 1961

WESTPHAL, SIEGFRIED, *The German Army in the West*, Cassell, 1951

and the regimental histories of those regiments which fought at Anzio

Index

Index

Index

French Expeditionary Corps 33, 232–33
Fulbrook, Lt.-Colonel E. 170, 178

Garigliano R. 19, 33–4, 53, 221, 232
German Forces:
  10th Army 32, 234, 241, 243
  14th Army 32
    15th Grenadier Regiment 175
    725th Grenadier Regiment 111, 150
    735th Grenadier Regiment 111
  65th Infantry Division 66, 84, 97, 111, 140, 161, 167, 169
  71st Infantry Division 66
  362nd Infantry Division 203, 205, 239
  715th Infantry Division 95, 97, 161, 165–67, 169, 180, 239
    168th Brigade 111
  Hermann Goering Panzer Division 32, 52, 55, 64, 66, 71, 161, 203, 220, 239
  114th Jäger Division 67, 161, 180, 203, 220
  Luftwaffe 25, 37;
    at Anzio, 44, 51, 53, 116, 165
    3rd Panzer Grenadier Division 32, 55, 57, 59–60, 66, 84, 97, 111, 127, 161, 163–65, 169, 203, 220, 224–25
    29th Panzer Grenadier Regiment 33, 45–6, 53, 57, 59, 95, 111, 140, 165, 169, 175, 180, 203, 206, 220, 234
    Infantry Lehr Regiment 161, 163–64, 167
    71st Panzer Grenadier Regiment 45, 52
  90th Panzer Grenadier Division 32–3, 45
  26th Panzer Division 66, 72, 77, 97, 111, 163, 169, 175, 203–5, 220
  1 Parachute Corps 53, 97, 203
  4th Parachute Division 33, 55, 66, 97, 140, 155, 235, 244
    11th Parachute Regiment 111, 223
Good, Lt.-Colonel I. R. 114, 116, 137, 183–84
Gordon-Lennox, Lt.-Colonel G. C. DSO 69
Gordon-Watson, Major D. M. L. 63, 99
Gothic Line 32
Gould, Captain T. G. 200
Gräser, Lt.-General Fritz-Hubert 97, 127, 137, 161, 164–65
Greenaway, Major H. 128
Green Bush Hill 238
Gregson-Ellis, Major-General P. G. S. 228
Grenadier Gully 125–26, 131
Grinley, Lieutenant P. M. 66

Index